Crisis and Decline

Crisis and Decline
The Fate of the Southern Unionists

R.B. McDowell

THE LILLIPUT PRESS
Dublin

First published in December 1997 by
THE LILLIPUT PRESS LTD
62-63 Sitric Road, Arbour Hill,
Dublin 7, Ireland.

A CIP record for this
title is available from
The British Library.

ISBN 1 874675 92 9

The Lilliput Press receives financial assistance from
An Chomhairle Ealaíon/The Arts Council of Ireland.

Set in 10 on 13 Sabon by Sheila Stephenson
Printed in England by Biddles Ltd

Contents

Illustrations between pages 118 and 119

Preface

RECEDING IMPERIALISM usually leaves behind those who have for generations staunchly upheld its authority and flourished under its aegis – Germans in Bohemia, Swedes in Finland, Loyalists or Tories in the American colonies, Greeks in Asia Minor, Muslims in the Balkans. Amongst those abandoned adherents of a lost cause were the unionists in the south and west of Ireland. From the time Home Rule became a serious issue in politics they strove to maintain the union enacted in 1800, and once the Treaty was signed they had either to emigrate (a depressing and costly option adopted by comparatively few) or adapt themselves to the new political environment. Of those who stayed on in the Irish Free State, some went into internal political exile, while many contrived to play an active part in the economic and social life of the country. All retained principles, prejudices and loyalties which challenged the preconceptions of contemporary Irish nationalism.

A community that had for so long played such a conspicuous and powerful role in Irish life and that, even in its decline, remained a distinctive and to a limited extent influential element in the south and west of the country, undoubtedly merits a measure of attention, at least on the level of a short study. Moreover, departed greatness tends to exercise a profound, uncanny fascination, encouraging in some a stern or sour belief that history inevitably metes out social justice; arousing in others a melancholy sense of loss –

> Lo, all our pomp of yesterday
> Is one with Ninevah and Tyre

– and reminding many of the transitory nature of things –

My name is Ozymandias, king of kings:
Look on my works, ye Mighty, and despair!

Nothing beside remains. Round the decay
Of that colossal wreck, boundless and bare
The lone and level sands stretch far away.

After I entered Trinity College, Dublin, in the early thirties, I moved in the ex-unionist world, enjoying its hospitality and imbibing its opinions and prejudices. Naturally, then, when working on Irish history of the first half of the twentieth century I have been repeatedly reminded of controversies, battles and personalities glimpsed from a distance long ago. Memory, I hope, has been at times a help in illuminating the results of research. However, to avoid being over-obtrusive, I have relegated my recollections of public affairs (the recollections of a person of no importance) to a section following the final chapter.

Acknowledgments

I AM GRATEFUL to Dr David Dickson for most helpful advice and criticism, and to other sometime colleagues in the Modern History Department, Trinity College, Dublin, for their encouragement. From Dr Elizabethanne Boran and Miss Olwen Myhill I have received valuable assistance. I must thank the Deputy Keeper of the Records, Public Record Office of Northern Ireland, for permission to use the material in his custody, and I am greatly indebted to the staffs of the libraries and repositories in which I have worked for the facilities and help they have readily afforded me.

1 Sanior Pars

DURING THE HOME RULE CONTROVERSY those who were advocating any degree of political autonomy for Ireland had to contend with one difficulty: the fact that a substantial number of the inhabitants of the country were not, in the political sense of the term, nationalists. About the beginning of the twentieth century unionists optimistically asserted that roughly one-third of the population supported the maintenance of the union. Admittedly this was a minority, but it was certainly a potent one, comprising, it was said, 'all that is best in Ireland, her enterprise, her industry, her intellect, her culture, her wealth' and, it might be added, 'the backbone ... and the fighting power of the country'. The Unionist party, a party distinguished by quality if not quantity, was the party of education and property – demonstrated for instance by an analysis of the reception committee of the great 1887 Dublin unionist demonstration: 101 deputy lieutenants and JPs, 124 barristers, 65 physicians, 28 fellows and professors of Trinity, the governor and directors of the Bank of Ireland, 34 directors of public companies and 445 merchants.[1]

The Irish unionists, at least 1,100,000 strong in 1914, were divided by geography, history, economic developments and religious demography into two sections, the Ulster or Northern unionists and the unionists in the other three provinces, the former centred on Belfast, the latter on Dublin. In estimating the numbers and distribution of Irish unionists the denominational statistics provided by the Irish census are exceedingly helpful, bearing in mind that generally speaking Protestants were unionists and

---

1 *Fortnightly Review*, lxxiv, p. 317; *Nineteenth Century and After*, xxi, p. 256; J. Atkinson, *Speech*, in Irish Unionist Alliance publications, iv; *Parl. Debates*, 3 series, ccciv, 1388-96; *The Times*, 14 Nov. 1887.

Catholics nationalists. The fastidious might deplore confounding the spiritual with the secular, but many keen partisans would, at least as regards their own side, regard this as a happy coincidence of religious and political virtue.

However, other strong but more broad-minded party men wanted their cause to be comprehensive rather than sectarian. Some intelligent unionists, anxious to prove that the union was widely recognized as most beneficial to Ireland, eagerly welcomed Catholics to their ranks. W.E.H. Lecky, for instance, once wrote, 'I have never myself looked upon Home Rule as a question between Protestant and Catholic. It is a question between honesty and dishonesty, between loyalty and treason, between individual freedom and organised tyranny and outrage.'[2] Nationalists were insistent that all Irishmen were in essence nationalists. It was only blind prejudice, narrow self-interest or invincible ignorance that prevented unionists throwing in their lot with their nationalist fellow countrymen. Wolfe Tone, regarded as one of the fathers of Irish nationalism, had expressed the wish to substitute the common name of Irishman in the place of the distinction of Protestant, Catholic and Dissenter. Tone of course was a man of the Enlightenment. Nineteenth- and twentieth-century Irish nationalists were faced with the problem of reconciling the liberal approach to religion and politics with the undeniable fact that, since the overwhelming majority of nationalists were Catholics, Catholicism and nationalism were closely intertwined. For many, indeed, Catholicism was an essential component of Irish nationalism. Nationalists seem to have solved the problem by assuming that for a Protestant nationalist, his Protestantism was a matter of assenting to certain dogmas and forms of worship and would not seriously affect his feelings and thinking about Ireland. But an Irish Protestant derived much of his religious tradition from England and Scotland, the Authorized Version and the Shorter Catechism being important elements in his heritage. Naturally then, the great majority of Irish Protestants were biased in favour of the British connection. There were, however, a small number of Protestants who, out of the belief that the union was crippling

2 *The Times*, 21 June 1892.

Irish development, enthusiasm for the Gaelic past and the Home
Rule future, generosity of spirit or sheer crankiness, were nationalists – 'rare birds', according to Carson, whom the nationalists
were 'fond of exhibiting'. Or, as the Church of Ireland Archbishop
of Armagh declared, 'a stage army', exploited on every occasion.3
The Protestant nationalists included some distinguished figures
such as Yeats, George Russell, Stephen Gwynn, a man of letters
who became a nationalist MP, Shane Leslie, a convert to
Catholicism, and T.W. Rolleston, 'an aristocratic nationalist'.
Rolleston admired the high-mindedness of Sinn Féin in its early
days, denounced the Irish parliamentary party as 'a damnable
gang of swindlers' and defended Lord Clanricarde's dealing with
his tenancy. He was both a strong Home Ruler and a fervent imperialist. 'Let us', he wrote, 'while steadily urging our national
demands, at the same time claim and hold that place at the centre
of authority of the Anglo-Celtic empire which the facts of physical
nature, of race and of history have assigned us.' Irishmen, he was
convinced, had qualities – broad-mindedness and a sympathetic
awareness of differing opinions and interests – that fitted them to
play an influential part in imperial affairs.4

Catholic unionists were more conventional and probably far
more numerous than Protestant nationalists. They included landlords, soldiers, lawyers, and a fair number of resolute supporters
of law and order, some who were instinctively conservative and
others who were unimpressed by the case for Home Rule; or, as a
unionist pamphleteer put it, 'all the Irish Roman Catholic gentry
(except Sir Thomas Esmonde), three-quarters of the Roman
Catholic professional men, all the great Roman Catholic merchants and half of the domestic class'.5

Catholic unionists may have deplored and even have been disconcerted by the way in which the Irish Catholic clergy tended to
identify Catholicism with Irish nationalism, their emphasis on 'Faith
and Fatherland'. But Catholic unionists could console themselves

---

3 *Parl. Debates*, 4 series, xi, 825; *Journ. General Synod*, 1912, p. xlvii.
4 C.H. Rolleston, *Portrait of an Irishman* (1930), pp. viii, 17, 31, 51, 117-18;
  T.W. Rolleston, *Ireland, the Empire and the War* (1900).
5 *Irish Unionist Alliance Publications*, vi, leaflet, 57.

by reflecting that through much of history and over much of the contemporary world the Church was a conservative force, upholding the status quo, ready to defend property and the existing order so long as the state abstained from attacking ecclesiastical rights. As Lord Fingall said at a great unionist meeting, 'if Catholicism had any political tendency it was rather towards the maintenance of the union'.[6]

Working on the assumption that denominational and political loyalties closely coincided, the Irish unionists fell into two sections, the Ulster unionists and the unionists in the other three provinces. But by the beginning of the twentieth century this line of division was found to be imperfect. Though the unionists definitely predominated in some parts of Ulster, in the province as a whole they outnumbered the nationalists by a very narrow margin, so when the question of excluding the North from the jurisdiction of a Home Rule parliament in Dublin arose, it was ultimately decided that 'political Ulster'[7] should be the six north-east counties. Therefore it is convenient when discussing the Southern unionists statistically to consider them as being the unionists in the three southern provinces together with those in Counties Cavan, Donegal and Monaghan (twenty-six counties in all).

In 1914, of the 1,100,000 Protestants in Ireland 327,000 were in the twenty-six counties, amounting to slightly over 10 per cent of the population of that area. Their distribution was highly erratic. In the city of Dublin under a fifth of the population was Protestant; in the three townships of Kingstown, Pembroke and Rathmines and Rathgar and the rural districts of Blackrock and Dalkey, prosperous sections of the Dublin built-up area though outside the city boundaries (and determined to remain so, their inhabitants being on this issue Home Rulers), Protestants amounted to over 60 per cent of the total population.[8] In the city and county of Dublin combined, Protestants (numbering 101,000) formed slightly over 21 per cent of the population. Protestants

---

6 *Unionist Convention ... Report of the Proceedings* [1892], p. 76.

7 *Irish Unionist Alliance Publications*, iii, leaflet 103.

8 The distribution and occupational composition of the Dublin Protestant population is treated in considerable detail by M.E. Daly in *Dublin, the Deposed Capital* (1984), chapter v.

amounted to 17 per cent of the population of County Kildare and 21 per cent of the population of Wicklow, so that a new 'pale', the city of Dublin and the neighbouring counties, included 127,000 Protestants, about one-third of the Protestants in the twenty-six counties. Another 70,000 were to be found in the three Ulster counties, where, as might be expected, there were substantial Protestant minorities – in Donegal 21.5 per cent of the population, in Monaghan 25.32 per cent, in Cavan 18.54 per cent. All this meant that there were comparatively few Protestants to be found in the rest of Leinster, Munster and Connacht. In Leinster minus the 'pale' they were just under 9 per cent of the population, in Munster 6 per cent (rising to almost 9 per cent in County Cork) and in Connacht under 4 per cent. In three urban centres they were comparatively numerous – in Cork 11.56 per cent, in Limerick 9.48 per cent, in Sligo nearly 9 per cent.

If the Southern Protestants' geographical distribution was distinctly uneven, the social composition of the community, as shown by the occupational tables included in the census, was remarkably top-heavy. In the twenty-six counties almost half the lawyers (a shade under 48 per cent), well over one-third of the medical men (37.7 per cent) and almost half the surveyors and engineers were Protestants. Turning to business, over one-fifth of the merchants (21.9 per cent), over 70 per cent of those engaged in banking, half the accountants, almost half the auctioneers and nearly one-third of the commercial clerks were Protestants. On the other hand only 7.4 per cent of farmers and 2.7 per cent of farm labourers and farm servants were Protestants.

Though the numbers of Protestant farmers (something over 21,000) and farm labourers (4000) in the twenty-six counties were relatively small, the Southern unionists could claim they had a substantial number of farmers (at least 21,000) in their ranks. These together with a sprinkling of farm labourers, servants in 'big houses', landlords' men, Protestant small shopkeepers, urban artisans and police and military pensioners, who all prided themselves on being supporters of the union, afforded some justification for asserting that Southern unionism embraced all classes in the community. That the party was both socially inclusive and had a strict sense of social propriety was demonstrated at a great Dublin anti-

Home Rule meeting held in the Rotunda. The body of the hall, it was reported, was almost filled by artisans and working men while members of the aristocracy and professional and mercantile men occupied the platform.[9] Shortly afterwards the Dublin Conservative Workingmen's Club emphasized class interdependency, calling on the government to take steps to restore to the landed interest 'their former capacity for employing the industrial classes'. The Club was strongly of the opinion that to avoid the struggle forced on them by the enemies of law and order would be 'to brand ourselves as moral and political poltroons'.[10]

The most conspicuous element in Southern unionism was the landed interest, peers, and baronets resident in Ireland and the landed gentry, the class which, according to a eulogist, formed 'the backbone of the country' from which had sprung Ireland's 'most distinguished sons'.[11] There was, another eulogist wrote, 'good stuff' in the descendants of 'the toughest breeds of the old Irish race' and of 'the hardier and more adventurous spirits of Great Britain or of a cross between these stocks'.[12]

Though the landed interest was clearly discernible, and in any neighbourhood there would be general agreement as to which families belonged to it, membership was not precisely defined. What made a landed gentleman was not merely the possession of landed property but rather varying combinations of birth, acreage, upbringing, profession, life-style and, very occasionally, the determination to be recognized as one. It would be impossible to state statistically the size of the landed world but a rough guide to membership is provided by the Commission of the Peace. The head of an established landed family almost automatically became a JP (and in each county about twenty landowners were appointed deputy lieutenants, an additional acknowledgment of their status). In the 1880s approximately 2690 JPs described themselves as a landlord or landowner (about 2270 in the twenty-six counties). Therefore the Irish landed world could be taken to number a few

---

9 *The Times*, 8 May 1886.
10 Minutes of the Conservative Workingmen's Club, Oct. 1887.
11 R. Burke, *A Genealogical and Heraldic History of the Landed Gentry of Ireland* (1904), preface.
12 *The Case of the Irish Landlords. By One of Them* (1903), p. 6.

thousand families.[13] Of course younger sons were to be found in the Church, the services and the law, and daughters sometimes married non-landed men, so many people all over Ireland cherished a connection, even if distant, with an indubitably landed family.

An Irish landlord was usually doubly a man of affairs – both managing his estate and taking part in public life as a JP, a poor-law guardian, a grand juror or a militia officer. An estate was, it has been said, 'a local industry',[14] with indoor and outdoor servants, bailiffs, gamekeepers and rent warners. Beyond the demesne walls there were tenants to be conciliated, encouraged, rebuked or on occasion evicted, and the landlord or his agent had to be familiar with 'files, rentals, ledgers and rent rolls ... head rents, ground rents, gale day and hanging gales, turbarys, free farm, fee farm and first, second, third term rent decisions'.[15] There were instances, fortunately comparatively rare, when a landlord involved in acute agrarian conflict might have to live under police protection, almost in a state of siege – the stresses and strains that might be sustained by a boycotted family being vividly portrayed in two novels of the early 1880s, *The Landleaguers* by Trollope and *A Boycotted Household* by Letitia McClintock, the daughter of a County Donegal landlord.

A landlord's economic and social status was clearly indicated by his residence, 'the big house', with outbuildings, gardens and plantations. Until early in the twentieth century these houses (and their equivalents elsewhere in Europe) were taken for granted; in fact to the hundreds scattered through Ireland, built on classical lines, there were added during the nineteenth century a number of Gothic mansions – suggesting a sublime unawareness of the impending land acts. Later, between 1921 and 1923, a number of Irish country houses were destroyed and others fell into ruin with

---

13 *Commission of the Peace (Ireland), Return* [Cd 200], H.C. 1886, liii. In 1870 there were about 5500 landed proprietors with over 100 acres and 5900 with under 100 acres (*Return for 1870 of Landed Proprietors in Each Country*, H.C. 1872, xlvii). In 1904 the executive committee of the Irish landowners convention referred to the 13,000 landowners in Ireland (*The Times*, 29 Nov. 1904).

14 *Irish Times*, 18 Nov. 1939.

15 S. Leslie, *Doomsland* (1923), p. 34.

the departure of their owners. Ireland in the 1930s, it was remarked, was covered with dilapidated mansions with 'unpainted and rusting gates and grass-covered drives'.[16] An extreme nationalist dismissed these as 'big garks of country mansions', built by a wastrel, spendthrift, rack-renting ascendency.[17] But in England there was a growing nostalgic interest in eighteenth-century architecture and in a way of life 'emphatically rejected in practical affairs' – 'there was never a time when so many landless men could talk at length about landscape gardening'.[18] This vogue spread to Ireland. The big house began to be seen as the embodiment of aesthetic values, grace, balance, craftsmanship and sensitive planning, and its past occupants were seen through a romantic haze, enjoying elegant leisure and indulging in delightful eccentricities. With the pre-1900 agrarian system receding into the distant past, Irish landlords became associated, not with harsh estate management, but with the creation of an architectural heritage that enriched the countryside, gave pleasure to people of sensibility and was an asset to the tourist industry.

Though the Irish landed world was sometimes viewed in a Leveresque light as being composed of hard-riding, rollicking eccentrics, a country gentleman with a strong sense of history pointed out that at the end of the nineteenth century the great majority of the Irish landed gentry were as 'sober, orderly and perhaps as dull as those who lived in England'.[19] The Anglo-Irish gentry, a member of the landed world explained, were endowed with a combination of 'levity and pessimism, of conscientiousness and good-natured laxity, of practical benevolence and abusiveness and of courage'.[20] They saw themselves contributing not only moral stamina but culture to Irish life. Landlords and ex-landlords, a County Longford country gentleman asserted, formed 'oases of culture, of uprightness and fair dealing in what otherwise would be a desert of dull uniformity'.[21] In all this there was perhaps a

---

16 *Irish Times*, 18 Nov. 1939.
17 *Catholic Bulletin*, xxvi, p. 668, xxvii, p. 846.
18 E. Waugh, *Work Suspended* (1943), p. 184.
19 *National Review*, xlii, p. 654.
20 E.O. Somerville, *The Enthusiast* (1921), p. 154.
21 Unionist Alliance papers, D989/A/II/II.

trace of excessive self-satisfaction. Still, in a deferential age, when a vast number of middle-class men and women aspired to be regarded as ladies and gentlemen and assiduously tried to practice the manners and rules of good society, the landed gentry were respected and looked up to as social exemplars, even by those who might differ from them in politics.

It goes without saying that the gentry were, with rare exceptions, staunch unionists. A hundred years earlier many of the leading landed families had been eager to win and preserve Ireland's legislative independence. But the parliament they had admired and cherished was one in which the landed interest preponderated. Circumstances had changed, and the imperial parliament was viewed as more likely to respect the rights of landed property than a Dublin assembly controlled by the representatives of a restive tenantry. Those landlords who were Protestants (the great majority) preferred to be in the United Kingdom than in a Home Rule Catholic Ireland. Finally, they were often connected with England by family ties, education and service in the forces, and shared many of the loyalties and prejudices of their English equivalents.

During the first three-quarters of the nineteenth century the Irish landlords possessed power and prestige. No doubt they had their critics, but it was taken for granted that they were an essential and permanent part of the Irish agrarian system and would continue living 'an ordered, dignified existence in their big old-fashioned houses', enjoying in their own orbit 'power, leisure and deference'.[22] Throughout the debates on the Land Act of 1870 it was assumed that, with some adjustments, the landlord-tenant relationship would continue to function successfully for the foreseeable future. But in ten years it had become conventional political wisdom that agrarian relations in Ireland were so unsatisfactory that the landlord must be removed from the system. As early as 1883 a future Conservative prime minister, Arthur Balfour, was advocating legislation to promote on an extensive scale the creation of a peasant proprietary, and two years later, Ashbourne, an Irish Lord Chancellor and a pillar of the Conservative Party in the Lords, was responsible for a land-purchase act, the first of a series which culminated in the

---

22 *Nineteenth Century and After*, lxxv, p. 177.

Wyndham Act (1903), 'that great treaty between rival agrarian interests in Ireland'.[23] The Wyndham Act embodied a scheme of land purchase that proved acceptable to both landlords and tenants, one feature of the scheme being that the bonus on the purchase price paid to the landlord came out of the imperial exchequer.

At the time they were being prised from their estates (at a price), the Irish landlords were also rapidly losing political power and influence. The Reform Act of 1884, enfranchising the rural householder, placed electoral power in most constituencies in the hands of the small farmers and labourers – 'the hovel electors', to quote one conservative – who, though they had many virtues, were 'ignorant, excitable and prejudiced' and absolutely unused to the duties and responsibilities of public affairs.[24] From 1885 onwards in the south and west a landlord, unless he was a Home Ruler, had little or no chance of winning a seat. In 1898 the gentry lost control of county government. The Local Government Act of that year, which Lecky called 'a great and perilous experiment' and glumly accepted as a political necessity, transferred local administration from the grand juries, landed oligarchies, to elected country, urban and rural councils. A landed gentleman could still expect to be a justice of the peace, but he had to rub shoulders with the chairmen of county and district councils who were ex-officio JPs, and the bench had already been diluted by the government's efforts to conciliate public opinion by granting the Commission of the Peace to, in the words of a strong unionist, 'persons possessing the confidence of the peasantry ... substantial, or let us say the less insubstantial small farmers'. He consoled himself by reflecting that 'the Irish rustic', though he will always have a certain ingrained respect for 'the quality', would have only contempt and distrust for '"Doran JP", who is little more than his equal'.[25]

At the beginning of the twentieth century the Irish landlord was an endangered and disappearing species. A sympathetic observer, George A. Birmingham, painted a pathetic picture of an Irish country gentleman, excluded from local affairs, if listened to politely,

23 *Parl. Debates*, 5 series, xxxviii, 427.
24 *Parl. Debates*, 3 series, cclxxxvi, 1572-3, 1586; cclxxxviii, 603.
25 A.D. Godley, *Reliquae*, ed. C.R.L. Fletcher (1926), ii, p. 14.

gazing from a window in his 'stately home' over a broad stretch of country and sighing, 'it is mine no longer'.[26] Birmingham, though a humourist who delighted a large readership by dwelling on the absurdities of life, especially Irish life, was fundamentally a serious-minded man who sadly concluded early in the twentieth century that there 'was no place in Ireland nor anywhere else for the gentleman in human affairs' (in 1922 he left Ireland and settled in England).[27] About 1913 'country gentlemen of moderate fortune', it was said, were migrating to the Dublin suburbs and seeking 'occupations which would provide a living wage for a man of refinement and good traditions'.

But there was another, less dramatic side to the picture. Land purchase could leave a landlord with his house, a fair acreage (demesne and home farm) and a chunk of liquid capital. He could still enjoy sporting and social life, and when he felt an urge to participate in public life he could be active in the Unionist Alliance or attend the General Synod. It is not surprising, then, to find that in the 1912 edition of Burke's *Landed Gentry of Ireland* the head of nearly all the families included is still recorded as residing in the traditional family seat. After all it was generally agreed, at least among public-spirited men who were connected with the landed world, that once the old agrarian system had been swept away, the sometime landlords would continue to play a stimulating and valued role in rural Ireland. John Redmond, when supporting the Local Government bill of 1898 and Wyndham's Land Purchase bill, expressed the hope that there would be ex-landlords (he was about to become one himself) who would remain in their own country and take part in the management of its affairs. It would be 'monstrous', he said, if men who had an aptitude for county business were excluded on narrow sectarian or political grounds. Irish landlords, Colonel Saunderson, a leading Southern unionist, assured the House of Commons, were very anxious to live 'in our own native land ... we are Irishmen as much as the tenants are ... we love our nation as much as they do', and, far from sulking, they

---

26 G.A. Birmingham, *Irishmen All* (1913), p. 108.
27 For a short but very perceptive study of G.A. Birmingham, see R.B.D. French in *Friends of the Library of Trinity College, Dublin, Annual Bulletin*, 1955, pp. 11-16.

would readily offer themselves for election to local bodies.[28] Horace Plunkett, concerned with economic regeneration, argued that if Ireland was to become a land of small farmers, it was undoubtedly desirable to have scattered through the countryside 'a certain number of men possessed of education, wealth, leisure and the opportunity for study and travel'. The sometime landlords, living on their demesnes and home farms, could introduce improved agricultural techniques and strive to make the country culturally alive – for example as a start arranging magic lantern lectures.[29] Another country gentleman, having pointed out that the gentry were near enough to the people 'in racial sentiment to understand and sympathize with their national aspirations', but 'remote enough to command their respect', wanted the gentry to both encourage cultural activities and battle against corruption in public life – unfortunately, he wrote, politics to the average Irishman was just a game.[30] The nationalist MP Stephen Gwynn, himself of landlord stock, reflecting in 1909 that Ireland had lost half her gentry, 'a great loss'; he too wanted the gentry to play an active part in a Home Rule Ireland, though he warned them it would be a democratic Ireland and that 'they must take their chances in the ruck'.[31] An optimist could even hope that with land purchase the legitimate political influence of the resident gentry would be revived and that their ex-tenants, converted into owner-occupiers, instinctively attached to the status quo, would vote unionist. But an experienced civil servant, who knew Ireland well, warned unionists who said they found farmers in the South indifferent or even hostile to Home Rule, that they should 'make allowance for the amiable tendency of the Celt when off the platform to say what will please'.[32]

With the Wyndham Act in operation it was hoped that land would cease to be an embittering issue in Irish politics. This, however, was not the case. Though at first land purchase under the act proceeded briskly, some landlords (especially those with heavily encumbered estates) were reluctant to sell out; there were tenants,

28 *Parl. Debates*, 4 series, cxxi, 1209; cliii, 1261, 1263; cxx, 218.
29 H. Plunkett, *Noblesse Oblige* (1908), pp. 24-33.
30 S. de Vere in *Nineteenth Century and After*, lxxii, pp. 620-2, 674-5.
31 *Nineteenth Century and After*, lxxii, p. 637; lxiii, p. 179.
32 *The Times*, 11 April 1914.

probably hoping for a further reduction in rents, who hesitated to buy; and trends in the stock market made it harder to finance land purchase. The result was that land purchase slowed up, and by 1914 the process of transforming the tenants into owner-occupiers was only about two-thirds of the way to completion. There was also the problem of evicted tenants, in the words of a nationalist MP 'the wounded soldiers of the land war'; 'loafers', according to a unionist MP, who should not be benefited at the expense of honest tenants who were being denounced as 'land grabbers'.[33]

By 1914 the Estates Commissioners had managed more or less to reconcile the claims of these two categories but bitter memories festered. Then, in the post-Wyndham era, the Irish land question emerged in a new guise. While many tenants were happily purchasing their holdings, land hunger was growing among landless labourers and poor farmers on uneconomic holdings. This appetite, it was felt, might be satisfied if stretches of grazing land, let on short leases by large farmers and landlords, were acquired by compulsory purchase at what agitators considered was a fair price and divided amongst the landless. To compel ranchers to sell and deter graziers from taking lands on short leases, boycotting, cattle-driving and other forms of intimidation were employed. A number of the landowners who were the targets of agrarian agitation were unionists, and Southern unionists in general were shocked to see, in the words of James Campbell, a hard-hitting lawyer and MP, the law of the land 'paralysed' in parts of the south and west.[34] Campbell may have exaggerated, but the disturbances reinforced a basic unionist conviction, that in a country prone in the south and west to lapse into agrarian violence the unionists were consistent and courageous supporters of law and order, in contrast to the nationalists, who either tended to be passive or even to condone extra-legal behaviour – a bad augury for what would happen under Home Rule.

Strong convictions, readily and confidently expressed, were a characteristic of Southern unionists, but unfortunately a systematic exposition of their political creed was never published. In their

---

33 *Parl. Debates*, 4 series, cxxiv, 450; 4 series, x, 1429, 1450.
34 *National Review*, xlviii, p. 896.

ranks were a number of men and women of intellectual power –
Ashbourne, Atkinson, Elrington Ball, Richard Bagwell, Edward
Dowden, C.L. Falkiner, John Healy, Emily Lawless, Lecky, David
Plunket, E.O. Somerville – but in their writings and speeches they
restricted themselves to dealing with immediate issues, making
penetrating comments on the play of events but touching only
briefly on general principles. Nevertheless their political beliefs are
easily perceived and outlined. The Southern unionists profoundly
believed that the union of Great Britain and Ireland was of the
greatest value politically, economically and culturally to Irishmen.
It enabled Ireland to share in the councils, activities and thought
of three other historic communities: the English, the Scots and the
Welsh, the four nations working happily together with each preserving its distinctive qualities and traditions, the United Kingdom
demonstrating how much vigorous variety could flourish within a
common political framework. Irishmen gained immensely from
being able to participate fully in the many-sided life of the United
Kingdom.

Moreover, the United Kingdom was the keystone of a mighty
empire, 'a great worldwide bond of English-speaking men', which
meant not only 'wealth and power for England but freedom and
happiness for all that lived under the protection of the imperial
flag'.[35] Nor, as Irish unionists were quick to stress, should the Irish
contribution to Great Britain and the empire be overlooked.
Catalogues of names could be recited – soldiers, Wellington,
Wolseley, Gough, Roberts, or administrators, Wellesley, Hastings,
Mayo, or men of letters, Swift, Burke, Goldsmith. Ireland, it was
asserted, brought three valuable strains into British and imperial
life: the Celtic, with a dash of audacity, the practical and constructive Anglo-Irish intellect and the Scottish, 'more solid than brilliant'.[36] It appeared to intelligent young Southern unionists that at
the opening of the twentieth century the Anglo-Irish or the unionist element was 'the most vital creative force' in the country. To
them Irish nationalism was 'a morbid inflamation which sought to

---

35 D. Plunket, *The Conservative Government and the Future of the Empire*
(1886), p. 10.
36 J. Healy in *Ireland Today* (1913), p. 59.

reject not only British civilization but world culture and progress'.[37]

Ireland, it was continually argued, had prospered under the
union. It was better for Irishmen to be seated at Westminster than
in 'a pettyfogging assembly in which Parnellite may squabble with
anti-Parnellite over the water and gas in Skibbereen'. A vast
amount of beneficial legislation for Ireland had been passed by the
imperial parliament. 'What', a fellow of Trinity asked, 'has the
United parliament left for an Irish parliament to do?'[38] Also, an
imperial parliament and government could view Irish problems in
a broad perspective and hold the balance fairly between contend-
ing sections – a vital matter for Southern unionists, who for all
their self-assurance were a small, scattered minority.

The disadvantages of belonging to a minority, more especially a
ci-devant privileged minority, were brought sharply home to
unionists by the workings of the Local Government Act of 1898.
In 1911 it was reported that of 707 county councillors in the three
southern provinces only fifteen were unionists, and this almost
certainly meant that unionists stood a poor chance when local
government appointments were being made.[39] Of course, it could
be argued that nationalist voters could scarcely be expected to
elect as their representative an avowed unionist. As Lord Mayo
explained in the House of Lords, when he stood for a district
council 'he was told, "If you say you are a Home Ruler we will
elect you at once" and of course I said I would not have anything
to do with it.'[40] As regards local patronage Patrick Foley, the
Catholic Bishop of Kildare, approached the question in what he
obviously thought was a reasonable way. 'Until', he said, 'the balance of disadvantage which told against Catholics in the past was
fully redressed, the question of justice to all parties, on the principle that the endowments as well as the burdens of citizenship
should be evenly distributed, could not arise.'[41] Fair enough in the

---

37 L. Robinson, *Bryan Cooper* (1931), p. 89.

38 *Unionist Convention ... Report of the Proceedings* (1892), p. 154; T.E. Webb,
The Irish Question (1886), p. 45.

39 *Notes from Ireland*, 1 Jan. 1911; and see *The Times*, 2, 5 Nov. 1912.

40 *Parl. Debates* (Lords), 5 series, xiii, 716.

41 *Irish Times*, 22 Feb. 1904.

Bishop's opinion. Nevertheless the disappointed unionist applicant (in his own eyes well qualified) may well have thought it inequitable to make him pay for his putative progenitor's good fortune.

Apprehensive unionists could of course be reminded by the advocates of Home Rule that it did not repeal the Union but merely modified it. Under the bills of 1886, 1893 and 1912, Westminster and the British government would still exercise a considerable degree of influence in Irish affairs. Such a division of powers and functions, unionists retorted, would be administratively and financially almost unworkable. Moreover, unionists, especially Irish unionists, continually dwelt on a much more fundamental objection to Home Rule: that it would be merely a prelude to complete separation from Great Britain. Once an Irish parliament and an Irish executive were established in Dublin they would be continually striving for further concessions ('no man', Parnell had declared, 'had the right to fix the boundary to the march of a nation') until Ireland obtained complete independence. If Home Rulers denied this they were either deluded or intent on hoodwinking the British public.

Fervently loyal to the union and the empire, Southern unionists were at the same time very conscious that their homes were in Ireland. It was the Irish landscape, Irish streets, roads and railways and the Irish climate that provided the background for their diversified activities. Bound to Ireland by ties of friendship and family and by institutional loyalties, it was there they had their property and their careers and enjoyed a way of life that was often very tolerable. 'I hate leaving my country,' an ultra-unionist Galway landlord wrote in 1920, 'there is no country like it, if it is properly governed – I am fond of stock breeding and there is no property in the British Isles like this for it'.[42] Referring in *Hurrish* to a fictional Irish landlord, Emily Lawless remarked, 'the sense of country is a very odd possession, and in no other country is it odder than in Ireland. Soldier, landlord, Protestant, Tory of Tories as he was, Pierce O'Brien was at heart as out-and-out an Irishman as any of his tenants.'[43] These feeling are warmly expressed in some artless

---

42 Ashtown to W. Long, 5 Aug. 1920 (Long papers, 142).
43 E. Lawless, *Hurrish* (1886), i, p. 84.

verses by two members of a County Clare landed family:

> I am only a poor West Briton
> And not of the Irish best
> But I love the land of Erin
> As much as all the rest
>
> I love the blue clad highlands
> Blue rimmed with sunset low gold
> Each ruined tower recalling
> The days and scenes of old
>
> But our little western island
> Could never stand alone
> And we share the greatest empire
> That the world has ever known
>
> To Celt and Scot and Saxon
> That empire was decreed
> 'Tis guarded by Irish solders
> Who fight in Britain's need.[44]

Southern unionists were well aware that they had wider loyalties as well as Irish ties and traits, but only in very rare instances does this seem to have caused distressing emotional or intellectual tension. Strong local affections and a commitment to the United Kingdom could for Southern unionists co-exist happily enough. To them, it was said, 'Ireland was a country not a nation'.[45]

To an Irish nationalist this attitude was anomalous if not outrageous. Irishmen, nationalists asserted, shared historic memories, material interests, ideals and aspirations. Ireland therefore was a community indubitably entitled to political autonomy, and people in Ireland who did not accept this were self-proclaimed aliens. To unionists, both in Great Britain and Ireland, this was an over-simplification. Nationality was a complex compound and it should not be held as axiomatic that a community possessing a sense of nationality required for its expression political independence. There were many communities, including the Scots and the Welsh, having the 'notes' of a nationality, that were content to be included

---

44 *In Britain's Need. By the Brothers Ross-Lewin* (1917), p. 51.
45 *Bell*, ii, no.6, p. 26, John Eglinton, *Irish Literary Portraits* (1935), p. 10.

in a large sovereign state. In addition, unionists contended that Ireland was a divided country, inhabited by more than one race – the term 'race' being used to denote a group intensely conscious of its traditions and outlook – and optimistic unionists hoped the time would come 'when the enlightened intelligence of the subject race or people' would see 'the advantages of the once-hated rule' and become reconciled to it.[46]

Conscious of belonging to a distinctive, vigorous, self-assured if small community, leading Southern unionists from time to time attempted to explain tersely how they were able to harmonize their dual loyalties, attachment to Ireland and a profound belief in the value of a close union, cultural as well as political, between Ireland and Great Britain. Edward Dowden, Professor of English in Trinity, in 1886 expressed it succinctly: unionists, though friends and lovers of England, were 'not the least faithful friends and lovers of this island of our birth'.[47] Earlier, in the seventies, at the very beginning of the long struggle for the union, the eloquent John Thomas Ball, MP for Trinity and later Irish Lord Chancellor in Disraeli's second administration, answering in the House of Commons the question, 'What had Ireland gained by the union?', replied, 'a participation in your greatness, to be sharers in your glory, the opportunity of being one and the same with you'. His aim was, he said, to raise his country to the British level and to eliminate, at least in the legislative sphere, differences between the two islands. Incidentally he regarded the bulk of the population of Ireland to be, like the old Gaels, 'an enthusiastic, susceptible and credulous people'.[48] Some ten years later, in 1886, a Tipperary landowner told a unionist meeting that 'they had a special local duty to Ireland' but he 'denied that England was not their country as well'.[49]

David Plunket, who confessed himself to be an Irishman born and bred, 'all of whose traditions and recollections of happier

46 J. Atkinson, speech delivered 7 March 1895 (*Irish Unionist Alliance Publications*, iv, p. 187).

47 *Unionist Convention ...Report of Proceedings*, p. 100.

48 *Parl. Debates*, 3 series, cxcix, 1462; ccxx, 729.

49 Robert Bagwell, reported in *The Times*, 9 Jan. 1886. Probably Robert was a misprint for Richard.

times are associated and intertwined with Ireland', endeavoured to distinguish between two schools of Irish patriotism. There was the old school of Irish nationalism, with 'its passion, poetry and real self-sacrifice' but romantic and impracticable. Then there was another school of patriotism, whose adherents were no less devoted to our country and its people, which 'desires to see them preeminent and successful within the limits of an empire they have built up'. Theirs was a patriotism that saw no shame 'in submitting to a parliament and an imperial power of which it is in itself an integral element and in whose greatness it has played a glorious part'.[50] Another successful lawyer and Trinity MP also contrasted the two forms of Irish patriotism. There was, he said, the understandable patriotism that wished to see Ireland an independent nation, and there was the other form of patriotism, 'as pure and worthy but infinitely more sensible and sound', which saw no dishonour in binding Ireland to her 'greater and stronger sister'. Ireland could under the union with Great Britain enjoy her freedom, be helped by her riches and join with her in making her laws, marching forward in her progress and in upholding 'the sceptre which sways her mighty empire'.[51]

An invigorating element in the Southern unionist outlook, especially strong among landed and professional people, was a comforting sense of superiority. They adopted a *de haut en bas* attitude to their nationalist neighbours; political tact muted their comments on their Ulster fellow unionists, whom they found dour and unpolished. To Southern unionists, whose political and social centre was Dublin, Belfast seemed an upstart creation of industrial power, dull and dreary, lacking distinguished public buildings and sadly deficient in culture and *joie de vivre* – yet, it had to be granted, virile and expanding. Even the English, with whom the Southern unionist felt so closely akin, were open to criticism. The regrettable fact had to be faced that many Englishmen supported Home Rule and that there were English conservatives who were so eager to kill Home Rule by kindness that they acted on the principle

50 *Parl. Debates*, 4 series, x, 1875-7; xvi, 1625.
51 J. Atkinson, 'Our appeal to England' (*Irish Unionist Alliance Publications*, ii, p. 46).

that it was better to please your enemies than to do justice. Also, some Englishmen were sadly deficient in *savoir-faire*. For instance, in Emily Lawless's *Hurrish*, Pierce O'Brien, a Clare country gentleman, thinks an RIC inspector, son of 'a well-to-do London tradesman', to be 'consequential and underbred with a cockney accent', and Lady Naylor, in Elizabeth Bowen's *The Last September*, is struck by how shallow English people are and how hard to 'trace': 'practically nobody who lives in Surrey seems to have been heard of, and if one does hear of them they have never heard of anyone else who lives in Surrey'.[52]

Of course it could be said that Pierce O'Brien and Lady Naylor condemned the inspector and the unfortunate inhabitants of Surrey not because of their national characteristics but because they were not, to use an old phrase, out of the top drawer. Two other Cork gentlewomen, Somerville and Ross, wrote that when they came in contact with middle-class English people they learned a lesson in 'honesty, level-headedness and open mindedness',[53] but Major Yeats, an intelligent, good-natured and gentlemanly Englishman in thir *Irish R.M.* stories, is frequently baffled by the mental agility and social ingenuity of the Irish rural world, gentry and country people alike.

Southern unionists felt that, owing to circumstances, they had developed qualities that the stolid English often lacked. England's faithful garrison in Ireland, living, working and keeping on reasonably good terms with their neighbours in an acutely divided country, had learned that it was politic to take into account even absurd social susceptibilities and that authority must often be exercised with tact and good humour. 'The Englishman', a Southern unionist MP wrote, 'in a clumsy, blundering way is making the world a better place to live in .... Dogged, stupid, if you like, he is doing great work. But he lacks understanding and that is what we Irish can give him .... If we live for ourselves alone we betray our destiny.' And another fervent admirer of the Anglo-Irish explained that their open-mindedness made them ideal cosmopolitans and enabled them to add 'a useful and truly imperial

---

52 *Hurrish*, pp. 79-83; E. Bowen, *The Last September* (1948), p. 83.
53 E. Somerville and M. Ross, *Irish Memories* (1917), p. 254.

tinge to the British rule' overseas.[54] Southern unionists were very conscious that they both dwelt in the empire's heartland, the British Isles, and as members of a loyal minority were stationed on the imperial *limes*. Significantly enough, the conception of Empire Day (24 May), a day dedicated to reminding citizens of the empire of their duties and responsibilities, was for years advocated by Lord Meath, a Southern unionist peer devoted to good causes. Meath was eager that all the communities under the British flag, 'free, enlightened, loyal', should nourish 'a sane patriotism', self-sacrificing, concerned with social reform and free from any taint of jingoism. His efforts were crowned with success when the government announced in the Lords on 5 April 1916 its recognition of Empire Day.[55]

Southern unionists were exhilarated by the imperial ideal and inspired by the history of imperial expansion, which, it could be said, had begun in Ireland. The study of Irish history, to which they made a substantial contribution, reinforced their political convictions. Needless to say, their version of Irish history differed markedly from the nationalist picture of the Irish past. Nationalists dwelt with pride on Ireland's heroic and golden ages, eras preceding the Norman invasion. From the arrival of the Normans, Irish history was for nationalists a long courageous struggle against conquest, confiscation and oppression. To a unionist historian Irish people had 'a pathetic delight' in dwelling on 'the gloomy recollections of their abortive past' – 'the contemplation of their own suffering and misfortunes had a morbid attraction for them'.[56] Historians with a unionist bias when surveying Irish history from the twelfth century tended to stress the constructive work and cultural achievements of the invaders and settlers, and to stress the value of the British connection. Even Bury, whose main interests, classical and Byzantine history, were far removed from Ireland, may to some extent have been influenced by his unionist background when he wrote a life of Saint

---

54 B. Cooper, *Collar of Gold* (1920), p. 104; John Eglinton, *Anglo-Irish Essays* (1917), p. 5.
55 Lord Meath, *Memories of the Twentieth Century* (1924), pp. 75-8, 269.
56 C.L. Falkiner, *Studies in Irish History and Biography* (1902), p. 156.

Patrick. The subject attracted his attention, 'not as an important crisis in the history of Ireland but in the first place as an appendix to the history of the Roman empire'. Saint Patrick's great achievement, it seemed to Bury, was to sweep Ireland into the ambit of Roman imperialism. Six years after Bury published his life of Saint Patrick the first volume of Goddard Henry Orpen's *Ireland under the Normans* appeared. Anglo-Norman domination, Orpen concluded, had been distinctly beneficial to Ireland. When the Normans arrived Ireland was lagging far behind the more progressive European nations, and the '*Pax Normannica*' had encouraged ecclesiastical reform, agricultural advance, urban growth, trade and architecture and had undermined Celtic particularism, with its primitive legal customs. When accused by a fellow medievalist of 'not displaying more sympathy with the Gaelic element', Orpen retorted by dwelling on the Gaels' dynastic wars, 'their raids of plunder and destruction', and argued that what was termed 'the Irish resurgence' had tended not to Irish unity but to chaos and retrogression in the fifteenth century. 'Well', he added, writing in 1923, 'they have got their great deliverance now, and all I can say is "Heaven help them".'[57]

Irish history from the beginnings of the Tudor era to 1660 was surveyed by a contemporary of Orpen, Richard Bagwell, a country gentleman who was a leading member of the Irish Unionist Alliance. An assiduous worker, he aimed at marshalling the facts with a minimum of comment. His five dense volumes offer a useful introduction to a long stretch of modern Irish history and his approach, if at times colourless or flat, is certainly objective. But the thrust of his work provides the Tudor conquest and the maintenance of English authority in the seventeenth century with the justification of historical inevitability. Though Irish nationalists would have heartily agreed with his statement that the Elizabethan conquest of Ireland was cruel, they would have found it hard to stomach his explanation – that the Crown was poor, so England could not govern Ireland as she governed India, 'by scientific administrators who tolerate all

---

57 G. Orpen to E. Curtis, 19 March 1923 (Curtis papers, TCD MS 2452). For Orpen's loyalty to the Irish landed gentry, see Orpen to Curtis 19 May 1921 and G.H. Orpen, *The Orpen Family* (1930), p. 190.

creeds and respect all prejudices'. Moreover his historical work (and his political experience) convinced him that 'Ireland has always suffered and suffers sorely from want of firmness'.[58]

Lecky, an Irish landlord and an outstanding historian, was a unionist, but his *History of Ireland in the Eighteenth Century* (1892) was marked by the qualities for which he was so widely and rightly admired: clarity, fair-mindedness and a consistent determination to comprehend and expound sympathetically the arguments of the supporters and the opponents of the union. However, in the last few pages of the work he abruptly changes gear, when he starts to discuss the unfavourable circumstances in which that 'great experiment', the union, had operated in the nineteenth century. The conciliatory measures that should have accompanied it had been delayed; Irish economic conditions until mid-century had been bad; the financial arrangements had seemed unfair, though recently the imperial parliament had placed 'the unrivalled credit of the empire' at Ireland's disposal; agrarian agitation and conspiracy had been rife; and finally, owing to the application to Ireland of the fashionable theory of democracy, the Irish unionists, comprising 'the great bulk of the property and the higher education of the country, the large majority of those who take any leading part in social, industrial and philanthropic enterprise', were in three provinces virtually disfranchised. In short, nineteenth-century Irish history taught 'the folly of conferring power where it is certain to be misused and of weakening those great pillars of social order on which all real progress ultimately depended'. Still all was not lost, there were strong forces working for the union. Belfast and the surrounding areas had progressed amazingly and in industrial development had reached 'the full level of Great Britain'; the country in general was growing more prosperous, a multiplicity of relationships – commercial, financial and social – were drawing Great Britain and Ireland closer together, and it was clear that 'the whole course and tendency of European politics is towards the unification and not the division of states'.

Strange as it may seem, Lecky came under fire from another Irish unionist, Dunbar Ingram, for being 'one of the anti-English

58 *Ireland under the Tudors*, i, preface, pp. ix-xi.

school'. Ingram, a man of considerable learning, after practising at the bar in England and India and holding a professorship in India, settled in Dublin and devoted himself to writing Irish history. An instinctive polemicist, he believed history properly deployed strengthened the unionist case. He dismissed Grattan's parliament as 'the most worthless and incompetent assembly that ever governed a country'. The union, he asserted, had given 'emancipation to the Roman Catholic, a poor law to the starving, education to the needy, medical assistance to all and a land code more favourable to their industry than that of any other country in the world'. For good measure he added that every blessing the Irishman enjoyed, 'save his religion, his bodily conformation, his soil and his climate', was the gift of England or Great Britain.[59]

A generation younger than Lecky, Caesar Litton Falkiner thought that 'the study of Irish history is a signal lesson in charity to all Irishmen'.[60] A unionist parliamentary candidate in an almost hopeless constituency (South Armagh) and an energetic member of the Unionist Alliance, as an historian he was balanced, lucid and lively, with a lightness of touch and a caustic turn of phrase. His interests were wide – political history, biography, topography, and parliamentary, social and administrative history – and the steady stream of essays and articles that flowed from his pen suggest that but for his untimely death he might have been one of the most distinguished historians of his day. He was especially interested in the activities and achievements of the eighteenth-century Irish ruling world and in the development of English institutions in Ireland, including its cities and towns. Most Irish towns, he pointed out, owed their origin to the Saxon invader, and he noted the significance of the fact that 'the succession of the viceroys is embalmed in the names of the principal streets of the Irish capital'.[61] A convinced unionist, he had a melancholy awareness that 'the descendants of the Catholic and Celtic elements' in Ireland remained 'inveterately opposed' to the British connection.[62] But at the opening of the twen-

---

59 T.D. Ingram, *A Critical Examination of Irish History* (1904), pp. 13-14, 298, 310.
60 *Studies in Irish History*, p. vi.
61 *Essays relating to Ireland* (1909), pp. 160, 186.
62 *Studies in Irish History*, p. 56.

tieth century he saw that several currents in Irish life were tending to weaken antagonism to the union.[63] Falkiner's exact contemporary and close friend Francis Elrington Ball was also an unsuccessful unionist candidate and was for a time secretary of the Irish Unionist Alliance. To Ball, 'Irish history was the history of the English in Ireland and of the civilization they had brought into that country',[64] and *con amore*, he produced an erudite edition of Swift's correspondence and a history of the judges of the superior courts, 'during the seven centuries when the authority of England was absolute in their appointment'. Having 'devoted the best years of my life to the defence of the legislative union',[65] in 1918 he left Dublin to reside in London, remarking a few years later that 'the destruction of the Record Office has broken my last ties with Ireland'.[66]

The nineties, a decade that for Irish unionists was marked by the resounding defeat of the second Home Rule bill, witnessed the beginnings of the Irish Renaissance, an extraordinary florescence of Irish letters – poetry, fiction and drama. Some of those who participated in the movement were not keenly interested in politics, others were idiosyncratic in their approach and some of those active in contemporary Irish intellectual life were unionists. Still, the Renaissance on the whole was bound to have an invigorating effect on Irish nationalism. Its leaders wrote on Irish themes: 'we would create nothing', Synge said, 'if we did not give all our thoughts to Ireland'.[67] Men of letters, caught up in the movement, strove to comprehend and explain Ireland and 'Irishness', minting epigrams and playing with paradox in their endeavours to discover the essence of the Irish being. This emphasis on Ireland's distinctive characteristics and on Ireland's outstanding contribution to civilization inevitably reinforced the demand for political independence. A well-known playwright declared, '*Cathleen ni Houlihan* and the *Rising of the Moon* made more rebels in Ireland than a thousand platform speeches and a hundred reasoned books.'[68]

---

63 *Edinburgh Review*, cxcii, p. 75.
64 See *DNB* notice on Ball.
65 *The Judges in Ireland 1221-1921* (1927), i, p. xxii.
66 F.E. Ball to Lawlor (Lawlor papers), n.d.
67 W.B. Yeats, *Essays* (1961), p. 320.
68 L. Robinson, *Curtain Up* (1942), p. 17.

One outstanding Irish man of letters, Edward Dowden, stood aloof from these developments. Dowden, Professor of English in Trinity, was a man with vast stores of literary knowledge who expressed himself with readable ease. His reputation was firmly based on his Shakespearian studies and a great life of Shelley but he wrote with understanding, sympathy and 'sanity' on an astonishing wide range of authors, European and American. Tall and bearded, with gravitas but not heavy, he was the quintessence of the eminent Victorian, high-minded and intensely interested in the flow and flux of thought, a man to whom the devoted study of literature was a pilgrimage to truth. Possibly a critic inspecting the corpus of his work would assume that Dowden practised a cloistered virtue. He would be wrong. Amongst Dowden's distinctions recorded in *Who's Who*, sandwiched between his presidency of the English Goethe Society and his membership of the Deutsche Shakespeare Gesellschaft, was his presidency of the Irish Unionist Alliance. All Dowden's 'combative instincts', a former pupil, John Eglinton, wrote, 'were aroused on behalf of the union, which had given him what Swift, Goldsmith, Berkeley never really felt that they possessed, a country'. Dowden, his pupil explained, was convinced that Ireland, by 'a luminous filling up of a hitherto blank space' would have a glorious opportunity of 'realising in these islands the perfect entelechy of an ideal for which he was ready to accept the name "English"'.[69]

A unionist, an imperialist and a liberal, Dowden was eager that the maintenance of the union should be supplemented by land purchase and local government reform; and in 1899 he was strongly in favour of measures that would 'settle once for all our mastery in South Africa'.[70] An assiduous committee man, he worked extremely hard for the Alliance; in January 1907, for instance, he was 'hammering away at unionist work' after writing articles on Elizabethan psychology and on Ibsen.[71] He persuaded the Provost, Salmon, to attend the great Dublin unionist demonstration of 1892 – Salmon had been hesitant, afraid that his attendance

---

69 John Eglinton, *Irish Literary Portraits* (1935), pp. 79-82.
70 *Letters* (1914), pp. 264-5.
71 *Letters*, p. 347.

might 'injure our centenary prospects'.[72] Dowden also edited
Songs for Unionists. When he was discussing that project with
Kipling the latter remarked, 'we need drilling a damned sight more
than doggerel'. Dowden's reply was that 'the two were not incompatible'.[73] It is scarcely surprising then that Carson looked forward to Dowden joining him at Westminster as one of the university members.[74]

In May 1886, after making a forceful speech at a unionist
meeting in the Rotunda – 'an impressive spectacle, so large and
heated a mass of human creatures' – Dowden attempted to analyse
his attitude to Irish politics. 'It is true,' he wrote, 'politics don't
penetrate to my individual centre of life, but I can throw myself
into a side which seems to me the right one for a while as if I were
a politician – and in fact I take a considerable interest in the maintenance of the union for I feel our moral and intellectual isolation
and provinciality would be increased by its repeal. I have no doubt
that it would precipitate a struggle between ultramontanism and
spiritual anarchy which would tend to efface the *mi-parti* in which
I think truth and wisdom chiefly reside.'[75]

It was the same quick reaction against provinciality which
influenced his attitude at the close of the century to the new tendencies in Irish literature. Willing to acknowledge that 'our
strength springs from the soil from which we grow', he immediately added that 'the spirit of man may inhabit an ampler space than
that in which his body lives and moves'. To him English, Scotch,
Welsh and Irish literature formed a unity, with each of the four
countries making its distinctive contribution. But though variety
was definitely desirable, no attempt should be made to 'whip up
deliberately and by artificial means the national spirit in literature.
Rather let Irishmen be eager to keep their country in close touch
with all currents of thought.'[76]

---

72 G. Salmon to E. Dowden, 9 June 1892 (Dowden Papers).
73 *Fragments from Old Letters* (1914), p. 383.
74 E. Carson to E. Dowden, 30 April 1890 and undated (Dowden papers, 964, 1199).
75 *Fragments*, p. 181.
76 *New Studies in Literature* (1902), preface. George Moore, in his nationalist phase, after meeting Dowden remarked that he was a TCD man 'who conceived

Dowden's approach to Irish letters was reflected for years in the writings of his pupils, William Kirkpatrick Magee (John Eglinton) and John Healy, the editor of the *Irish Times*. Just after Dowden's death in 1913, the *Irish Times*, while granting that Ireland was 'pulsating with intellectual activity', complained that 'we take ourselves and our new movements too seriously' and that 'our gloomy enthusiasts' shut themselves up within the four walls of Ireland. Few of the old school survived, and Trinity sheltered most of them. It was essential, the *Irish Times* asserted, to give our young men a broad and generous outlook.77 A year later the *Irish Times* indicated its own breadth of outlook by publishing a review of Lady Gregory's *The Irish Theatre*, in which it judiciously pronounced that 'the founders of the theatre have done a big thing even if it were not so big as some of their fulsome admirers would have us believe', along with a lengthy, enthusiastic review of Lord Mayo's *History of the Kildare Hunt*.78

John Eglinton, unlike Dowden, was according to himself 'a political agnostic', and as a civil servant (in the National Library) he was debarred from political activity. But as he took his opinions from the *Irish Times*, denounced Sinn Féin as 'warped intellectually and tinged with obscurantism', praised (in 1920) the Ulster plantation as 'an adventurous and fruitful enterprise', and after the Treaty of 1921 went into 'self-imposed' exile in Great Britain, he may be regarded as a unionist.79 Convinced that literature, far from being the product of nationality, was an individual response to life, an expression of character and temperament, he was quietly dismissive of efforts to root modern Irish literature in the Celtic Gaelic past.80 Yeats and A.E., he said, were not capable of mastering Old Irish and soon found the symbolic value of Irish legend to be less than they had expected.81 Eglinton, convinced that in the seventeenth century the 'centre of gravity' of Irish nationality had

---

Ireland as a distant English province' (*Letters of George Moore*, ed. J. Eglinton [1942], p. 85).

77 *Irish Times*, 5 April 1913.

78 *Irish Times*, 6 Feb. 1914.

79 *Irish Statesman*, 1919, pp. 61, 648; 1920, p. 493; *The Times*, 11, 17 May 1961.

80 *Literary Ideals in Ireland* (1899), p. 11; *Irish Statesman*, 1919, pp. 13, 121.

81 *Confidential* (1951), p. 7.

passed from the old Irish race to the Anglo-Irish, was proud to be a modern Irishman or Anglo-Irishman. He exhorted the Anglo-Irish world to assert its distinctiveness and to remember the achievements of its own heroes Ormonde, Molyneux, Berkeley, Grattan and even Parnell.[82] Incidentally, he was disturbed to see that Trinity College and Protestant society in general were 'left out of the account altogether' in what 'the new world' of James Joyce and Eimar O'Duffy 'calls Ireland'. The idea that England and Ireland were bound closely together by eight centuries of history, Eglinton judged, was repugnant to these young men.[83]

In their different ways, Eglinton thought, Bernard Shaw, an Irishman who adopted England as his country, and Swift, an Anglo-Irishman who chose Ireland, suggested that there was little real 'race' distinction between the two countries.[84] His own country, he once wrote, was 'an indeterminate region, taking in the English lakes, with bits of Scotland and Wales, in the midst of these was set Ireland'.[85] Though in 1917 he asserted that the 'Modern Irishman', while accepting the British connection, felt himself to be 'far more distinct from the Anglo-Saxon than he is from the mere Irishman', twenty years later he had come to the conclusion that it was possible to be a good Irishman and 'yet not to feel in oneself a much greater difference from an Englishman than an Englishman of Lancashire feels from one of Devon'.[86]

Since most Irish writers were to some extent influenced by English, European and classical literature, trying to distinguish their 'Irishness' from these outside currents of thought and their own, often very powerful, individuality, is a difficult and thankless task. However, Dowden and his disciples provided, for those Southern unionists who wanted it, an approach to English and Irish literature that accorded with their political presuppositions and enabled them to take a possessory pride in and enjoy Yeats and Synge, Hardy and Kipling, Lady Gregory's plays and Gilbert and Sullivan.

---

82 *Irish Statesman*, 1920, pp. 37, 445; *Anglo-Irish Essays*.
83 *Irish Statesman*, 1920, p. 253.
84 *Irish Statesman*, 1920, p. 469.
85 *Confidential*, p. 8.
86 *Memoir of AE* (1937), p. 97.

One facet of the Renaissance, the Gaelic revival, had considerable political significance. From early in the nineteenth century the Irish language had been steadily declining, and by 1900 only 14 per cent of the population, mainly concentrated in poor areas in the south and west, was Irish speaking. But the foundation of the Gaelic League, a popular movement with many branches, marked the beginning of a crusade to turn the linguistic tide. Supporters of the League emphasized that Irish, a rich, subtle and beautiful tongue, with a literary tradition strong in legend and poetry, enabled present-day Irishmen to share the ideals and emotions of their ancestors, preserving the continuity of a race that, it was pointed out, 'once held possession of more than half Europe'.[87] It also was the language through which Irishmen could best express themselves. It accorded with the patterns of Irish thought and feeling. The use of English, it was said, was bound to paralyse the Irish mind and weaken Irish spirituality. But a Gaelic-speaking Ireland would be at ease with itself and abounding in creative power. Theoretically the movement was non-political and a unionist could be a Gaelic Leaguer (presumably being able to put his case more eloquently in his native tongue). But the members of the League were overwhelmingly nationalist and Catholic, and even those nationalists whose knowledge of Irish was scanty must have realized that Ireland's claim to political autonomy would be greatly strengthened if it was in the process of becoming a Gaelic-speaking country with a distinctive Gaelic culture. 'Most of all the Irish language', an enthusiast wrote, 'is one of the things which distinguishes us from England. It is a mark of the separateness which it is the business of every nationalist to maintain and to emphasise on every possible occasion.'[88] To those striving for the revival of Irish, the enemy, the dry rot in Irish cultural life,[89] was anglicization, and almost inevitably their efforts to spread the use of Irish was accompanied by strident attacks on English manners, modes and morals. England, the author of a pamphlet published by the Gaelic League declared, had 'a mind without God ... it is a fleshly spirit bent

---

87 Douglas Hyde, address to the Irish Literary Society: E. Curtis and R.B. McDowell, *Irish Historical Documents* (1943), pp. 310-13.

88 *Irish Statesman*, 1919, p. 273; *Irish Review*, iii, p. 216.

89 Gaelic League pamphlets (U.C.D., MSS department), pamphlet 35.

towards earth, a mind unmannerly, vulgar, insolent and bigoted'.[90] Gaelic Leaguers, as they struggled to master Irish grammar and acquire a vocabulary, were convinced that they were helping to restore a vital, vigorous civilization and could feel an intense sense of cultural and moral superiority over alien peers and landowners and those Irishmen of all classes, shoneens, snobs and West Britons, who slavishly and meanly admired English ways (including music-hall songs, popular magazines and cheap newspapers).[91]

To a leading unionist, the aim of the Gaelic League seemed to be 'as much to foster hatred of England and all things English as to foster love of Ireland', and Caesar Litton Falkiner remarked that the League at times was 'more concerned with politics than philology'.[92] Falkiner himself sympathized with those who were trying to preserve Irish as a spoken language in the areas where it survived, but he did not think that its revival in districts where it had died out would be 'productive of any national benefit'. Another Southern unionist, a distinguished Celtic scholar, condemned the language movement as divisive. 'It laid bare', he wrote, 'the conflict of races which lies at the bottom of all Irish questions ... deepens the old division between native and settler – invigorates the old antagonism to all institutions and habits of English origin ... and awakens in the Irish Protestant the consciousness of his Anglo-Saxon descent.' He admitted that a few Protestants had been attracted to the movement out of intellectual curiosity, or sympathy with an ancient civilization or because they found in Gaelic Ireland 'a piquant contrast to the formal traditions of the English public school'.[93] Those unionists who might have been alarmed by the assertiveness of the Gaelic League were reassured by the *Irish Times*, which pointed out that if since the Tower of Babel mankind had been afflicted by a diversity of tongues, the trend of modern progress was towards the spread of the larger languages at the expense of the smaller.[94]

---

90 Gaelic League pamphlets, pamphlet 24.
91 For the views of a fervent supporter of the revival stated with uncompromising force, see D.P. Moran, *The Psychology of Irish Ireland* (1908).
92 *National Review*, xliv, p. 380; *Edinburgh Review*, cxc, p. 80.
93 E. Gwynn in *Ireland Today* (1913), pp. 138-46.
94 *Irish Times*, 18 March 1905.

11 The Mobilization of a Minority

THE SOUTHERN UNIONISTS were held together by a number of organizations. In the political sphere the most outstanding was the Irish Unionist Alliance, founded in 1886 as the Loyal and Patriotic Union, changing its name in the early nineties. The Alliance had constituency, later replaced by county, branches, and local branches, of which there were about 220 in 1900. The county branches elected a General Council and there was an Executive Committee, composed of the president, the vice-presidents, forty members elected by the General Council and thirty co-opted members.[1] The Alliance collected information from all over Ireland, and published a large number of short pamphlets and leaflets on the Irish situation, composed largely of quotations from nationalist speeches and writings with pungent comment. In 1909 it published a work of two hundred pages on the Home Rule question. When the 1893 Home Rule bill was being debated the Alliance distributed two million leaflets and arranged five hundred meetings in Great Britain. In the 1895 general election it distributed seven million leaflets.[2] When the 1912 Home Rule bill was introduced the Alliance took an office in Manchester and had 'missionaries' touring England. It may be added that at least one local branch – the Gorey branch, with 320 members – sent Irish unionist newspapers to England and supported financially the Alliance's intervention in English by-elections, 'as one of the best ways of educating the electorate on the Irish question'.[3] The

---

1 Annual report of the Irish Unionist Alliance, 1904 (D 989/8/3/38), and List of Branches, D 989/A/5/1.

2 *Irish Unionist Alliance Publications*, vii, leaflet 83; *National Review*, xliv, p. 375.

3 For the Gorey branch records, see Courtown papers, TCD MSS 238-9, and Unionist Alliance papers, D 989/A/8/2/27, 31.

Alliance was an all-Ireland body, but as its headquarters was in Dublin and the Ulster unionists from 1905 had their own powerful representative body, the Ulster Unionist Council, the Alliance came more and more to speak for Southern unionism.

There were also in the twenty-six counties eighty Orange Lodges, including thirty-eight in the three Ulster counties and ten, together with the Trinity Lodge, in Dublin. The order, Protestant and conservative, provided its members with political inspiration and social life. It manifested itself in the twenty-six counties in the border areas (Cavan, Monaghan and Donegal) by colourful parades on 12 July. A distinguished Oxford classical scholar, born in County Cavan, described one of these demonstrations on the Cavan-Leitrim border affectionately, and after referring to 'the Dorian and Phrygian moods of drums and fifes and brazen instruments', pronounced that 'anything deserves to be kept alive which tends to isolate the stronger race and prevent it being absorbed'.[4]

In Dublin there were the City and County Conservative Club (providing some club facilities) in Dawson Street, and the Dublin Constitutional Club and the City of Dublin Unionist Registration Association, both concerned with the registration of electors and both having premises in 10 Leinster Street. The same building also housed the Dublin Women's Unionist club, an active body, with 3000 members in 1914. (Incidentally, early in 1905 Mrs Dockrell, whose husband was later to be a unionist MP, was a candidate for the chairmanship of the Blackrock urban council. On another unionist being elected, she declared, 'it is not party … it is sex prejudice'.[5]) There was also the Unionist Association in Grafton Street, which kept in touch with the Ulster Unionist Council. Finally there was the City and County of Dublin Conservative Working Men's Club, founded in 1883, whose membership embraced many middle-class men, a fair number of clerks, civil servants, a commercial traveller, and a dentist. It provided its members with the amenities of club life, concerts and political lectures and, most important of all, took considerable trouble over the registration of electors.[6]

---

4 *Report of the Grand Lodge of Ireland*, December 1914 (1915); A.D. Godley, *Reliquae* (1926), ii, pp. 15-25.
5 *Daily Express*, 4 Jan. 1905, 1 Apr. 1914.
6 City and County of Dublin Conservative Working Men's Club Minutes.

There was a large and zealous unionist newspaper press. In Dublin there were *The Irish Times*, the *Dublin Daily Express* and *The Evening Mail*. The *Irish Times* (founded in 1859) aspired with some success to be the Irish equivalent of *The Times* – providing for its readers a broad coverage of United Kingdom and foreign affairs, finance, sport and literature. Its first editor was a classical scholar and this was reflected in the tone of its editorials, which with Olympian dignity and apparent detachment vigorously expounded unionist orthodoxy. The *Daily Express*, 'Protestant and constitutional', declared that its mission was 'to promote loyalty and peace in Ireland, to maintain the imperial connection, to cultivate a cordial and friendly intercourse with Great Britain and to give a practical tone and direction to the national sentiment'. *The Cork Constitution*, which 'circulated amongst the nobility, the gentry, landed proprietors and mercantile classes', forcefully advocated the unionist cause in the South, and scattered throughout the twenty-six counties there were about twenty local weekly or bi-weekly newspapers, mainly filled with local news and advertisements, that proudly claimed to be upholding the conservative or unionist cause.[7]

In addition to the unionist organizations that have been mentioned there were a number of institutions, ostensibly non-political but overwhelmingly unionist in membership, that bound Southern unionists together, giving them companionship, cohesion and confidence. These included the Irish Landowners Convention, founded in 1887 to defend the interests of landlords when land purchase was being debated; the Church of Ireland, with its general synod, diocesan synods and its rectories, nearly always diffusing an air of gentility; the other Protestant Churches; the Masonic order, with its awesome rituals, its charities and social dinners; three leading Dublin clubs; the country clubs; a number of sporting clubs; the Protestant schools; and Trinity College. In fact a Southern unionist when not at work could spend almost all his time with those who shared his opinions and prejudices.

Trinity College, 'the college of the Anglo-Irish breed', according to a provost, 'the one really successful English institution in

---

7 *Newspaper Press Directory*, 1914.

Ireland',[8] with its squares and park in the very centre of Dublin, prided itself on its traditions and achievements. A critic might suggest that pride could easily develop into complacency, but at the time of its tercentenary in 1892 the College had much to be complacent about: a galaxy of brilliant scholars on its staff, a long list of famous graduates (often readily recited) and an excellent reputation for teaching and research. The medical school was associated with the great names of Graves and Stokes; the College had close links with the Irish bar (in 1914 of the fourteen high court and appeal court judges ten were Trinity graduates) and the Divinity school supplied the Church of Ireland with most of its clergy (in 1914 of the eleven bishops ten were Trinity graduates). Life *intra muros* was full and vigorous and Trinity dons and undergraduates could participate in the varied activities of a lively city. It is, then, scarcely surprising that Trinity men and (from 1904) women were passionately loyal to the College. The College itself was fervently unionist. It had been founded as an Anglican and anglicizing institution; now it prided itself on being open to all creeds at a time when the Catholic Church was emphasizing that for Catholics education at all levels should be strongly influenced by Catholic doctrine. The College had officially declared its opposition to the Home Rule bills of 1886 and 1893, and in 1885 the then provost, J.H. Jellett, a man in his seventies, had set an example by going down to Cork to vote against a Home Rule candidate.[9]

The university MPs were always unionists. The ten men who sat for the university constituency between 1880 and 1918 included two unionist cabinet ministers, a unionist solicitor-general for England (Carson) who was to be a member of the War Cabinet, and Lecky, one of the leading unionist intellectuals. Many of the graduates worked in England or joined the imperial services; those who remained in Ireland were often leading local unionists. As for the undergraduates drawn largely from the Irish unionist world, they tended to be exuberantly unionist, for instance on the occasion of Joseph Chamberlain's visit to Trinity in Black Week to receive an honorary degree, a party of undergraduates seized the

8 *Ireland Today*, p. 59; *National Review*, xxix, p. 404.
9 *The Times*, 9 Jan. 1886.

green flag floating over the Mansion House and tore it to pieces. Meanwhile the older generation seated in the Public Theatre, applauded loudly when they detected amongst the public orator's polished Latin phrases a reference to Chamberlain's consistent support of the union.[10]

When the Home Rule bill of 1912 was introduced Trinity did not pronounce officially on the measure. It might have been felt that it was unnecessary to do so – the two sitting MPs, both unionist, had been returned unopposed in 1910. Moreover, there might have been a growing sense that academic detachment (a fashionable concept) dictated that the College as an institution should abstain from intervening in politics, though its members of course could hold and express strong views. When the bill was in committee, James Campbell, one of the Trinity MPs, proposed at the request of the senior fellows that Trinity College should be exempted from the jurisdiction of the impending Irish parliament. But even strong unionists felt that an extra-territorial status for the College would have been a standing provocation to an Irish parliament sitting on the other side of College Green and, given that the Irish executive would be in nationalist hands, an ineffective safeguard. The Board (apparently reluctant to oppose Campbell) approved of his proposal by nine votes to two with one abstention. Eight junior fellows promptly signed a letter against the amendment and a meeting of fellows and professors rejected Campbell's proposal by twenty-four votes to thirteen.[11] A compromise was reached. It was provided in the bill by general agreement that the property and constitutions of Trinity College and the Queen's University of Belfast should not be interfered with by the Irish parliament without the consent of the institution concerned. It would be a mistake to assume that the opposition in Trinity to Campbell's amendment implied that the College's unionism was weakening. But it does suggest that there were those in Trinity who were beginning to accept reluctantly that Home Rule was a distinct possibility and that they must consider realistically how the College, by adapting itself to changing circumstances, could continue to flourish in a Home Rule Ireland.

---

10 *The Times*, 19 Dec. 1899.
11 *The Times*, 23, 25, 28 Oct., 12 Nov. 1912.

Though socially influential, the Southern unionists were electorally weak. From 1886 to 1918 they were never able to return more than two MPs – in addition to the Trinity representatives, who will not be taken into account in what follows. In 1886 the Southern unionists fielded eleven candidates and failed to obtain a seat, though two liberal unionists, Sir Edward Sullivan, a Dante scholar and bibliophile, and J.T. Pim, a poplin manufacturer, fared reasonably well in the St Stephen's Green division of Dublin and South County Dublin (which included the prosperous suburbs) respectively; and in North Monaghan Sir John Leslie of Glaslough secured nearly 40 per cent of the vote. In 1892, encouraged by the success of Salisbury's government in combining firmness with remedial legislation and the Parnellite split, the Southern unionists fought no fewer than thirty-four seats but won only two – St Stephen's Green and South County Dublin, the successful candidates being William Kenny, a Catholic barrister standing as a liberal unionist, and Horace Plunkett, the fervent advocate of agricultural co-operation. In the 1895 general election, though they fought fourteen constituencies the unionists only retained the two seats they had won three years earlier. By the next general election, 1900, Irish unionists were apathetic or highly critical of a unionist government that seemed to them over-eager to conciliate nationalist opinion. They were especially irritated by the highly intelligent and idiosyncratic Plunkett, who had been appointed vice-president of the newly created Department of Agriculture and Technical Instruction. Plunkett, who was progressing from being a unionist to a very moderate nationalism, had appointed as secretary of the department T.P. Gill, who ten years earlier had played a leading part in the Plan of Campaign, in the opinion of unionists an outrageous defiance of law and order. Plunkett had also, his detractors declared, been insufficiently emphatic in supporting the government's South African policy. As a result an independent unionist candidate, the historian Francis Elrington Ball, stood against Plunkett in South Dublin. 'Electioneering', it was said, 'was outside the scope of his abilities'[12] and he received only 1500 votes to 2800 for Plunkett, the result being that a nationalist with

12 *The Times*, 9 Jan. 1928.

only 3660 votes captured the seat. The Nationalists also secured the St Stephen's Green division, defeating J.H. Campbell QC, who had succeeded Kenny in 1898.[13] As a slight compensation for these losses the unionists at a by-election won Galway city by a slender majority, their candidate being Martin Morris, member of an old Galway family and the son of a very popular judge. During the next few years Irish unionist disillusionment with the Conservative government deepened and in January 1906 the Southern unionists contested only three seats: two in Dublin city, neither of which was won, and one in South County Dublin for which Walter Long, a Chief Secretary, who in contrast to his colleagues had won the approval of Irish unionists, was returned. In January 1910 the Southern unionists fought five seats – South County Dublin, East Donegal, North Monaghan and two in Dublin city. They won only South County Dublin, where Bryan Cooper, a Sligo country gentleman, had a majority of sixty-six in a total poll of ten thousand. December 1910 was disastrous for the Southern unionists. They fought four seats – St Stephen's Green (Dublin), South County Dublin, North Monaghan, East Wicklow and gained none, though Cooper was defeated by only sixty-seven on a poll of over ten thousand and Lord Herbert won about 45 per cent of the vote in the St Stephen's Green division. Thus from 1910 to 1918, during a series of momentous debates on Irish policy, the Southern unionists were represented at Westminster by only the two Trinity MPs, one of whom (Carson) was from 1911 closely identified with the Ulster unionist cause. But the Ulster unionist MPs were ready to draw attention to Southern unionist grievances, and four of them, who were members of the Irish bar, had homes in Dublin.

There were also some British MPs who had strong links with Southern Ireland: Wilfred Ashley, a conservative whip who had inherited the Palmerston estate in the west of Ireland; Lord Kerry, a soldier and author, prevented by 'a certain constitutional delicacy' from attaining the place in public life which his abilities warranted;[14]

---

13 See A. Jackson, 'The Failure of Unionism in Dublin 1900' in *IHS* xxvi, pp. 377-95.

14 *The Times*, 7 March 1936.

Pretyman Newman, a County Cork landowner, who sat for a Middlesex constituency; Edward Goulding, an influential back-bencher; J.G. Butcher, the son of a Bishop of Meath, a successful barrister, 'an uncompromising tory', a man of rigid principle, 'too stiff, too insensitive' to adapt himself to changing circumstances;[15] and two sons of the first Lord Iveagh, Rupert and Walter Guinness. The elder brother took little part in debate but Walter Guinness, later a cabinet minister, with a lucid mind 'tragically free from illusions',[16] between 1908 and 1922 paid close attention to Irish politics.

In the House of Lords the Southern unionists were much better represented. In 1914 sixty-eight of its members who described themselves as conservatives or liberal unionists had a residence in the twenty-six counties. A few of them – Devonshire, Fitzwilliam, Lansdowne, Midleton – certainly had their main residence in England, and Lansdowne, as leader of the opposition in the Lords, was bound to be somewhat detached from the Irish unionist peers. On the other hand Atkinson and Rathmore (David Plunket), who now resided in England, had in the past been active Southern unionists. Self-assured and unconstrained by constituents, a num-ber of the Irish peers expressed with candour and individuality their views on Irish problems, and in a chamber where the conserv-atives predominated they were assured of a sympathetic audience. From about 1914 the Southern unionists' principal spokesman in the Lords was Lord Midleton. With a strong sense of duty, he was, according to the critical Lady Oxford and Asquith, a loyal friend and one of those rare people who always tell the truth – another contemporary rated him as remarkably tactless. Outspoken, with, he believed, an awareness of political realities derived from years of parliamentary and official life (he had been a cabinet minister for five years), he could at times display an irritable and nagging impatience with those – Irish unionists or British cabinet ministers – who had not the sense to agree with him.[17] Devoting a considerable

---

15 *The Times*, 1 July 1935.
16 *The Times*, 16 Nov. 1944.
17 *The Times*, 16 Feb. 1942; *The Crawford Papers*, ed. J. Vincent (1984), pp. 75, 104, 137, 276, 393.

amount of time and thought to Ireland, he scarcely realized that as an intermittent, if fairly frequent visitor, he might fail to appreciate subtle but significant changes in the Irish situation.

Powerful, self-assured and occupying commanding ground in economic and social life, Irish unionists, especially in the south and west, were bound to feel apprehensive when they contemplated the changing balance of forces in Ireland. Disestablishment and the agrarian revolution had demonstrated how well-planned efforts could bring down pillars of the temple, and with the democratization of local government unionists believed they were getting a foretaste of what would happen under Home Rule. The nationalist leadership was skilled in the arts of manoeuvre and propaganda and the Irish Parliamentary Party, reunited in 1900, had the backing of the nationwide National League, with its local branches which, unionists believed, could exercise considerable coercive pressure at the parochial level. The National League was reinforced by the Ancient Order of Hibernians, a popular benefit society. According to an ultra-unionist peer, the 'Hibernians' were the most recent manifestation of a prolonged and determined effort to drive the English government out of Ireland that had expressed itself in the past through the Whiteboys, the Defenders, the Ribbonmen and the Molly Maguires. Though the historical case for continuity between all these movements may be faulty, the Ancient Order of Hibernians was undoubtedly fervently Catholic and nationalist – and very efficiently organized.[18]

Not only were Irish nationalists politically well-organized but they were, in the eyes of apprehensive unionists, closely allied with the Catholic Church, with its masterful hierarchy, large clerical army and devoted laity, a most powerful and pervasive force in Ireland. Its vitality and vigour were manifested in numerous directions by many associations and societies, parochial, religious, educational and charitable, and by hundreds of impressive buildings, neo-Gothic cathedrals, parish churches, monasteries, seminaries and convents and schools. Even a severe critic would have to admit that Irish Catholicism in the post-Vatican I era, untroubled by doctrinal doubts and difficulties, was characterized by the zeal

---

18 [Lord Ashtown], *The Unknown Power behind the Irish Nationalist Party* (1907).

of its clergy, the loyalty of its laity, and the sustaining piety of many of its members. Protestants, of course, considered it had unattractive features. It seemed to them that Irish Catholicism was aggressive and obscurantist. Catholic ecclesiastics were avaricious and power-hungry, ready to work hand in hand with time-serving local politicians. To unionists the Catholic Church appeared a potent force in the drive for Home Rule. Admittedly the hierarchy would not subordinate the interests of the Church to those of the nationalist party, and Irish nationalists at times resented and resisted ecclesiastical domination. But many Catholic clergymen were active in the Home Rule movement and most nationalists assumed that their religion and their patriotism went together.

At the beginning of the twentieth century some Southern Protestants viewed with alarm the claims of the Church to regulate the rules of marriage for its members and to control Catholic educational policy – claims which might, if they were respected by a Home Rule government, affect Irishmen who were not Catholics. For instance, Trinity College might be reduced to being a small, sectarian institution. The dangers that unionists feared they faced were illustrated at the very beginning of the twentieth century on an immediate and mundane level by the noisily advertised programme and activities of the Catholic Association, a body of laymen based in Dublin with branches elsewhere. Pointing to the disproportionate share of power and patronage possessed by Protestants in Irish business and professional life, the Association called on Catholics to tackle 'the bigotry question' by giving their custom, when possible, to fellow Catholics (or *faut de mieux* to liberal Protestants). 'When there is a question between the Gael and the Pale, give the Gael every chance you can.' The Association conceived itself to be involved in a social and cultural as well as an economic battle. Protestants had not only the jobs but social prestige – they represented 'the generally understood idea of social respectability' – and 'tame' Catholics, afraid of being betrayed by their accents or lack of 'tony qualities', eagerly sought to ingratiate themselves with Protestants, a potent 'anglicizing agency'. It was urgently necessary to restore the social morale of Catholic Ireland, to make it 'a self-contained and self-independent' entity, so that 'we shall be subject to the Ascendancy class in absolutely nothing'.[19] Or, as a popular Catholic magazine put it, 'we want to get on top'.[20] Towards these ends the Association recommended collecting information, surveillance and putting pressure on business firms. It also suggested that there should be Association dinners, decorum being assured by the presence of the clergy. At first the Association received a measure of episcopal support, but in January 1904, after William Walsh, the influential Archbishop of Dublin, denounced its activities as unchristian and inexpedient and likely ultimately to damage Catholics, it apparently ceased to function. The failure of the Association demonstrated that tolerant goodwill and business links were far stronger in Southern Ireland than a demanding, narrow determination to advance denominational interests in every possible sphere. But Protestants and many Catholic unionists must have been alarmed by the bitter resentment expressed in the Association's publications and wondered how far it reflected a widespread, if often silent, dislike of Protestants and unionists as a privileged and consciously socially superior group.[21]

Irish unionists were not only confronted by open foes. They were also very conscious they had candid friends by whom their position could be undermined. Unionist ministers, anxious to ensure peace and quiet in Ireland and to gain credit for having helped to solve the Irish question, might make concessions at the expense of their Irish supporters, 'a policy of doles and sops', which would leave the nationalists unappeased. The period of unionist parliamentary predominance, it was glumly noted, was marked by a Land Purchase Act that irritated the Irish landlords and provoked an Irish peer to remind Lord Salisbury that the Irish Unionist Alliance, which had done so much for him, was largely organized by landlords;[22] by the

---

19 *Handbook of the Catholic Association.*
20 *Irish Rosary*, Sept. 1902.
21 Protestant antagonism to Irish Catholicism was nourished by the writings of discontented Catholics, such as *Priests and People in Ireland* (1992) by M.J.F. McCarthy and *Father Ralph* by G. O'Donovan, which depicted Catholic ecclesiastics as domineering, intellectually unprogressive and oppressive, determined to control as much of Irish life as they could and excessively eager to obtain financial support for Church purposes.
22 *Parl. Debates*, 4 series, xliii, 1226.

Local Government Act of 1898; by Plunkett's appointment of T.P. Gill to the secretaryship of the Department of Agriculture and Technical Instruction – a good illustration in Dowden's opinion of 'the new unionist policy of facing both ways';[23] by a failure in unionist eyes to maintain law and order in the face of agrarian agitation; and by faulty administrative decisions, as for instance in the case of Constable Anderson, 'the Irish Dreyfus'.[24] Finally there were well-founded suspicions that the Chief Secretary, Wyndham, viewed sympathetically the attempt by a small group, led by Dunraven, to evolve an Irish policy that would conciliate moderate nationalists while leaving the union substantially unimpaired. Early in 1905 Wyndham was succeeded as Chief Secretary by the solid and politically highly orthodox Walter Long, to Irish unionists a most reassuring replacement. Though it could not be forgotten that leading British unionists, once in office, were liable to display a dangerous pragmatic flexibility when approaching Irish issues, at least they would stop short of Home Rule; at the 1906 General Election, the Liberals, concentrating on the defence of free trade, implied that if victorious they would not introduce a Home Rule bill during the lifetime of the coming parliament. So after the great Liberal landslide, Irish unionists could relax and wait confidently for the workings of the political cycle to restore the Unionist Party to office in a few years' time.

23 Dowden in a vigorous article summed up the grievances of the Irish unionists at this time (*National Review*, xliv, pp. 373-81).
24 *Parl. Debates*, 4 series, cxxxix, 738.

III Home Rule and the War

NINETEEN HUNDRED AND TEN was an ominous year for Irish unionists. The result of the general election of January 1910, almost duplicated in December, was that the Liberal government remained in office but without its overall parliamentary majority and dependent on the support of the Irish nationalists – 'Faust in the grip of Mephistopheles'.[1] Then, with the enactment of the Parliament Bill in August 1911, a Home Rule bill could reach the statute book, in spite of the unbending resistance of the House of Lords, during the lifetime of the parliament elected in December 1910. So by the normal laws of political mechanics Home Rule seemed to be inevitable. Also there had been a marked change in the political climate. For ten years or so after Gladstone's conversion to Home Rule, the Irish question had dominated British politics. But by 1910 other issues had come to the fore and British unionists, though of course still committed to the maintenance of the union, were now intensely concerned with tariff reform, social policy, imperial development, foreign policy and defence problems. Instinctively they wanted to get the Irish question out of the way if they could do so decently. They were not prepared to consider complete capitulation but they might, after exhausting conventional parliamentary methods, be ready to entertain a compromise. It did not require a great effort of the imagination to see the outlines of a possible compromise – Home Rule for the south and west where the nationalists predominated, with all or part of Ulster remaining under the Act of Union.

But tempers on both sides of the House had been sorely tried by the angry debates on the 1909 budget and the Parliament Act, so when the King's speech in February 1912 announced a measure

---

[1] Letter from Villiers Stanford in *The Times*, 9 April 1914.

for the better government of Ireland unionists braced themselves for the coming conflict. The Northern unionists were already organizing a sustained and spectacular opposition to Home Rule. They had the advantage that as a compact, distinctive community with strong feelings about their political destiny they could claim on democratic grounds that their demands should be respected. Moreover, they did not only appeal to principle but took good care that their wishes should not be ignored and overridden. They selected as their leader Sir Edward Carson, a Southern unionist, who combined passionate conviction with compelling oratorical power and a flair for grasping the realities of a situation. Funds were raised, a provisional government formed, contingency plans for passive resistance drawn up, a large volunteer force recruited, drilled and armed, and great gatherings held at which Ulster unionists pledged themselves to stand together to defend their cherished position of equal citizenship within the United Kingdom. Liberals and nationalists professed to be shocked by an avowed intention to defeat an act of parliament by extra-legal methods. Carson to some extent agreed with them. 'All doctrines of resistance, passive or active', he stated, 'tend to anarchy and that is why no man without a just or righteous cause ought ever to dare to preach to any of his fellow citizens anything tending to a breach of any law that passes the imperial parliament.' But he dared the attorney general (Rufus Isaacs) to lay down that free men must submit to any act because it has been passed by the government of the day. For himself, to submit to Home Rule would mean betraying his countrymen, not only in Ulster but in all Ireland.[2] The more extreme nonconformist opponents of the 1902 Education Act and the suffragettes would have understood his position.

The Southern unionists also campaigned energetically, striving to bring home to the public in the whole United Kingdom their unalterable opposition to Home Rule. Throughout the South unionist clubs were formed, social groups that supplemented the Unionist Alliance. A junior branch of the Alliance was formed and the Unionist Women's Committee, which had been dormant for

---

2 *The Times*, 2 Oct. 1912.

some years, was revived in 1911 and busied itself in sending literature to England and arranging lectures. In October 1911 a major
unionist demonstration was staged in Dublin.[3] At the Rotunda
Skating Rink six thousand unionists from the south and west met,
under the presidency of Lord Ardilaun, and enthusiastically
adopted 'a protest'. It stated that the creation of an Irish parliament, 'whether independent or subordinate', would endanger
commercial relations between Great Britain and Ireland, produce
social confusion, probably lead to civil war, imperil personal liberty by handing Ireland over to a party that had repeatedly defied
the law and displayed an utter disregard of the 'elementary principles of honesty and justice', and deprive them of their birth rights
as subjects of the Crown and citizens of the empire.

They also expressed their feelings by singing lustily a song
written for the occasion by Colonel Dudley Sampson:

> Brothers shall we sever,
> Never, never, never,
> But we'll cling for ever to the Union and the King.
> No home rule shall bind us,
> But traitors ever find us
> For union and the King.[4]

During 1912 the Southern unionists showed the flag by holding
meetings in a number of provincial centres – Carlow, Cork, Galway,
Kilkenny, Limerick, Tralee, Tipperary, Sligo and Waterford. In
Sligo, the Women's Unionist Association was addressed by a couple
of leading unionist barristers; in Cork 1200 Munster unionists,
meeting in the Assembly Room, were addressed by Midleton. So
many were present that an overflow meeting in the Gregg Hall was
attended by another six hundred and 'in addition to these meetings,
young men, engaged in business as clerks, who were unable to come
in the afternoon, held a meeting for themselves and filled the hall
(about 1200 being present) to protest against the bill'.[5] In Limerick

3 *Irish Unionist Alliance, Report 1911-12* (D989/C/3/38); *Irish Times*, 9 March
1914; *The Times*, 16, 22 Jan. 1912.
4 *Irish Times*, 11 Oct. 1911.
5 For Cork unionism see 'Southern Irish Unionism: a Study of Cork Unionists
1884–1914' by I. D'Alton in *Proc. RHS*, 5 series, xxiii, pp. 71–88.

a Unionist Alliance meeting, addressed by George Wyndham, was followed by a riot, stones being flung at the secretary's house and the police drawing their batons. A Carlow unionist gathering was warned by Sir Henry Blake that Home Rule meant the disruption of the empire and by Arthur Samuels that it would involve greatly increased taxation. In Galway, 'all that was best in Ireland and Galway' crammed into the ballroom of the Railway Hotel, were told by Sir William Mahon that a quarter of the population, the loyal minority, paid half the taxes. A unionist meeting in Tipperary was addressed by Richard Bagwell, the historian, and Darby Scully, a Catholic landowner. The former explained that Home Rule would transfer power to men who had learned the art of politics in Tammany Hall, the latter argued that any legislation urgently required could be secured from the imperial parliament.[6]

In the following year (1913) the last great Southern Unionist demonstration was held in the Theatre Royal, Dublin, where four thousand unionists from the south and west gathered to hear Bonar Law. Every member of the audience was supplied with a Union Jack, and when these were unfurled, 'the effect of them fluttering from floor to ceiling' was most impressive. Bonar Law delighted his audience with a pugnacious speech, pouring ridicule and scorn on the government's handling of the Irish question. But a perceptive Southern unionist would have heard with some apprehension his announcement that the unionist leadership was ready to consider any proposal by the government that would avert civil war and by his emphasis on the need to protect the interests of Ulster.[7]

The Southern unionists, though they could not, as Midleton said, appeal to the sword, admired and commended Ulster's resistance to Home Rule. Ulster's aims, the *Irish Times* declared, were the salvation of the state as well as the defence of her own rights

---

6 *The Times*, 11 March, 22 April, 11, 17, 21 Oct. 1912; *Irish Times*, 21 May 1912; *Galway Express*, 1 June 1912; *Parl. Debates* (Lords), 5 series, xii, 772.

7 Bonar Law's energetic opposition to Home Rule invigorated his party and raised its hopes of victory in the next general election. But of course the government might well have been able to postpone a dissolution until 1915 (see J. Smith, 'Bluff, Bluster and Brinksmanship', in *Hist. Jr.*, xxxvi, pp. 161–78).

and liberties, and Ulster unionism, 'popular and democratic', was fighting an unlawful and unconstitutional tyranny.[8] Southern unionists might have been somewhat embarrassed by the methods employed to prevent Churchill speaking in the Ulster Hall, but they conceded that the Ulstermen should decide on what should be done, and the *Irish Times*, admitting that the Larne gun running was unlawful, argued that it was not a breach of the King's peace.[9] The Dublin women's unionist clubs helped to equip an ambulance for the UVF, an organization greatly admired by the *Irish Times*, and a Cork Orange Lodge declared that they were willing to stand side by side with their Ulster brethren.[10] There were indeed, as might be expected, unionists in the South who did not thoroughly approve of the political tactics employed by the Ulster unionists. The Church of Ireland bishops in the southern provinces decided not to suggest that there should be special services in their dioceses to mark the signing of the covenant and, according to the Bishop of Cork, who had spent all his life in the south-west, the majority of the laity in his diocese strongly objected to being in any way identified with the Ulster movement. But lukewarm opinion tends to be ineffective.[11]

Optimistic unionists hoped that Ulster's refusal to accept Home Rule would wreck the bill. Carson told the Southern unionists: 'If Ulster succeeds Home Rule is dead. Home Rule is impossible without Belfast.' Home Rule without Ulster, Midleton wrote, was financially impossible and administratively absurd – a view heartily endorsed by the *Irish Times*.[12] But there was another possibility deeply perturbing to Southern unionists. The bill might not be wrecked but merely amended, by the exclusion of all or part of Ulster. Mathematically, exclusion would prove disastrous to Southern unionists. From being part of an all-Ireland minority amounting to about 25 per cent of the population, they would find themselves a minority of about 10 per cent in the Home Rule

---

8 *The Times*, 15 April 1914; *Irish Times*, 27 March 1913, 4 May, 17 June 1914.
9 *The Times*, 16 Jan., 9 Sept. 1912; *Irish Times*, 27 April 1914.
10 *Irish Times*, 11 March 1914; *Daily Express*, 13 Feb. 1914.
11 Archbishop of Dublin to the Bishop of Ossory, 5 Sept. 1912 (J.H. Bernard papers, Add. MS 52782).
12 *Irish Times*, 11 Oct. 1911, 17 June 1914; *The Times*, 15 April 1914.

area. Naturally they continually stressed the unity of Irish unionism. Unionists, north and south, Shaw, the secretary of the Irish
Unionist Alliance emphasized, had the same policy of unvarying
opposition to Home Rule, and he trusted to the chivalry of the
Northern unionists to ensure that no agreement was come to
which ignored the scattered unionist minority in the South who
could not contemplate the use of physical force, 'save in defence
of our lives'.[13]

The *Irish Times* in January 1913 was thankful that an amendment to the Home Rule bill exempting Ulster from its operation,
proposed by Carson, who did not fail to stress he was opposed to
the bill 'root and branch', had been rejected. For Southern unionists, the editor declared, 'an Irish parliament containing a substantial and vigorous minority from North-east Ulster, would have a
few redeeming features'. The Northern unionists, it emphasized,
must 'stand or fall with the whole of unionist Ireland'.[14] A year
later the *Irish Times* argued that the exclusion solution was
impossible – Ulster unionists and nationalists could never agree
over the area to be excluded. Exclusion would be 'permanently
fatal to every Irish hope and every Irish interest ... it would condemn our country to an eternity of national weakness, industrial
impotence and sectarian strife'. Moreover, it involved the sacrifice
of the unionists of the south and west and the 'betrayal of loyal
friendships'.[15] Healy, the editor of the *Irish Times*, writing privately
to Robinson, the editor of *The Times*, in October 1913, expressed
himself forcefully against exclusion, which he refused to take seriously. Redmond, he pointed out, could not accept it, Nationalists
would not tolerate it, Home Rule was impossible without the
industries of Ulster and a three-province Ireland with its farmers
overtaxed would soon be bankrupt. Carson and his friends could
not desert their fellow unionists: 'the idea of Carson throwing to
the wolves the university for which he sits in parliament is incon-
ceivable'. Furthermore, an Ulster parliament, unleavened by the
conservatism of the south of Ireland, would be dominated by

13 *The Times*, 8 April 1914; *Daily Express*, 9 April 1914.
14 *Irish Times*, 2 Jan. 1913.
15 *Irish Times*, 19 Feb. 1914.

socialism. Healy argued that the Ulster townsman, by nature an extreme radical, was kept unionist by his fear of the Pope. On the other hand a Dublin parliament 'unleavened by the character and brains of Ulster would be another Tammany Hall'. Finally, exclusion would destroy the prospect of a peaceable final settlement. Healy would abide by the result of the general election. If there was a deadlock it should be followed by a conference and settlement by consent – the English unionist leaders making it clear to Carson that they would not support further Ulster resistance. Healy's own plan was for four provincial councils under an Irish parliament with safeguards against discriminatory taxation. Three of the councils were not really needed but Ulster should not be 'singular'. With this form of Home Rule, he prophesied, the unionist minority would be the most powerful party in the Irish parliament in ten years.[16]

While they may have differed significantly in their attitude to exclusion, all Irish unionists were united in urging a simple, satisfactory way out of the impasse – a general election. It could be argued that Home Rule was not distinctly before the electorate in 1910, and more plausibly that if Ulster received special treatment, the meaning of Home Rule was fundamentally changed. Unionists were of course well aware that it was highly unlikely that the Liberals could win four general elections consecutively, and by-elections seemed to show that the pendulum was swinging in the right direction. The *Irish Times*, which continuously called for an appeal to the people, admitted that a unionist victory at the polls would not *ipso facto* settle the Irish question. It would be a difficult task to clear up the mess left by the Liberals. Still the unionist party would be ready with a policy of 'justice and appeasement'.[17] However, in the early summer of 1914 there were no signs that Asquith, heading a confident and talented administration, backed by a large if composite House of Commons majority, was convinced that he ought to seek a new mandate.

The steady progress of the Home Rule bill to the statute book, the growing possibility of exclusion and the realization that the

---

16 J. Healy to G. Robinson, 3 Oct. 1913 (*The Times* archives).
17 *Irish Times*, 15 May, 2 July 1914.

unionist leadership, while fighting in parliament to the last, might accept Home Rule accompanied by exclusion as a *fait accompli*, forced some thoughtful Southern unionists to reconsider their attitude to the Irish problem. Monteagle, a keen advocate of agricultural co-operation, 'an Irishman before I am a unionist', rather favoured a federal solution and urged that a conference should be held 'to seek means of avoiding the hateful operation of "exclusion"'. Townley Balfour, a well-known County Louth landowner, supported the suggestion, stating that a large number of unionists outside Ulster thought that opposition to Home Rule was futile. A Kerry country gentleman argued that the majority of Irish unionists, unsympathetic towards 'the parochialism and religious animosities of the North', should throw in their lot with the new order, which would encourage the whole Irish race to take part in the development of the imperial system. Another Kerry gentleman, Morgan O'Connell, a landlord and unionist, argued that separation had been 'buried' by the nationalists' acceptance of the Home Rule bill[18] and some well known unionists, including Fingall, Dunraven and Sir Hutchinson Poe, were among the signatories to a letter urging that the question of the future government of Ireland should be lifted out of the sphere of party politics.[19]

While some Southern unionists were beginning optimistically to hope that widely diffused vague goodwill would create an atmosphere in which apparently intractable constitutional conundrums would be solved and sternly conflicting interests reconciled, others thought that the time had come to face unwelcome probabilities. If, as a Roscommon gentleman exclaimed, the Southern unionists were going to be 'thrown to the wolves'[20] or, as Bryan Cooper put it less emotionally, the unionist leaders in the Lords were going to demand the permanent exclusion of Ulster, it behoved the Southern unionists to think about 'safeguards' for themselves in a Home Rule Ireland. Cooper himself proposed several: the judiciary and the police were to be reserved services; the Irish parliament was to be debarred from repealing the Malicious

---

18 *The Times*, 8, 13 July 1913, 21 May, 14 Oct. 1912.
19 *The Times*, 21 Oct. 1912.
20 *The Times*, 20 July 1914.

Injury acts and from imposing discriminatory taxation; and all civil service appointments were to be by competitive examination, so as to prevent 'the Hibernianization or Tammanization' of the civil service. Finally steps should be taken to ensure that the unionist minority should have adequate representation in the Dublin parliament.[21]

A very influential group of Southern unionists was brought face to face with the urgent need for safeguards for the minority in the South, when in March 1914 the government introduced in the Lords a bill providing that any Ulster county that voted for exclusion would be exempted from the operation of the Home Rule bill (then approaching the statute book) for six years. The official opposition attitude was stated by Lansdowne: exclusion of all Ulster and no time limit. Naturally the Southern unionist peers were despondent. They saw, as Oranmore and Browne expressed it, rising from 'the altar of compromise the smoke of a hetacomb of unionist victims from the south and west'. A number of peers from the South of Ireland emphasized that the union must be maintained. Barrymore, the veteran leader of the Munster land-lords and a pillar of Southern unionism, called on the government to withdraw both the Home Rule bill and the amending bill and then to try to discover 'some saner, sounder, safer solution for the Irish question'. Meath suggested a solution on federal lines and Arran, a covenanter, who fervently believed that he was pledged against Home Rule for any part of Ireland, attacked the English unionists for 'giving up the essence of their being – the union' and the Ulster volunteers for being prepared to sacrifice the welfare of Ireland and the empire for their own safety. Wicklow, however, 'against ... the principles of the party to which I belong and almost against my own convictions', was prepared to accept exclusion. Both he and Midleton, while demanding that the bills be submitted to the electorate, were anxious to insert in the amending bill safe-guards for the Southern minority. This was accomplished when the bill was in committee, it being provided that the Irish judiciary should be appointed not by the Lord Lieutenant but by the Crown; that the RIC, land and land purchase should be

---

21 *The Times*, 6 July 1914.

reserved subjects; and that a form of proportional representation should be employed in elections to the Irish parliament.

During July 1914 a series of dramatic events – massive 12 July demonstrations in Ulster, the Buckingham Palace conference, the landing of arms at Howth followed by disturbances in Dublin – fastened attention on Ireland, the most urgent political problem. Then, suddenly, at the beginning of August all domestic issues were completely dwarfed by the outbreak of a European war involving five great powers. The government, parliament and the public immediately became absorbed in the war effort, and though the Home Rule bill was enacted in September 1914, the Suspensory Act provided that it would not come into operation until the end of the war.

For the Southern unionists this was their finest hour. They were able to throw themselves wholeheartedly into serving the empire in a time of peril, proudly sharing the fears, hopes and sacrifices of their fellow subjects in Great Britain. 'The Irish gentry more than maintained the immemorial traditions of the Anglo-Hibernian breed,' and almost every unionist family in the south and west was represented in the services. Some indication of the community's contribution is afforded by the Trinity College War List, a copy of which, the *Irish Times* declared, would replace the Book of Kells in pride of place amongst Trinity's possessions. The latter illustrated 'the glories of a remote Irish civilization, the former held between its covers the hopes, the sorrows, the pride of a great university'.[22] Those Southern unionists who stayed at home were very active in Red Cross work, war charities, providing comforts and entertainments for the forces and in recruiting. In these activities they sometimes found themselves on surprisingly good terms with some of their nationalist neighbours. On 3 August 1914 Redmond had in an eloquent speech ranged Ireland alongside Britain in the European crisis. The Southern unionists, an intelligent observer remarked, viewed Redmond's declaration from 'their peculiar standpoint of slightly cynical detachment, they had seen many dawns of better days ... a half humorous

22 *Irish Times*, 23 July 1915, 15 April 1916, and see 'T.C.D. and the War' by L. Dooney in *Ireland and the First World War* (1988), ed. D. Fitzpatrick.

smile came easier to them than any kind of sentiment'.[23] However in the south and west unionists and those nationalists who followed Redmond's lead appeared together on recruiting platforms, though there were differences of emphasis in their appeals, nationalists urging Irishmen to enlist in defence of small nations, unionists calling on them to rally to the defence of the empire. Nevertheless, it was widely felt that co-operation in the war effort and the fellowship of the trenches might transform the political outlook in Ireland. Old prejudices would vanish and a new consensus on Irish, British and imperial problems emerge.

But early in the war recruiting revealed a wide gulf in thought and feeling between the Southern unionists and large sections of Irish opinion. From the middle of 1915 Healy, the editor of the *Irish Times*, was concerned about the apathy with which the recruiting problem was regarded in some areas and by some social groups, an apathy illustrated by the failure of two-thirds of the local authorities to form recruiting committees and by 'the promenade slackers' to be seen in Bray.[24] Two classes, in Healy's view, had conspicuously failed to do their duty – farmers' sons and shop assistants. He brushed aside the plea that the former were engaged in food production; thousands of them were engaged raising cattle, 'a leisurely occupation', and could well be spared. As for the shop assistants, they should be told by their employers that they could be replaced by female labour.[25] In October the *Irish Times* displayed prominently the King's letter calling for recruits, loyally commending it in an editorial. When the Military Service bill of 1916 was being debated the *Irish Times* regretted what James Campbell termed 'the unexplained and unaccountable exclusion of Ireland from the bill', stating that it inflicted 'ignominy' on Ireland. The *Irish Times* also deplored Redmond's (comparatively mild) speech against the bill and a few weeks later was asking why was the Irish Parliamentary Party as a whole not taking part in the recruiting campaign and why was the machinery of the National League not working at full pressure to obtain recruits. When, a week or

23 J.O. Hanney in *Nineteenth Century and After*, lxxviii, pp. 396-400.
24 *Irish Times*, 8 July, 28 Aug. 1915.
25 *The Times*, 23 July, 11 Aug. 1915; *Irish Times*, 11 Aug. 1915.

so later, the *Irish Times* mediatively remarked how the war had thrown into relief the trivialities of public life in Ireland, its meaning was clear.[26]

From early in the war unionists, with their eyes fixed intensely on the fluctuating fortunes of the far-flung imperial battle line, were aware of disquieting symptoms on the home front. A fervent minority in the Irish Parliamentary Party had repudiated Redmond's attitude to the war, believing that Irishmen should abstain from taking sides in the conflict but be ready to take advantage of England's difficulties. As a result the National Volunteers (the nationalist equivalent of the Ulster Defence Volunteers) had split, the wing dominated by the extreme nationalists, the Sinn Féiners, organizing a force formed on military lines, the Irish Volunteers, and conducting a vigorous anti-recruiting campaign. Unionists naturally called for the prosecution of anti-recruiting speeches and publications and between the autumn of 1915 and mid-April 1916 their views were conveyed to the authorities by Midleton, 'acting as the mouthpiece of a small but influential body of businessmen'. In a series of interviews with the Prime Minister, the Chief Secretary, the Under-Secretary and the Lord Lieutenant, he emphasized that the government was allowing a potentially dangerous situation to develop unchecked. He suggested that serious offences against the Defence of the Realm Act should be tried by court martial, that seditious publications should be suppressed and the Irish Volunteers banned. In short what was required was firm government.[27] The chief secretary, Birrell, an urbane man of letters as well as a politician, believed that fanaticism thrived on persecution. An energetic counter-attack on sedition (which he was aware was widespread) would provide the seditious with good publicity and cheap martyrdom, and win them the support of all those in Ireland who were inherently against the government. Left to themselves the Irish Volunteers would go on drilling and parading but would not resort to direct action. If Midleton was for the 'nip it in the bud' policy, Birrell saw himself as the personification of masterful inactivity.

---

26 *Parl. Debates*, 5 series, lxxvii, 1231; *Irish Times*, 4, 13 Jan., 19, 26 Feb. 1916.
27 *Parl. Debates* (Lords), 5 series, xxi, 965.

At the end of April 1916, a week after Midleton had his last interview with leading members of the Irish administration, an insurgent force, composed of Irish Volunteers and men of the Irish Citizen Army seized a number of buildings in Dublin and proclaimed that an independent Irish Republic was in being. The insurrection lasted a bare week but profoundly influenced British and Irish opinion. Irish unionists were deeply angered by an action that not only challenged the authority of the Crown and the supremacy of the law but struck a blow at the allied cause when the battle of Verdun was raging. The insurgents were not only unprincipled but displayed a lamentable lack of political perspective and proportion. Unionist opinion was accurately reflected by John Healy (the editor of the *Irish Times*) when he described the insurrection as 'a brutal, bloody and savage business', with innocent civilians butchered in cold blood and unarmed policemen and soldiers shot down. Its suppression had been one of the most difficult and dangerous duties that British soldiers had ever had to perform, marked by 'fierce and bloody street fighting which our army had not known since the Peninsula war'. Still, the insurrection had at least 'exposed the elements of disaffection' and 'if the government wills they can be crushed out of existence'.[28]

On 3 May the *Irish Times* declared that though 'the country has no desire that punishment should be pushed to the point of mere revenge', it demanded that 'stern justice should be inflicted on the authors of one of the most deliberate and far-reaching crimes in Irish history'. A few days later it declared the surgeon's knife must not be stayed until the whole malignant growth had been removed.[29] At the same time, Bernard, the Church of Ireland Archbishop of Dublin, wrote a short pungent letter to *The Times* pointing out that martial law was the only security for life and property in Dublin, that stern measures were required to avert the danger of another insurrection and that 'this is not the time for amnesties and pardons, it is the time for punishment swift and stern'.[30] Both Healy and Bernard wanted a strong chief secretary,

---

28 *The Times*, 1, 2 May 1916.
29 *Irish Times*, 3, 5, 6 May 1916.
30 *The Times*, 5 May 1916.

who would provide Ireland with 'a firm, just and powerful government' and do his best to help, not hinder, the police. Other suggestions made by Southern unionists were that arms should be swept up, that Irish primary school teachers should not be permitted to teach what history they pleased, that primary school children should be taught to take pride in the empire and in the gallant Irishmen who had built it up, that sedition, 'however much it may be froth and bubble', should be 'taboo' in Ireland during the war, and that the rank and file of the insurgents who had been taken prisoner should be permitted to join the army – 'they would return to Ireland with larger views of their duties'. Conscription, the *Irish Times* pronounced ten days after the insurrection ended, would have a steadying effect on the country; a few months later the paper stated that it was impossible to produce a respectable justification for the failure to extend conscription to Ireland and that the Irish Parliamentary Party had done practically nothing to encourage recruiting.[31] Some months later Archbishop Bernard approached the question of extending conscription to Ireland from a cost-effective standpoint. 'I am one of those', he wrote,

who start from the premiss we must win the war and that we cannot do this without using every available man. Therefore I hold that compulsory service must come. But I am satisfied from my own knowledge of the country that it cannot come without bloodshed. How then, you may ask, can I recommend it? The answer is that the sacrifice of 500 or 1000 lives (I do not anticipate it will cost as much as this) is worth while if we can thereby shorten the war by a single day and sooner or later the intended insurrection will come in Ireland. It is better it should come at once.

Having endured the shock of the 1916 insurrection, the Southern unionists would have been content to continue concentrating on the war, postponing the consideration of constitutional change until the conclusion of hostilities. But the British government was very conscious of Irish discontent, dangerous in wartime and damaging to British prestige in the USA and the

---

31 *Parl. Debates* (Lords), 5 series, xxi, 970; *Fortnightly Review*, cvi, p. 442; *Irish Times*, 11, 17 May, 3 Aug. 1916; J.H. Bernard to Wimborne (draft), 24 Nov. 1916 (Add MS 52782).

Dominions. Also it was under pressure from the Irish Parliamentary Party, now engaged in a desperate struggle with the militant republicans for the hearts and minds of nationalist Ireland. So at the end of May, Lloyd George, 'a dynamic force', was entrusted by the cabinet with the task of discovering a basis for an Irish settlement. A persuasive and resourceful negotiator, Lloyd George managed after some weeks to get the Irish Parliamentary Party and the Ulster unionists to accept a scheme – the immediate implementation of Home Rule with the six northern counties excluded. As might be expected the Southern unionists disapproved of the scheme. It seemed to them that 'the whole world of their political convictions, sentiments and loyalties had fallen away beneath their feet'. 'Their brilliant and faithful services to the empire', the *Irish Times* declared, deserved better than political annihilation. Though prepared 'to go a long way towards surrendering the form of government from which their name is derived', they regarded partition as ruinous economically and Home Rule as handing over the twenty-six counties to Sinn Féin.[32]

The Southern unionists sent deputations to London to put their views before the Prime Minister, Bonar Law and Lloyd George, and a number of unionist MPs. Barrymore and F.S. Stewart, a land agent on a large scale, explained to the Colonial Secretary, Arthur Long, that the Lloyd George proposals were repugnant to unionists and would satisfy nationalists only in the short term. Precipitate action must be avoided.[33] James Campbell, who had just been appointed attorney general for Ireland, thought that the Lloyd George scheme would be regarded as a reward to Sinn Féin and in the future would make it difficult to carry a Home Rule measure for the whole of Ireland or a plan of imperial federation. He advised the prime minister to postpone the question until the end of the war and to entrust the administration of Ireland in the meantime to a committee composed of leading Home Rulers and unionists.[34] Robinson, the vice-chairman of the

32 *Irish Times*, 19, 23, 24 June 1916.
33 *Irish Times*, 27 June 1916; *The Times*, 28 June 1916; G.F. Stewart to A. Long, 31 May 1916 (Long papers, 191).
34 J. Campbell to W. Long, 10 June 1916 (Long papers, 173).

Local Government board, a civil servant of decidedly unionist leanings, thought that all the Irish situation called for was a fair and courageous chief secretary who would back the RMs and the RIC. He recognized there might be trouble – resolutions from local bodies and cattle-driving – but they had been through all that before and discontent was only serious when there was 'a milk and water' administration.[35]

When early in July it looked as if Lloyd George's proposals might soon be implemented, the executive committee of the Unionist Alliance formulated the safeguards they thought should be included in the scheme. There was to be a strong senate representing 'property, industry and commerce', the imperial government was to have a veto on Irish legislation, the judiciary was to be appointed by the imperial government, and the right of appeal from the Irish courts to the House of Lords was to be retained. Land legislation, public loans, education and the law relating to malicious injuries were to be reserved subjects. The Irish parliament was to be debarred from imposing disabilities or granting privileges on religious grounds. The Irish parliament when making laws relating to commerce and taxation was not to differentiate between any classes of persons or property, its powers over income tax were to be limited, and 'tacking' was forbidden. Finally, civil-service appointments were to be made on the results of competitive examination. This long, comprehensive list of safeguards, which severely limited the already limited powers of the Irish parliament under the Home Rule act, vividly indicates the intensity of Southern unionist apprehensions. But by the end of July their fears were lulled by the failure of Lloyd George's bold attempt to dispose of the Irish question – his proposals being severely criticized by unionist cabinet ministers and finally rejected by the Irish Parliamentary Party when it realized that exclusion might be permanent.[36]

The Southern unionists, content with the status quo, were strongly in favour of postponing the consideration of constitutional change until after the war or, if possible, to the Greek Calends. But

---

35 H. Robinson to W. Long, 27 July 1916 (Long papers, 331).
36 R.B. McDowell, *The Irish Convention* (1970), pp. 54-5; G.F. Stewart to W. Long, 15 July 1916 (Long papers, 363).

the government could not ignore the *damnosa hereditas* of Irish discontent, voiced bitterly by the Irish Parliamentary Party and even more vehemently by the extreme republicans. So in the spring of 1917 the war cabinet tried a new approach. A gathering of representative Irishmen, a convention, was to endeavour to hammer out an agreement and if a scheme secured substantial support in the convention it would be implemented by the government.

Midleton in the Lords said that the Southern unionists were prepared to take part in the convention if 'the loyal element' was adequately represented, and the Irish Unionist Alliance, while depreciating 'the opening of the question' of Irish self-government during the war, appointed a committee to select delegates to the convention.[37] These were Midleton, Sir Henry Blake, a retired colonial governor, Andrew Jameson, the head of a famous firm of distillers, F.S. Stewart, a land agent, and J.B. Powell, a Catholic barrister. If Bernard, the Archbishop of Dublin, two unionist peers (Mayo and Oranmore and Brown) and E.H. Andrews, the chairman of the Dublin Chamber of Commerce, are included, the group numbered nine; and it may be added that two independently minded peers and Mahaffy, a political maverick, might be regarded as Southern unionists in a wide sense of the term, giving that section a dozen representatives in an assembly of ninety-five members.

The Archbishop of Dublin, John Henry Bernard, who in 1919 was to succeed Mahaffy as provost of Trinity, was a man of formidable intellect and impressive presence. In politics he was a pessimistic realist. He accepted that Home Rule was on the statute book (in a democracy *Vestigia nulla retrorsum*) and that Ulster had been promised exclusion. But after the 1916 insurrection Home Rule was overshadowed by the Sinn Féin demand for a republic, something Great Britain could never concede. Thus the immediate choice lay between order and anarchy. All this boded ill for the unionists of the south and west, who had always steadily obeyed the law and during the war 'gave all they had to give'. In a partitioned Ireland they would find themselves 'under the heel of an angry, disappointed and hostile majority'. Still, Bernard did not

---

37 *The Times*, 2 June 1917.

despair. He thought it possible that a consensus might be achieved favouring a self-governing, united Ireland, closely connected with Great Britain and having effectual safeguards – a conservative second chamber, an Ulster veto on legislation for the whole of Ireland – for the minority.[38] He was to meet with a series of setbacks but persevered with wearied resignation.

The Convention deliberated for over seven months (from July 1917 to the beginning of April 1918). At first the Southern unionists tended to be silent but after a time they began with characteristic self-assurance to try to persuade the Convention to agree to a plan that would maintain the connection with Great Britain, satisfy a wide spectrum of Irish opinion, including the Northern unionists, and provide safeguards for the minority. Convinced of the virtues and value of the union, they were acutely aware that a Home Rule measure was on the statute book and that, given the evolution of opinion in Ireland and Great Britain, it would be impossible to repeal it. Therefore what they aimed at was the acceptance by the convention of a Home Rule scheme that would preserve the British connection and provide important safeguards for the Irish unionists. There was to be a second chamber, constituted on highly conservative lines, and the unionists were to be guaranteed initially 40 per cent representation in the Irish House of Commons (it was calculated that in a joint sitting of both houses they would have 50 per cent of the votes). The contentious issue of the control of customs and excise was to be decided by the imperial parliament after the end of the war. The scheme secured support from those nationalists who were prepared to water down Home Rule for the sake of Irish unity. Also there must have been nationalists who were prepared to accept Home Rule as a satisfactory enough solution of Anglo-Irish relations, reconciling their Irish patriotism with their appreciation of many aspects of British life. Though they might on a platform express romantic enthusiasm for those who had in the past fought for Irish freedom, nevertheless they energetically participated in English intellectual and cultural life, sometimes joined the imperial

---

38 *National Review*, lxviii, 212-21; Memorandum to W. Long (c.1919) (Add MS 52783).

services, enjoyed London and, if elected to parliament, took part with gusto in the proceedings at Westminster.

The scheme strongly advocated by the Southern unionists was accepted in the convention by narrow majorities, the Ulster unionists voting against it and the nationalists splitting. But the publication of the convention's report coincided with the issue of Haig's 'backs to the wall' order of the day, and though the government considered granting Home Rule to Ireland, a more immediate issue was the enactment of a second military service measure which could be extended to Ireland by order in Council. The *Irish Times* thought there were two courses open to the government: either it should say it was afraid to enforce conscription in Ireland or it should extend conscription to Ireland, enforcing it immediately and impartially. The two Church of Ireland archbishops publicly expressed the hope that the country would accept conscription cheerfully,[39] and a public-spirited Queen's County landlord told Arthur Long, the Colonial Secretary, that conscription could be enforced easily enough after the harvest. No one, he wrote, respected the law more than an Irishman when he found he could not break it with impunity, and he had told neighbouring farmers that if Germany won the war their farms would be given to Germans for whom they might find themselves working as serfs (a warning already issued by the *Irish Times*).[40] But nationalist Ireland was firmly united against conscription; Carson and James Campbell warned the prime minister that an attempt to enforce it would lead to bloodshed and that 'the number of men worth getting whom it would yield would be very small'. By September 1918 even the *Irish Times*, though it believed that the arguments for conscription were logically unanswerable and that those who regarded it as only a *Brutum fulmen* were living in a fool's paradise, for the moment simply expressed the hope that the recruiting campaign, which of course it enthusiastically backed, would raise the men required from Ireland.[41]

---

39 *Irish Times*, 8, 18 April 1918.
40 R.A.G. Crosby to W. Long, 22 July 1918 (Long papers, 189); *Irish Times*, 27 Nov. 1915.
41 D. Lloyd George, *War Memoirs*, v, p. 2667; *Irish Times*, 18 Sept. 1918.

From the outbreak of the war unionist activities in the south and west seem to have been almost completely suspended, with many keen unionists joining up or devoting themselves to war work. A survey of the state of the party in thirteen counties in the south and west by a vigorous unionist in 1916 suggested that the unionists in those counties were ill-organized and often politically pessimistic. In Roscommon the unionists were 'quiescent', in Galway and Sligo 'dormant' and in Sligo a federal settlement was being talked about. In County Waterford the unionists were 'few and scattered', many having gone to the war; in Tipperary, 'everyone who used to support the cause has gone to the front'; in Leitrim the unionists were 'negligible'; in Longford 'ardent' but few and scattered; in Limerick and Mayo, 'the practicably submerged' unionists felt Home Rule to be inevitable though they might dislike it as much as ever; in Clare, though there was no weakening in their faith they had not held a meeting since the beginning of the war; in Wexford it was reported 'nothing doing' and that some unionists were less afraid of Home Rule than they had been. In Cork unionism was dormant but unionists 'had not thrown up the sponge' (it was said that nationalists, with jobbery rampart, regretted their absence from local bodies); and in Kerry such unionists as there were remained faithful and a ladies branch had recently been founded.[42]

But the convention's proceedings and report seem to have stirred things up, at least among the politically concerned, with the result that an almost inevitable division in the Southern unionist ranks emerged between the *non possimus* section and those who favoured a flexible response – arguing that opposition to Home Rule could, as Lord Iveagh, expressed it, be combined with 'a prudent preparation for eventualities'.[43] Early in 1918 it was proposed at a meeting of the Executive Council of the Irish Unionist Alliance that the convention delegates should be instructed to consult the General Council before taking definite action.[44] This resolution was rejected

42 Reports on recruiting and political attitudes in thirteen counties in the south and west by J.M. Wilson, Jan.-March 1916 (Long papers, 388/2).

43 *The Times*, 3 Oct. 1918.

44 *The Times*, 29 Jan. 1919.

and at the beginning of March a group of twenty-two southern unionists issued a 'Call' to unionists in which they demanded the maintenance of the legislative union together with firm and just government, the development of Ireland's natural resources, the completion of land purchase and the extension to Ireland of the burdens and obligations imposed by the war on the rest of the United Kingdom.[45] In May the Council of the Irish Unionist Alliance discussed the delegates' policy but adjourned without coming to a decision, and in June, when the General Council elected twenty members to the Executive Committee, the Call section secured sixteen seats.[46] Midleton was convinced that his supporters must fight to retain control of the Alliance and he suggested the formation of a small committee (Desart, Donoughmore, Oranmore and Browne and Iveagh) which would make a tremendous effort when it came to co-opting members to the Executive Committee. If they were successful they should then take steps to exclude the Ulster delegates from the General Council.[47] When in July the executive co-opted a number of members, Midleton's supporters were victorious, according to their opponents by whipping up vice-presidents. Midleton himself characterized the 'Call' section's tactics as 'Tammany'.[48] Certainly the ultras seem to have taken steps to revive the Alliance's local machinery and use it to muster their supporters. For instance in County Wexford, a leading country gentleman having pointed out that the county branch with its two secretaries in France had been since the beginning of the war inanimate, pressed for the election of a 'sound' county committee that would take steps to prevent the Alliance falling into the hands of a Dublin clique. Incidentally, he remarked that in Wexford 'the ladies' were more energetic than the men.[49]

Emboldened by his July victory, Midleton at a meeting of the General Council of the Alliance in January 1919 launched a bold attack on his critics, strongly supporting a motion to the effect

45 *The Times*, 4, 5 March 1918.
46 *The Times*, 10 June 1918.
47 Midleton to G.F. Stewart, 12 June 1918 (Midleton papers PRO30/67/39).
48 *Daily Express*, 10, 11 July 1918; Midleton to R. Bagwell, 25 Oct. 1918 (Midleton papers, PRO30/67/39).
49 C.M. Doyne to Courtown, 7 July 1918 (Courtown papers, P50/4/89).

that when a scheme for the government of Ireland that involved the exclusion of any area was being considered, delegates from the excluded area should not speak nor vote. It was unfair, it could be argued, that when the interests of the Northern and Southern unionists diverged, the former should not only possess their own organization but have a voice in a predominantly southern body. Jellett retorted that the motion recognized partition and it was overwhelmingly defeated. According to Midleton a considerable number of Northern delegates voted; according to one of his opponents there were only forty-six Ulstermen in an assembly numbering four hundred.[50]

Midleton and his supporters – in the opinion of Sir Hugh McCalmont, 'the gang which have been the prime cause of all the trouble'[51] – promptly seceded from the Alliance and formed the Unionist Anti-partition League. The membership of the League included a number of peers (amongst them Barrymore, Desart, Donoughmore, Iveagh), Archbishop Bernard and some leading businessmen (Sir William Goulding, Sir Harold Nutting and Sir John Arnott) and it was treated with respect by the *Irish Times*. The Alliance elected as its new chairman Lord Farnham, recently returned from the war, and had amongst its members several peers who had not been very prominent in public life, two able barristers, Jellett and J.E. Walsh, grandson of a master of the rolls and a conveyancer, Harry Franks, a well-known land agent, General Sir Hugh McCalmont, the historian Richard Bagwell, and McKay Wilson (brother of Sir Henry Wilson), who had been Conservative candidate for Longford in 1885. It had the support of two popular newspapers, the *Dublin Daily Express* and the *Cork Constitution*, and it aimed, according to Pretyman Newman, an active member, to represent 'not only a small coterie of peers and commercial magnates' but 'the small farmers, the shopkeepers and rural clergymen in remote Kerry and Clare'.[52] Richard Bagwell, writing to Fitzwilliam Starkie, a senior civil servant with whom he

50 *The Times*, 25 Jan. 1919; *Daily Express*, 25 Jan. 1919; draft circular, 3 Jan. 1919 (Midleton papers, PRO30/67/4).

51 Sir H. McCalmont to W. Long, 28 Jan. 1919 (Long papers, 300).

52 *Daily Express*, 5 July 1918.

had co-operated in educational work, denounced those unionists who had surrendered their principles from fear of chaos or a Labour government. The union, Bagwell argued, had not broken down: 'it only requires efficient administration', and a Labour government would not necessarily lack a sense of responsibility. Moreover, 'in view of the enfranchisement of women it was not certain what the future form of government would be like'. These arguments impressed Starkie, a unionist, who in any event had 'little sympathy with ratters'.[53]

The Alliance saw the League as composed of about ninety peers and rich businessmen, activated by loyalty to Midleton. Members of the League dismissed the Alliance as led by 'nonentities' – Jellett, admittedly, was a sound man but lacked a consistent policy and his speeches were composed of platitudes.[54] The League of course stood for maintenance of the union, but was very much aware that if a Home Rule measure was going to be enacted it was important to preserve the unity of Ireland, prevent the establishment of an Irish republic, preserve the closest possible connection with Great Britain and secure safeguards for unionists. All this required the balanced judgment and negotiating skills which the men of affairs who belonged to the League were sure they possessed. The Alliance had a less sophisticated policy. The only choice was between the union in its integrity and separation, any degree of self-government for Ireland would soon eventuate in an Irish Republic. Divided on strategy, the Southern unionists faced a political abyss.

---

53 Starkie diary, 19 March 1918.
54 Report on a visit to Ireland, January 1920 (Long papers, 420); draft of circular (Midleton papers, PRO30/6/39).

IV The Fourth Home Rule Bill

AT THE OPENING OF the post-war era the Southern unionists were confronted by two dangers: Home Rule – the Home Rule Act of 1914 was on the statute book – and, even more disturbing, the demand for an Irish republic, voiced by Sinn Féin. Ten days after the Armistice the unionists were abruptly reminded that Home Rule might soon be operative. In their joint election manifesto, issued in November 1918, the prime minister and Bonar Law, the leader of the Unionist party, promised 'to explore all practical paths which might lead to the solution of the Irish question', ruling out only the coercion of Ulster and the complete severance of Ireland from the empire. This promise produced an immediate reaction from the moderate Southern unionists. At the beginning of December they issued a statement signed by four peers (Donoughmore, Desart, Mayo and Oranmore and Browne) and three leading businessmen (F.S. Stewart, Sir William Goulding and Andrew Jameson) declaring that in the present condition of Ireland, with a large section in the South aiming at complete independence, an attempt to introduce Home Rule would endanger the United Kingdom. Moreover Ulster could not be coerced, and without Ulster Home Rule would not be a success.[1]

In the 1918 general election the Southern unionists contested nine constituencies: Dublin University, St Stephen's Green in the city of Dublin, three of the four County Dublin constituencies, East Wicklow, North Monaghan, East Donegal and Cork city. In Trinity there were three unionist candidates: Arthur Samuels, one of the sitting members (his colleague Edward Carson, after representing Trinity for twenty-six years, now preferred to stand for a Belfast constituency); William Morgan Jellett, an uncompromising

---

1 *The Times*, 7 Dec. 1918.

unionist; and Sir Robert Woods, an independent unionist. There was also a nationalist, Stephen Gwynn, the well-known man of letters. Woods, a surgeon, was primarily interested in public health and he impatiently declared that what Ireland needed was 'a settlement by consent', though as 'a man of the world' he admitted events had rendered such an outcome 'remote'.[2] It might be thought that Samuels, as attorney general a member of the government, would have been embarrassed by the coalition's Irish policy enunciated in the Lloyd George/Bonar Law manifesto. In fact he avoided dwelling on it and privately explained that he was able to subscribe to it because it meant an end to Home Rule. Ulster would never yield and partition would never be accepted by nationalists and Southern unionists: 'Ergo Home Rule is finished'.[3]

In the Stephen's Green division the unionist candidate was Henry Hanna, a KC and author of *The Pals at Sulva Bay*. He was in favour of the punishment of war criminals and making Germany pay, and he robustly declared that his Nationalist and Sinn Féin opponents could each pack all their property in a suitcase.[4] The three unionist candidates in County Dublin were all leading businessmen, Sir Maurice Dockrell, Good and Sir Thomas Robinson. The unionist candidates in Wicklow and Monaghan were respectively Parker Keene, a tenant farmer, and William Knight, a solicitor. Generally speaking the candidates all agreed that the unity of Ireland must be preserved, that Ulster must not be coerced and that any measure of self-government would deliver Ireland, 'the key to British sea power' into the hands of Sinn Féin. Therefore the maintenance of the union, 'fairly, strongly and properly administered', was 'the one sane policy'. There was an alternative to Home Rule – 'reconstruction', 'a policy of progress and productivity'.[5] There was plenty to be done regarding social reform, health, housing, railway extension, exploitation of mineral resources, agricultural development, the improvement of private bill procedure and the admission of women to the professions (the last point was made by Samuels).

---

2 *Daily Express*, 7 Dec. 1918.
3 A. Samuels to J.H. Bernard, 12, 19 Nov. 1918 (Bernard papers, Add MS 52783).
4 *Daily Express*, 3, 5 Dec. 1918.
5 *The Times*, 22, 23 Jan. 1919.

The unionists naturally enough retained the two university seats, Samuels (with 1273 votes) and Woods (with 793 votes) being returned. Jellett secured 631 votes. (When in July 1919 Samuels was placed on the bench Jellett was elected to the vacant Trinity seat unopposed.)[6] Gwynn, though a strong candidate, the son of a Regius professor with three brothers fellows of Trinity and with war service, obtained only 257 votes. The unionists won one of the South County Dublin seats, Rathmines, in which Dockrell, fighting a Nationalist and a Sinn Féiner, secured just over half the vote. In two other County Dublin divisions and in Monaghan, the unionists secured nearly a third of the votes; in Wicklow their share of the vote amounted to a quarter; in the Stephen's Green division it was just under a fifth; in East Donegal, the unionist candidate, a County Londonderry landlord, won over 38 per cent of the vote; and in Cork city the two unionist candidates – an analytical chemist and a businessman active in municipal affairs – obtained just over 8 per cent.

While the Southern unionists held three seats Sinn Féin won seventy-three, and at the beginning of January a number of Sinn Féin MPs meeting at the Mansion House, Dublin, constituted themselves Dáil Éireann (The Parliament of Ireland), which on 21 January issued a declaration of independence and nominated ministers to form a provisional government. Dublin unionists must have been more impressed by the luncheon, held at the Mansion House on the same day, to welcome four hundred repatriated prisoners of the Royal Dublin Fusiliers, the whole of Dawson Street being 'a blaze of Union Jacks'. Southern unionists and the respectable Irish world in general probably scarcely noticed another event that occurred on 21 January – the shooting by an armed band in County Tipperary of two policemen. An incident which marked the beginning of what would develop, during the next twelve months, into widespread guerrilla warfare against the Crown forces.

Though great changes were taking place in the climate of opinion

---

6 There was the possibility of Jellett being opposed by a Midleton supporter, T.S. Battersby, who was however 'too late in the field'. T.S. Battersby to Midleton, 23 Nov. 1921, and J.H. Bernard to Midleton, 23 Nov. 1921 (Midleton papers, PRO30/36/48).

and the balance of political forces in Ireland, for a year or two many Southern unionists continued to think and argue along well-worn lines. The Irish problem seemed to them to be a purely sentimental one, not based on concrete grievances. The union assured fair play and justice 'to both sections of a people of distinctive race, religious belief and attitude towards England'. It might not satisfy those who 'regarded their imperial citizenship as servitude' but certainly satisfied the many who prided themselves on that citizenship. It was impossible to reconcile the disloyal, irresponsible Irish, so why go on trying to do so? Home Rule would only alienate Great Britain's friends in Ireland, without conciliating her enemies, whose aim was complete separation. The union was essential to the safety of the empire and if it was unflinchingly upheld 'the Irish problem would virtually disappear'.[7]

Many Southern unionists would have agreed with the editor of the *Irish Times* that, considering the general condition of the country, political experiments should be postponed. 'The maintenance of order', he wrote early in 1920 'is more important than the manufacture of a constitution.' Reconstruction should take precedence over Home Rule and, if all went well, supersede it. Increased powers should be given to Irish government departments together with substantial treasury grants – 'a species of economic self-determination'. Walter Guinness approached the Irish question along the same lines. Early in 1919 he pointed out that if an Irish parliament were set up it would be dominated by Sinn Féin, which was no longer run by a harmless literary coterie but was now strongly anti-British and anarchistic. The government, he argued, by social reform, for instance improving the health services, could cut the ground from under the negative policies of Sinn Féin.[8]

A fortnight later his approach received support from an unexpected quarter, the novelist George Moore. Moore when visiting Dublin in the summer of 1918 had inscribed his name in 'the book' at the viceregal lodge, 'to confirm my sanity in a country where there are so many in a dream'. Now, early in 1919, he boldly

---

7 *The Times*, 28 March, 10, 14, 24 April 1919.
8 *Irish Times*, 22 Feb., 14 June 1919, 13 April 1920; *Parl. Debates*, 5 series, cxiv, 1523-7.

declared in a letter to *The Times*, 'develop Ireland commercially …
and you will kill at the source Sinn Féin and all it stands for'. He
wanted a naval station and a great commercial port to be established at Galway, linked by improved railway communications to
Great Britain. This would make Ireland a great highway for traffic
between the eastern and western hemispheres and, 'enlisting men's
minds in a romantic adventure', would divert them from 'the bar-
ren field of anti-English politics'. Moore also pressed for the completion of land purchase, educational reform and the exploitation
of Ireland's mineral resources. Give Ireland the benefits of the
union and she will be loyal to the union; 'don't abandon your
friends to the Irish Bolsheviks'.[9] A similar policy was favoured by
C.T. Rolleston, who by 1918 had evolved, practically speaking,
into a unionist. Home Rule, he urged, should be replaced by a
more urgent programme – co-operation, the reform of elementary
education, the construction of a tunnel between Great Britain and
Ireland and large-scale drainage.[10]

The stern, unbending unionists who now controlled the
Unionist Alliance embodied their Irish policy in a series of defiant
statements. Bedrock principles must be asserted. The choice lay
between union and separation. Anything else was a makeshift policy, based on 'the futile theory of a half-way house', 'an attempt to
placate the implacable'. Home Rule, whether the 1920 bill or
Dominion Home Rule, would hand the South of Ireland over to
'the declared enemies of England', to whom 'the imperial idea was
anathema', and to a labour movement applying Bolshevik principles. All this would lead to the empire being weakened, the loyalists betrayed and conflicts between Ulster and the rest of Ireland
and between Sinn Féin and labour intensified. The government
should drop Home Rule and take firm steps to restore order.[11]
These views were enunciated verbally with considerable vigour,
when in May 1919 a deputation from the Alliance met a number

---

9 J. Hone, *Life of George Moore* (1936), p. 348; *The Times*, 18 April, 1 May
    1919; *Daily Express*, 30 Nov. 1918.
10 C.H. Rolleston, *Portrait of an Irishman*, pp. 127-31; *Irish Times*, 22 Feb., 11
    March 1919.
11 *Cork Constitution*, 15 Nov. 1919; *Daily Express*, 22 July 1920, 18 Feb. 1921;
    Dublin Evening Mail, 15 Nov. 1919; *The Times*, 8 Jan., 20 May 1920.

of MPs at Westminster. The deputation dwelt on the prevalence of disorder and agrarian trouble in the South and West, with raids by masked men on loyalist homes – Roman Catholics, Jellett asserted, were not raided, 'except in one case the man being a member of the Irish Unionist Alliance'. Sinn Féin and Bolshevism, it was explained, were allied to bring about the dissolution of law, the destruction of private property and the fall of the British Empire. The deputation urged that steps should be taken to complete land purchase, and to improve education, transport and the housing of the poor. But 'you must grasp the thistle and the nettle firmly', a Dublin businessman declared, and protect loyal people, a policy strongly advocated by Bagwell, the historian of Tudor and Stuart Ireland. 'Ireland', he said, never respects anybody who 'if she gives occasion for knocking her down, does not knock her down'. If England had committed a crime against Ireland, it was the failure to govern firmly. 'Tenderness', he added, 'was no cure for the Irish question.' Clare, he pointed out, was never so happy, as when recently law and order was being enforced by a large military detachment.[12]

The Southern unionists would have been satisfied with a policy of *Quieta non movere*, but the government, though beset by a multiplicity of problems at home and abroad, felt that it could not maintain a *non possimus* attitude to the nationalist demand for Irish self-government. Its approach, outlined by the Prime Minister in December 1919, was not strikingly original – a Home Rule bill on familiar lines but with two Irish parliaments. When the fourth Home Rule bill was being debated early in 1920, Asquith pejoratively described it as 'a large, cumbersome, costly, unworkable scheme', which was not supported by any section of opinion in Ireland. It was indubitably a large measure, its seventy-six clauses and nine schedules ultimately occupying sixty-seven pages of the statute book. Broadly speaking an amalgam of the 1914 Home Rule act and the amending bill, it provided that there should be two Irish parliaments, the parliament of Southern Ireland (twenty-six counties) and the parliament of Northern Ireland (six counties), each responsible for domestic affairs in its own area. Both parliaments by agreement could establish a parlia-

12 Unionist Alliance papers, D989/C/2/7; *The Times*, 30 May 1919.

ment for the whole of Ireland, and there was to be a Council of Ireland, with its membership drawn equally from the parliaments of Southern and Northern Ireland. This body would deal with private bill legislation, the administration of the Irish railways and any other matters which the two parliaments by identical acts might delegate to it. The financial provisions were highly complex – the outstanding feature being that customs, excise, income tax and supertax were to be under imperial control, though the Irish parliament could vary the rates of income tax and supertax. Ireland was to be represented at Westminster by forty-two MPs.

The bill was rejected out of hand by all sections of nationalist opinion. The Northern unionists accepted it as 'a judicious child accepts a dose of castor oil because it thinks it may do it good'.[13] Basing themselves, in Carson's words, 'on the strict logic of reason', the Ulster Unionist Council at a meeting in March pronounced that while they still supported the legislative union, they considered the present bill better than the 1914 act since it exempted them from the jurisdiction of a Home Rule parliament sitting in Dublin. As for the area to be excluded, they realized with 'sorrow and sadness' that better 'a strong Ulster of six counties ... than a weak, tottering fabric of the whole nine counties'. This acceptance of the six-county area aroused the indignation of the Cavan unionists, who complained that they had not had a fair hearing at the March meeting, and the leading Cavan unionist, Lord Farnham, pointed out to Carson that they were being handed over to a Dublin parliament by 'an organization which had made use of our money and our time'. How, he asked, could a covenant be broken for expediency's sake?[14]

The Southern unionists agreed in condemning the bill. The Unionist Alliance, while recognizing Ulster's claim to separate treatment, reaffirmed its determination to resist Home Rule.[15] The more flexible unionists were concerned about safeguards and

---

13 *Parl. Debates*, 5 series, cxxxvi, 1162.

14 *The Times*, 9, 11 March 1920; *Parl. Debates*, 5 series, cxxxvi, 770; W. Reid to W.D. Bates, 19 April 1920, Farnham to E. Carson, 19 April 1920 (Carson papers, DA 1507A/35/2, 3, 10).

15 *The Times*, 11 March 1920.

deplored partition, which, the Unionist Anti-partition League asserted, removed the last hope of a loyal Ireland.[16] Partition, the *Irish Times* declared, was ridiculous, ruinous, unnatural, burdensome to the Irish tax payer, unpopular in Ulster, hateful to nationalists, and disregarded 'the services and interests of nearly 500,000 of His Majesty's most loyal and enlightened subjects'. Nevertheless it admitted that the Ulster unionists were justified by logic, common sense and expediency in accepting the 1920 bill, which saved their peaceful, prosperous corner from ruin by establishing a 'Tudor pale' (with 500,000 loyal subjects outside it). The editor could not forbear to remark, however, that the three hundred Spartans had not surrendered Thermopylae without a blow. When the bill was on the statute book, though he looked forward to reunification of Ireland, he wished the Northern Ireland parliament well. The best policy for the immediate future, in his opinion, was co-operation between North and South, and he warned Southern Irishmen that not all their piety and wit, still less their bombs and revolvers, could undermine Northern Ireland.[17]

A week or so before the debate on the second reading of the Home Rule bill began, Midleton, Oranmore and Browne and a group of MPs – two of whom had Southern unionist backgrounds – approached Bonar Law and requested him to convene a meeting of unionist MPs to consider the bill (and presumably to halt its progress). Bonar Law refused to summon a meeting and told them that if they were opposed to the bill they should have said so earlier. He pointed out the Home Rule act was on the statute book and could not be repealed and that the alternative to the government's Irish policy was to retain Ulster in the United Kingdom and permit the rest of Ireland to set up a Sinn Féin Republic or 'go to the devil'. Incidentally he remarked that there was no difference between Irish independence and dominion status which 'would leave Ireland at liberty to cut the painter'. Shortly afterwards, writing to Midleton, he said that the government was ready to consider suggestions for the protection of the minority in the South but that 'the difficulty of giving any real protection by way

---

16 *The Times*, 2, 9, 15 March 1920.
17 *Irish Times*, 27 Jan., 3 Sept., 11 Oct. 1919, 11 March, 10 April 1920, 21 Jan., 2, 10 April 1921.

of representation to a minority so small as that in the south and
west is very great' – except possibly in a second chamber.[18]

In the House of Commons all three Southern unionist MPs
voted against the second reading of the bill. Dockrell in a jocular
speech – he suggested that the Council of Ireland should meet on
the Boyne viaduct – dismissed the measure as 'a beautiful dream'.
Jellett in a passionate speech declared that the choice lay between
the union and total separation, and that the latter would mean
entrusting Ireland to men hostile to England, who had been allied
to Germany and now looked to Russia. What, he asked, was to be
the fate of the Southern unionists, the loyalists, those who

through evil report and good report ... have steadfastly stood by their
King and their constitution. They had never wavered. They did their duty
and more than their duty in the war ... Now apparently they are going to
receive their reward and what is it – they are to be handed over to the
tender mercies of those who fought against them. Those who drew the
sword to defend you are to be handed over to those who drew the dagger
in the hour of your great agony and stabbed the empire in the back.

Pretyman Newman, MP for Finchley, speaking as a Southern
unionist, rejected the bill in toto, arguing that the only way to
protect the minority in the South was to maintain the union.[19]

The task of trying to amend the bill to make it slightly more
palatable to the Southern unionists was undertaken by Walter
Guinness. He believed that Sinn Féin and the Ulster unionists were
archaic; what he wanted was a united Ireland with safeguards for
Ulster, including possibly a local parliament. He proposed that
there should be an Irish senate, conservative in composition,
which would form a second chamber for both Irish parliaments.
Such a senate would provide a bulwark against revolutionary legislation inspired by Bolshevism, which he believed was a strong
element in Sinn Féin. He also proposed that forty-five MPs should
be added to the Southern Irish parliament, elected on a property
or religious franchise (the India Act of 1919 included communal
representation). Both these proposals were rejected but Guinness

---

18 Notes on interview 17 March 1920, B. Law to Midleton, 1 April 1920
   (Midleton papers, PRO30/67/42).
19 *Parl. Debates*, 5 series, cxxvii, 1306, cxxxiv, 928.

managed to have the number of Irish MPs that were to sit at Westminster raised from forty-two to forty-six (the four additional MPs being allotted to the Irish universities). He also urged that divorce should remain a reserved subject; otherwise people in Ireland would be in a difficult position if the Irish parliaments refused to pass divorce bills. He was assured that under the provisions of the Government of Ireland bill, private bills could still be introduced into the imperial parliament.[20] Finally, he slightly strengthened the Council of Ireland by giving it control over fisheries. It may be added that when the bill was in the Lords an amendment empowered the council to administer the Diseases of Animals Act.

In the House of Lords thirty unionist peers connected with the South of Ireland voted against the bill on its second reading and a dozen of them attacked it in debate. Generally speaking they still believed in the union, but, accepting that Home Rule was inevitable (Donoughmore pointed out that 'the will of the predominant partner is not what it always was'), they regretted the division of Ireland and argued that if it was for the immediate future inevitable, why create a parliament for the six counties remaining in the United Kingdom? Several peers, considering it obvious that the bill would not satisfy the nationalists, asserted that further concessions were necessary. Midleton, for instance, suggested that fiscal autonomy should be granted. Since this implied representation without taxation, Midleton ingeniously defended the retention of Irish MPs at Westminster by pointing out that Irish trade would in fact be controlled to a great extent by the imperial parliament. There was of course another approach to the bill: reject it and maintain the union. Farnham, representing 'the outposts of British civilization', condemned the utter futility of any Home Rule proposals. Mayo declared it was not the moment to grant responsible government to Ireland, and Killanin, in a stimulating and sparking contribution, implied that the union was the best possible solution for Ireland's problems. He castigated the Irish nationalists for continually ignoring Ulster unionist views and feelings. 'Irishmen have a great gift for denying the existence

20 *Parl. Debates*, 5 series, cxxix, 150, 1954, 1959, cxxx, 1166.

of anything they dislike' – and he was sure that if two parliaments were established they would steadily move further and further apart. 'If', he remarked, 'the parliament in Dublin ... makes Irish a compulsory language, in ten years it will not be any good these parliaments coming together because the members will not understand one another.'

When the bill was in committee the Southern unionist peers made determined efforts to obtain 'safeguards', and in the event they managed to insert in the bill some important amendments that were accepted by the Commons. It was provided that each parliament should be bicameral, and that the Southern Irish senate should be highly conservative in its composition. The Irish parliaments were forbidden to take any property without compensation. In the bill the Irish parliaments were empowered to increase or reduce the rates of income tax and supertax on individuals domiciled in Ireland, a provision that greatly alarmed some leading Southern unionists. 'In no country', Walter Guinness stated, 'do income tax lines so clearly follow political lines as in Ireland.'[21] They were reassured by a Lords amendment striking out the power to increase income tax and supertax rates, though the Irish parliaments were permitted to afford relief from those taxes.

21 *Parl. Debates*, 5 series, cxxxiii, 2161.

v The Victory of Sinn Féin

WHILE THE THIRD HOME RULE BILL was slowly moving through parliament it was being rapidly rendered obsolete by dramatic developments in Ireland. From early in 1919 an alternative government dependent on Dáil Éireann was being organized. Loans were raised by the Dáil Department of Finance; local authorities were directed to correspond with Dáil Éireann, ignoring the Local Government Board; republican courts were set up with criminal and civil jurisdiction. An indignant Cork unionist described the members of a court as youthful, ugly and large-eared, but had to admit that solicitors were prepared to appear before it[1] (however the Dáil minister for Home Affairs, seeking for judges, found the Irish bar 'worthy of the bad tradition it always had', with scarcely a dozen patriots in its ranks).[2]

Non-violent opposition to the Irish administration based in Dublin Castle was supplemented by armed insurrection. From early in 1919 the Volunteers, now known as the Irish Republican Army, began attacking policemen and small RIC barracks in some areas in the South with the aim of obtaining arms. Sporadic attacks developed into a widespread campaign, to a limited extent directed by headquarters in Dublin. Individual policemen were shot, small patrols ambushed and barracks suddenly besieged and sometimes captured. Early in 1920 many of the smaller barracks were evacuated and the police concentrated in towns and large villages, with the result that the King's writ ran only intermittently over large stretches of country. Though large parties of police and military scoured disturbed areas, investigating outrages and searching for arms, a man might find himself, Midleton complained,

---

1 *Parl. Debates*, 5 series, cxxx, 2080.
2 *Dáil Éireann Debates*, p. 67.

twelve to fifteen miles from a police barracks,[3] and law-abiding people were compelled to seek protection from the Sinn Féin courts and police. During 1920 and the first half of 1921 IRA attacks on the Crown forces escalated, large-scale ambushes – styled in the press 'battles' – were mounted, roads were trenched, bridges blown up, government buildings (including court-houses and tax offices) destroyed. Justices of the Peace were ordered to resign their commissions and witnesses and jurymen were intimidated, so that in the south and west the courts could hardly function (ironically it seems that in some counties the assize judges were presented with the customary white gloves, no true bills having been returned).[4] Prominent supporters of law and order and persons suspected of having given information to the Crown forces were shot.

It took some time for the government to realize that what it was facing was not a serious rise in recorded crimes and outrages but an organized, sustained attempt to overthrow Crown authority in Ireland, and it was not easy for the constabulary and the military to adjust to rapidly changing conditions. Traditional police tactics, even those evolved during periods of acute agrarian disorder, were futile in the face of strong, well-planned armed attacks, and the military, after the long-drawn-out struggle on the western front, had forgotten the lessons learned in South Africa. However, from the middle of 1920 the government began to respond vigorously to the situation in the south and west of Ireland. English ex-servicemen were recruited for the RIC, and an auxiliary division of the RIC was formed, 1500 strong, composed of ex-officers, companies of which were used to strengthen the police in seriously disturbed districts. Steps were taken to co-ordinate the activities of the Crown forces and to increase their mobility; the Restoration of Order Act passed in August 1920 widened the jurisdiction of courts martial; and in December 1920 and January 1921 eight counties and two county boroughs in the south and west were placed under martial law, the competent military authority being empowered to take whatever measures were necessary to suppress rebellion.

---

3 *Parl. Debates (Lords)*, 5 series, lx, 203.
4 *Parl. Debates*, 5 series, cxxvii, 959.

Members of the Crown forces and their civilian supporters felt they were fighting 'a one-sided war'[5] against adversaries, usually indistinguishable from ordinary civilians, who would strike unexpectedly and then quickly merge with the mass of the population. On occasion, 'maddened by the cold-blooded slaughter of their comrades',[6] as the *Irish Times* expressed it, soldiers and policemen committed acts of violence against persons and property – reprisals. Later, when martial law was in force, houses of persons suspected of strongly sympathizing with the insurgents were destroyed on the order of the competent military authority – official reprisals. Reprisals naturally produced counter-reprisals – the IRA burning the houses of known government supporters. Reprisals by the Crown forces, official and non-official, shocked some English conservatives who had an inherent respect for law and order, and English liberals who loathed militarism. The editor of the *Irish Times*, though he insisted that discipline should be preserved, emphasized that when it had broken down, this was due to extreme provocation. In June 1920 he wrote that young soldiers were undergoing a test that would strain the temper of the most seasoned troops. A large section of the Irish press was subjecting them to abuse and ridicule and Irishmen were claiming that war could be waged on the limited-liability principle – the IRA could employ every weapon of guerrilla warfare but the British government was not at war with Ireland.[7] His admiration for the Crown forces was unstinted. War, he declared, 'without any of the amenities of decent warfare', was being waged against the RIC, 'loyal men who have bred loyal sons and daughters'. As for the army, surely, he wrote, the warriors of the Great War have not been transformed into devils by their transplantation into Ireland, and if it could not be denied that the auxiliaries had faults, it was unjust to treat their 'lapses' as an excuse for an attack on the force.[8] The auxiliaries were also defended by Bernard. 'It is to be regretted', he wrote, 'that some members of the auxiliary police are desperate men, but they were appointed to

---

5 *Parl. Debates (Lords)*, 5 series, xli, 889.
6 *Irish Times*, 3 Nov. 1920.
7 *Irish Times*, 29 June 1920.
8 *Irish Times*, 29 Oct. 1919, 5, 24 March 1920, 22 Feb., 2 March 1921.

do desperate work, and if it were not for their activity in the south and west of Ireland no Protestant could live in security.'[9]

During the conflict between the Crown forces and the IRA, and during the civil war that succeeded it, the bulk of the population displayed a dogged determination, often combined with some ingenuity, in continuing to pursue their accustomed routine of work and pleasure. They might be reminded that conditions were abnormal by hearing shots, by being raided or held up and searched by either the IRA or the military, or when travelling, being delayed by broken bridges or striking railway men. But while all this could be frightening or exasperating, it was only incidental to the daily round – though in later years it provided plenty of anecdotal material. After all guerrilla warfare is sporadic and the degree of disturbance varied in time and between areas. Between 1 January 1919 and 11 July 1921 the Crown forces lost 1263 killed and wounded.[10] 'A ghastly total', the Chief Secretary stated, but an average of about twelve a week in a country of over 32,000 square miles. By a similar accounting, between January 1919 and May 1921 the Crown forces lost in killed 651 (80 per cent being members of the police force),[11] and of these fatal casualties, 70 per cent were sustained in Munster. Again, if between 1919 and the middle of 1923 at least two hundred country houses were destroyed, hundreds survived; and if the centre of Cork was burned out in January 1921, the devastated zone was only a small proportion of the total built-up area. The Irish newspapers printed lists of outrages – shootings, ambushes, raids, murders – often with vivid details. But, as an able historian said, 'you would get an entirely distorted view of Ireland if you were to take your opinions entirely from the daily budget of incidents'.[12] During these disturbed years the newspapers were packed with accounts of sporting events, theatre and cinema programmes and advertisements for shopping bargains. At the beginning of June 1921, when the conflict against Crown authority was at its height, a leader in

9 J.H. Bernard to A. Martin, 14 March 1920, 22 Feb., 2 March 1921 (Bernard papers, Add. MS 52783).
10 *Parl. Debates*, 5 series, cxl, 463.
11 *Parl. Débates*, 5 series, xliii, 2172.
12 *Parl. Debates*, 5 series, li, 1422. See also *The Times*, 5 April 1920.

the *Dublin Evening Mail* pointed out that there was something for everybody in the sporting events to be decided that day.[13] The Royal Dublin Society continued to hold its great annual horse show – the *Irish Times* compared its council to the Roman consul who refused to despair of the Republic[14] – and on the evening before the Custom House was destroyed the Royal Society of Antiquities listened to a paper on 'Murchertach O'Brien, High King of Ireland and his Norman son-in-law'. Sometime later, on 28 June 1922, the day before the Irregulars in the Four Courts surrendered to Free State forces, Bernard, provost of Trinity since 1919, recorded in his diary 'a day of street battle' and that the Postmaster General had called to settle about College hospitality for the Canadian athletes visiting Dublin in August, 'a great nuisance'. On 4 July he was present at Commencements and at the dinner in Hall 'to welcome' the honorary graduates. Some months earlier, an old political ally of Bernard, Andrew Jameson, a most public-spirited man, having remarked that the country seemed to be slipping into anarchy, went on to say that he had taken a stretch of fishing in the West – 'with a little fishing and shooting, and a few friends to play golf and bridge with, what a nice world it would be'.[15] Understandably then, Sir Nevill Macready, the Commander of the forces, and Dan Breen, the well-known guerrilla leader, when surveying the period 1919-21 were struck by the apathy that characterized many of their nominal supporters.[16] Dan Breen in retrospect wrote that 'the truth is that our war policy was not popular ... the public did not want the war ... but as it developed in intensity the vast majority of the people stood with us' – which suggests a somewhat passive form of support. Macready considered that loyalists in general did not exert themselves enough in support of law and order, for instance failing to supply

---

13 *Evening Mail*, 3 June 1921.
14 *Irish Times*, 10 Aug. 1920.
15 Bernard Diaries, A. Jameson to Midleton, 30 March 1922 (Midleton papers, PRO30/67/49).
16 N. Macready, *Annals of an Active Life* (1928), ii, pp. 555-61; D. Breen, *My Fight for Irish freedom* (1924), pp. 150-7. In a novel dealing with the 1919–21 conflict it was stated that in a small southern town 'even those who approved of Volunteer activities had wanted them to happen elsewhere, fearing the vengeance of the Black and Tans' (F. Carty, *The Irish Volunteer* [1932], p. 275).

the forces with information (he ungratefully overlooked the occasions on which loyalists, at considerable risk to themselves, gave useful information to the RIC or the military). At this point in parenthesis it should be said that from 1918 'unionist' as a political label was being supplemented or superseded by 'loyalist', the latter term resonant and implying adherence to high principle, covering not only unionists but those constitutional nationalists who avowedly supported Crown authority.

With the IRA taking the offensive and in many areas the Crown forces unable to protect the law-abiding, many loyalists must have been sorely tempted to keep their heads down. But for some, principle and circumstances forbade this easy option. In the face of Dáil Éireann's efforts to set up an alternative government and the IRA's campaign of violence the government was determined to keep the administration functioning and to ensure the King's writ ran throughout the country. It was desirable then, indeed almost essential, that the justices of the peace should perform their magisterial duties. JP had long been a coveted suffix, an indication of status or success. Now republicans made it clear that remaining a JP signified a willingness to assist in maintaining British rule. The response of some JPs was to resign; others refrained from sitting on the bench. But there were those who, undaunted, continued to act as magistrates. For instance in County Cavan, one JP – in his own opinion 'the largest unionist and Protestant landowner in the district' – continued to adjudicate to the end. Another Cavan JP, a land agent and auctioneer, attended the last petty sessions court held in Belturbet, guarded by thirty auxiliaries. He was on crutches because he had been wounded and after the Truce he left for England.[17] In Donegal a Catholic businessman with a remarkable variety of business interests (spirits, hardware, a bakery and coal), who 'strongly identified himself with the followers of racing and horse breeding, continued to supply a nearby military camp and refused to resign the Commission of the Peace. On one occasion he was put up against his yard wall and told he would be shot, his children were shunned in school and his wife ignored. His business was almost ruined, his staff

17 CO762/14JHB, CO762/157DG.

being reduced from ninety to nine.[18] In County Longford a large farmer, according to a District Inspector (DI) 'the most fearless and outspoken supporter of the Crown I have ever met with', continued to act as a JP – his cattle were driven and his lands seized for two years. In Meath, a merchant-tailor living in Navan stated that when the RM was on sick leave, 'practically all the magisterial work fell on my shoulders', the police being continually in and out of his house. He was subjected to a severe boycott but lived it down.[19] In Queen's County a retired colonel, living on a property that had been in his family from 1549, 'up to the end', according to an RM, carried out the duties of the law 'fearlessly and well'. 'My wife and I', the colonel wrote, 'lived in a constant state of terror, never knowing what the night might bring forth.' Another Queen's County JP, a large farmer, refused to resign and when four local court-houses were burned down arranged for courts to be held in his own house. He was boycotted and cattle, sheep and horses driven into his crops. In the same county, a draper, who as a JP refused to resign, gave the RM every assistance, and a well-known land agent continued to act as a JP, in the last six months sitting alone.[20] In the neighbouring King's County, a large farmer who continued to act as a JP and who supplied the boycotted police, was described by an RIC sergeant as 'one of the best gentlemen I have ever met, his scorn of rebel fear was so marked'. In 1922 after being dragged from his house and told he would be shot, he sold out and left Ireland to farm in Somerset. Another large farmer in King's County, who claimed that his ancestors had come from England in 1651, continued to sign summons when all the other JPs for miles round had either resigned or left the county. Another King's County JP, who had been on the bench for forty-eight years and who had been an active magistrate in Land League days, continued to sit. He had to repel an attack on his house and was assaulted at a fair. In County Kilkenny 'a retired army officer, 'an outspoken unionist who attended all the meetings', acted as a JP 'up to the very last' and was high sheriff for 1922.[21]

18 CO762/200JC.
19 CO762/110EMW, CO762/38JCP.
20 CO762/110WHF, CO762/128RKC, CO762/122HF.
21 CO762/68HNW, CO762/134AFH, CO762/61WJH-T, CO762/11/JJEP.

In County Tipperary a land agent, 'a man of heroic consistency', who sat when no other JP would attend, was murdered in January 1921.[22] In County Cork Lord Bandon and a well-known country gentleman both steadily attended quarter sessions. They were kidnapped and held for some weeks and their houses destroyed. In West Cork, a draper, who was the proprietor of the *Skibbereen Eagle*, assisted the RM in holding petty sessions, and in Cork city, a cycle agent who was a JP and who refused to resign was murdered in August 1922.[23] In County Mayo an RM could rely on a county surveyor with a son in the RAMC to attend courts. 'There was nothing of a trimmer about him,' the RM wrote, 'no man viewed the passing of the old order with more sorrow.' In Galway a landowner whose family, he said, had been British army officers for generations, 'flatly refused' to resign the Commission of the Peace and continued to attend Tuam petty sessions – he was the only JP to do so. Another Galway landowner, a man of about eighty, whose brother had been Chief Justice of Bombay and who kept the Union Jack flying over his house, was 'a fearless magistrate'. The only loyalist for fifteen miles round, he was fired at and boycotted, partly because he would not surrender his land to his tenants.[24] In County Sligo a Protestant farmer, owning well over two thousand acres, continuously took his place on the bench – graves were dug on his land with crosses attached to them bearing his name and those of his two herds. In Sligo town, a Protestant flour merchant functioned as a JP to the last moment and when travelling about the country obtained information about IRA activities which he passed on to the police; 'with the supremacy of the empire always in the forefront of his thought', he scorned to hide his patriotism. In Westmeath a landed gentleman, a cousin of Sir Henry Wilson, sat as a JP and openly showed his hostility to Sinn Féin. When he was staying in the Hibernian in Dublin a couple of men entered his room but when they found he had a guard of auxiliaries they abruptly retreated.[25]

There were other ways in which loyalists helped to keep the

22 CO762/175LEF.
23 CO762/82CS-K, CO762/27RS, CO762/59EDC.
24 CO762/71GJ, CO762/162AEE, CO762/26WJF.
25 CO762/9C, CO762/195GR, CO762/124JGW.

legal machinery functioning. Another cousin of Sir Henry Wilson, who was high sheriff for County Kildare in 1920, arranged that a machine-gun should be available for the protection of the assize judges – his house was raided and his cattle stolen.[26] In Cork city Sir Harley Scott, at the request of Lord French, accepted the office of high sheriff 'in defiance of rebel pretensions'.[27] Crown solicitors in many counties performed their duties unflinchingly. The Crown solicitor for County Cork, who often prosecuted before courts martial, was, he said, sentenced to death by the republicans three times, but 'the most peculiar aspect of that was that all three of my would-be executioners afterwards became my warmest friends'. The deputy Crown solicitor for Sligo, who regarded with contempt 'passive loyalists', claimed to have prosecuted hundreds for sedition and to have been sentenced to death by the IRA. The Crown solicitor for Limerick when attending an out-lying court made a point of going and returning by different routes. On one occasion, motoring to an inquest on members of the IRA shot in action, he sat, 'unarmed', between the CI and a DI, both armed and with steel armour under their tunics. The Crown solicitors for Leitrim and Galway lost most of their private practice by refusing to attend Sinn Féin courts. After the Treaty they both emigrated, the former to Belfast, the latter to Canada, with, though he was a Catholic, a letter of introduction to the Grand Master of the Orange Order in Canada.[28] Some solicitors prided themselves on not appearing in Sinn Féin courts, one of them, a Protestant, living in Tralee, sadly reflecting that 'even old loyalists who were shop-keepers went to Sinn Féin solicitors'.[29] Some grand jurors attended the assizes in spite of threats and there was a Tipperary farmer who in June 1921 was the only juryman to attend the assizes at Nenagh – he considered it his duty to do so as a loyal citizen of the British empire.[30] Witnesses were often reluctant to come forward but in Cork a medical man, late RAMC, often gave evidence

26 CO762/117AWW.
27 CO762/71HS, CO762/71HS.
28 CO76/54JTW, *Cork Examiner*, 16 Sept. 1952, CO762/167WHA, CO762/ 179JSG, CO762/58RAC, CO762/88JG.
29 CO762/129ARQ, CO762/92FCP.
30 CO762/155EE.

for the prosecution before courts martial. 'He has', it was remarked, 'what some people would call too much pluck.' At an inquest held in Westport on an RM who had been shot, when ten members of the jury wished to bring in a verdict of 'Died from gunshot wounds', a Protestant hotel proprietor, who had served in the RIC, insisted on a verdict of 'wilful murder'. He was backed by another Protestant and after some hours of heated discussion, 'as some of the jurors were businessmen with urgent business', the hotel proprietor prevailed. Later, as he would 'not bow down to rebels', he was compelled to emigrate to Liverpool.[31]

Loyalists were naturally very ready to afford aid and comfort to the Crown forces. Being friendly with the army and the constabulary was, they repeatedly asserted, normal social behaviour for unionists and loyalists. Many Irishmen had served in the forces, others had close relatives in the army or the RIC, and soldiers and members of the RIC were welcomed by different levels of loyalist society in their homes, at hunt balls, in the county clubs and in public houses. This openly displayed goodwill brought many loyalists into direct and sometimes dangerous conflict with republican sentiment and policy. The republican campaign against the police and army included a sustained effort to isolate them from Irish social life. The RIC, in quiet times acceptable and popular enough members of the local community, were to be treated as pariahs – in July 1920 the IRA in Donegal gave notice that 'all intercourse is strictly forbidden between citizens of the Irish republic and that portion of the army of occupation known as the RIC'.[32] The army, for which Ireland was an easygoing place with a very pleasant social and sporting life, was to be left lonely and bored in barracks. This policy was expected to both weaken morale and deprive the forces of the intelligence that was of such vital importance in guerrilla warfare. Loyalists, who regarded the Crown forces as integral and valued sections of Irish society, ignored the boycott. As a country gentleman put it, he entertained the auxiliaries just as he had entertained the army. A gentlewoman in County Kerry, 'a Protestant loyalist', whose brother 'and all

31 CO762/120CN, CO762/29JO'C.
32 CO762/148RN.

connected with us fought in the Great War', 'kept open house for the forces of the British government'; she was boycotted and her land seized. Another Kerry landowner, Sir Arthur Vicars, a some-time Ulster King-of-Arms, was on very good terms with the con-stabulary, regularly sending illustrated magazines to the local RIC barracks. On an April morning he was taken from his house and shot, a notice worded, 'Spy. Informers beware. The IRA never for-gets', being affixed to his body. The headmaster of a well-known 'loyalist and Protestant' school, the Abbey, in Tipperary, provided cricket and bridge for the army.[33] In Carlow a solicitor, who had in the past represented the Unionist Party before the revising bar-rister, had army officers to tennis and shooting parties. In 1921 his house was raided but he and his sons armed with revolvers drove the raiders off. However, soon afterwards he sold his practice. A land agent in King's County gave refreshments to the military; after this shots were fired into his drawing room and his cattle dri-ven. A farmer in Kildare took auxiliaries out shooting over his land; his cattle were driven and his fields left 'more like a common than a cultivated farm'. A large farmer in Louth, 'an out and out unionist', who had fought in the Boer War, entertained 'the com-mandant of the Black and Tans [presumably of the auxiliaries]'. In 1923 armed men gave him five minutes to get out of his house before it was burned. 'I had to go as I left my bed save that I put on a dressing gown.'[34] A Tipperary JP, a Catholic, a large farmer, a racehorse-owner and a gentleman rider, who according to a DI, followed 'the British ideal as distinct from the purely Irish one', was active in recruiting and in Red Cross work – his wife organiz-ing a Red Cross bazaar. They seem to have frequently entertained army officers because their maids were notified 'your time could be turned to better account than cooking for those swell army officers who have ravaged our land at the point of the sword'. The farmer himself was warned that 'the boys you call murderers have enough lead to blow you to atoms', and he was raided and boycotted.[35]

A doctor's wife in Carrick-on-Shannon made her house a sort

---

33 CO762/61HC, CO762/60EB, CO762/71GFS, *The Times*, 15 Apr. 1921, CO762/169GF.
34 CO762/89ESM, CO762/75RD, CO762/93ICG, CO762/78JAAC.
35 CO762/177JP.

of club for army and RIC officers, preparing meals for those returning from raids and organizing entertainments at the barracks, setting, her rector said, 'an example of loyalty in a very hostile community'. The rector himself was praised by an army officer for doing all he could to keep the troops happy in very dismal surroundings. The rector of Mountrath in Queen's County made the RIC honorary members of the parochial hall and raised from his parishioners money to buy a billiard table for their use. Another Church of Ireland clergyman, a County Galway rector, when accused by raiders of offering hospitality to the Black and Tans, replied that as they were his parishioners it was natural to ask them to the rectory. A Clare farmer, a woman, helped to provide a reading room for the troops and had an officer's wife as a paying guest – 'why she was not burned out', the local rector wrote, 'is a marvel to me'. The Grand Mistress of an Orange Lodge in County Galway raised money to provide comforts for the troops; raiders put stock on her land and she had to retreat to Cavan. A Church of Ireland widow in Cavan, a dressmaker, made her house a home for young English RIC men, and when two were killed placed wreaths on their graves.[36]

Loyalists not only swept members of the Crown forces into their social life, providing them with relief from their monotonous and perilous duties and incidentally adding to their own enjoyment, but on occasion they gave practical help. A number of businessmen and shopkeepers supplied the military and police at the risk of being boycotted. As a butter and egg supplier in Kerry, who had always been 'in the most friendly intercourse' with the gentry, put it, he would not obey the IRA order to stop supplying the Crown forces because, 'apart from the same being illegal I thought it tyranny of the worst form if a man could not have what friends he wished'. He continued supplying the police, 'a decent body of men', was boycotted and was 'just able to keep floating but no more'.[37] In Listowel a public house run by an RIC man's widow was said to be one of the few places where the police were

---

36 CO762/148EB, CO762/143JCB, CO762/140RB, CO762/21DEB, CO762/66EJ, CO762/174LA, CO762/103RW.
37 CO762/35DO'S.

safe. It was referred to by republicans as 'the den of the enemy'. In Youghal the IRA tried to get a public house, patronized by the police, closed at 10 p.m. but the proprietor, an ex-soldier, secured a military guard and kept it open.[38] A Nenagh grocer declared that 'I catered for them [the RIC] in the kindest possible manner'. After the Treaty her store was broken into and her customers intimidated. The manager of a flour-mill in Waterford, a Protestant, supplied the military with food. He was harassed, his employer thought it advisable to dispense with his services, and he found himself a bus conductor in England, 'very different work to which I was accustomed'.[39] The owner of a motor business in Carlow gave the use of his cars free to the military. A garage proprietor in Ballina allowed his premises to become the military headquarters for the area. A motor trader in Donegal lent his cars to the military and when he accompanied them on 'a sunt' wore uniform to prevent the IRA identifying him. After the Truce he left for Belfast. Another Donegal garage proprietor, a Catholic, both drove for the RIC and provided cars for the funerals of men killed by the IRA. He was boycotted and, from being reasonably well off, was reduced to keeping a boarding-house in Bundoran.[40] A Galway landlord arranged for an army intelligence officer to use his house when he did not wish to visit the police barracks.[41] A Cavan cattle-dealer who had served in the war carried provisions for the RIC in spite of threats. 'Of course I made nothing out of these transactions', he wrote, 'as I only carried the goods.' At the end of 1921 he fled to the North and joined the Special Constabulary. A Protestant farmer drove an army sergeant, whose lorry had broken down, to Fermoy. 'That night', he wrote, 'I was well afraid of myself.' A commercial traveller, living in Cork, carried despatches for the RIC. In 1921 he was ordered to leave Ireland. 'I am not what might be called easily frightened,' he said, 'but I considered it discretion when a revolver was placed at my head and retreated to Belfast.' A Kilkenny farm labourer, whose brothers had served in the army and whose wife did washing for

---

38 CO762/64MC, CO762/35RB.
39 CO762/64NH, CO762/119HP.
40 CO762/38GBJ, O762/88JW, CO762/44DKK, CO762/89LWM.
41 CO762/133LAL.

the military, gave the military his carrier pigeons 'to help them in the struggle with the murderous gang'.[42] In Leitrim the freemasons allowed a military detachment to camp in their hall. The member of the Lodge principally responsible for this decision was a draper, who refused to close his shop when there were political strikes. He was boycotted and left for England where he was very successful in his investments. A wholesale grocer in Mayo surrendered his gun to the RIC. There were, it was stated, 'twenty more people in his district having guns, and not one of those, some of whom were Protestants, had the pluck to follow Mr M——'s example but all of them gave their guns to the Sinn Féiners'. He was raided and lost £300 in cash. A Protestant farmer in Kerry, 'well known as an imperialist', both assisted the Crown forces and tried to combat Sinn Féin propaganda. He was raided, and after receiving a warning from Austin Stack, whom he had known in his youth, he fled to England and opened a bookshop in London.[43]

A farmer's widow in Longford sheltered wounded auxiliaries after an ambush. She was boycotted and could not get men to work for her. The widow of a DI who ran a stationary shop in Thurles went to the assistance of a mortally wounded DI in 1919. She too was boycotted and left for England. A publican in Kerry who took two badly wounded soldiers into his house was boycotted and warned: 'If your miserable soul is not pledged to Satan like your slimy body to Dublin Castle, then look to it.' A farmer in Cork, who 'entertained and was entertained by the officers in Kanturk', sheltered soldiers after a major ambush at Clonbarren. A retired colonel in Westmeath in January 1921 when a DI and two constables took refuge in his house motored for help to the nearest police barrack. Immediately a military force was sent to rescue the RIC party – and afterwards the colonel was fined £500 by the IRA. A shopkeeper in Youghal, a prominent Orangeman, when the Hampshire's band was ambushed, sent out 'his girls' to take tea to the troops, he was boycotted and stones were flung at him. 'I don't believe', he declared, 'that the Armenians were worse treated than we were.'[44]

42 CO762/127WS, CO762/111CB, CO762/97JHH, CO762/116JO'B.
43 CO762/22TM, CO762/161ET, CO762/42GD.
44 CO762/14KS, CO762/125DJR, CO762/143KGP, CO762/62EF, CO762/27JHL, CO762/51ED.

When chatting with friends and acquaintances in the army and the RIC, loyalists must have talked about politics, the conditions of the country and what was happening in the neighbourhood. Much of what they said would have helped the police and the army to grasp the situation in which they were operating. Moreover, keen supporters of Crown authority sometimes gave the authorities specific information concerning IRA activities. Frequently, in fact, the insurgents' plans must have been seriously disrupted as a result of information received from loyalists. For instance a farmer in Leitrim, a Protestant, seeing an ambush being prepared near his home, informed the police. He had to hide in the woods for six weeks and was 'severely boycotted – 'even the woman I was going to marry was afraid to speak to me and married someone else'. Another Leitrim farmer and his wife during 1919-20 told the military where they would find wanted men. Their house was frequently raided and the family moved to Belfast, the husband joining the B Specials.[45] In the same county a Protestant gamekeeper supplied the soldiers guarding a railway with food and the police with information. A medical man in Leitrim, a TCD graduate, passed on the authorities information about an impending ambush which had been given to him by a Protestant farmer. The farmer was taken out of his house and shot, leaving a widow and six children. She migrated to Belfast and the doctor hastily left Ireland to practice in London.[46] In Donegal, according to a DI, the fifteen-year-old son of a Catholic businessman passed on to the authorities information about an intended ambush which 'saved a hundred lives'.[47] In Roscommon a police pensioner who was an ex-soldier gave his old companions 'all the information I could possibly command regarding their enemies'. In 1920 returning from an ex-servicemen's meeting he was waylaid and beaten and for months had to sleep in ditches and crocks of hay. A cattle dealer in Cavan gave information to the police and became, he said, 'a marked man'. A farmer in the same county, 'a Protestant and a loyalist as his family had been for hundreds of years', gave information about republican

45 CO762/149TC, CO762/38D & A McN.
46 CO762/169GD, CO762/69CP, CO762/4L, CO762/174ET, CO762/98TA.
47 Co762/205EM.

courts; his tractor was seized and his flour-mill boycotted. A small farmer in Westmeath, a Protestant, buried RIC men after an ambush and gave what information he could to the Crown forces. After being raided and prevented from cutting turf he departed to the North. Another Protestant farmer in a neighbouring county, Meath, informed the military about a projected ambush. He was raided and threatened, a revolver being thrust into his mouth.[48]

A saddler in Kildare was fortunate. From raiding the mails the IRA discovered he was writing to the police, but because they only found this out after the signing of the Treaty, they reluctantly decided not to shoot him, instead ordering him to leave Ireland.[49] In Tipperary a Church of Ireland clergyman who continually entertained army officers and who on 11 November 1918 had flown the Union Jack and removed a Sinn Féin flag from his school, constantly informed the police about intended ambushes, on one occasion driving in his trap seventeen miles, 'to avoid ambush patrols'. After an attack on his rectory in 1922 which was beaten off, the doors having been strengthened, he left for Bournemouth.[50] In the same county a farmer twice saved the police from running into an ambush. The wife of the Crown solicitor for Clare, having discovered that an ambush was being prepared for a cavalry patrol, informed her husband who telephoned the police and the patrol was alerted. Her house was burned and she had to leave for England. Another loyalist lady, the owner of Finsborough House, having been told by her foreman that a road along which a military party was going to travel had been mined, went at once to the barracks with the information. The result was an engagement in which two insurgents were shot. Shortly afterwards in July 1921 her house was burned down and she had to take refuge in a nearby wood.[51]

About the same time in West Cork, Mrs Lindsay, an elderly widow living near Coachford, and her chauffeur-butler, while motoring home saw a number of men preparing an ambush. She at once turned back and drove to the nearest police barrack, 'in the hope', she said, 'of saving some poor fellows'. As a result a military

---

48 CO762/20JJMcE, CO762/60HT, CO762/173TN, CO762/188JS.
49 CO762/192JO'D.
50 CO762/37LEH.
51 CO762/124H&TO'B, CO762/81FWG, CO762/75FMD.

detachment surprised the ambushers and captured five who after trial by court martial were sentenced to death. Mrs Lindsey and her chauffeur were kidnapped and charged with being spies. Mrs Lindsey was compelled to write to the general commanding in Cork, pointing out 'the consequences to herself should the men be executed'. 'In accordance with the settled policy of the authorities', it was decided to ignore her letter and after the men were executed she and her butler were shot, Cathal Brugha, the Dáil Minister of Defence, pleading that 'stern necessity' dictated this 'drastic action'.[52]

For loyalists, to supply information to the authorities which might lead to the prevention or punishment of criminal acts was simply the duty of a good citizen. Though some of the less prosperous informants may have received payment for their intelligence work they were probably influenced by loyalty and comradeship (if ex-soldiers or police pensioners) rather than money. To republicans, giving information to the British forces was treason and, with intelligence of vital importance in guerrilla warfare, treason of a most dangerous kind – and a number of civilians suspected of giving information were shot. Since the victim was often described as 'Convicted spy' on a notice pinned to his body, presumably some attempt was made to assess the degree of guilt before execution. Indeed in April 1921 the adjutant general of the IRA stated that a convicted spy should not be executed until the conviction and sentence had been ratified by the brigade commander of the district. But the process for deciding a suspect's fate must have been very rough and ready. Persons suspected of supplying information were executed all over the country, in County Galway, Kerry, King's County, Limerick, Leitrim, Longford, Monaghan, Cork. In Cork, Commandant Tom Barry took vigorous action against 'the bloodhounds who were nosing out victims for the British murder gangs', arranging for twelve suspected spies to be shot early in 1921, including two Methodist businessmen, two large Protestant farmers and, later, a retired colonel with a fine war record.[53]

52 E.C. Wylly, *History of the Manchester Regiment*, ii (1925), pp. 309-12; *Parl. Debates*, 5 series, cxlv, 1605-8. An appreciation of Mrs Lindsay was published in the *Morning Post*, 13 August 1921.

53 *Parl. Debates*, 5 series, cxlvi, 1624, cxxxviii, 1262, cxxxiv, 71; T. Barry, *Guerilla Days in Ireland* (1949), p. 105.

Between 1919 and the Truce at least 130 civilians were shot by the republicans in the twenty-six counties. Of these approximately forty-seven were shot as spies, including ten ex-servicemen[54] – 'all ex-soldiers', a retired major wrote, 'were looked upon as spies'.[55] Incidentally, according to military intelligence the IRA frequently described (usually by a notice on the body) a victim who had not been an informant as a spy, so as to convince the public 'that they had almost miraculous powers of tracing a traitor'.[56] In addition twelve civilians who were shot were known to be friendly with the Crown forces – for instance an ex-soldier in Longford who 'would speak to a policeman if he knew him', a Tipperary butcher who supplied the RIC and who was 'friendly with the Crown forces to the extent of having drinks with them', and a Dublin hotel porter who visited the Castle 'to pass the time of day with the police'.[57] The other victims included three RMs, four women shot when accompanying members of the Crown forces,[58] a few young men who were considering joining the Crown forces, two farmers who refused to attend Sinn Féin courts, two Protestant farmers in Longford who refused to surrender their guns, Captain G.B. O'Connor, a Cork JP who had been a unionist parliamentary candidate, the retired Church of Ireland Dean of Leighlin, who was shot when his family house was burned down (it was believed it was going to be occupied by the Crown forces),[59] a land agent near Bandon who was 'a Protestant and one of the staunchest loyalists

---

54 These figures are based on newspaper reports and the reports of military courts held in lieu of inquests in WO35. C. Townshend in *The British Military Campaign in Ireland* (1975) provides a valuable critique on the latter sources. The government stated that between 1 Jan. 1919 and 31 March 1921 92 civilians were murdered in the twenty-six counties and that between 1 Jan and 31 Apr. 1921 73 civilians had been deliberately murdered by Sinn Féin assassins, (*Parl. Debates*, 5 series, cxl, 463, 2086). Of course it is sometimes difficult to be sure why an individual was shot, widespread disorder offering opportunities for ordinary crime and personal malignancy.

55 CO762/51CJJL.

56 WO35/150DF; O. Winter, *Winter's Tale* (1953), pp. 299-301.

57 WO35/142ATB, WO35/147BTC, WO35/149A.

58 Miss Barrington, Mrs Blake, Mrs Hunt and Miss E. Seales (for the last named see WO35/159A).

59 WO35/149B JF.

in his neighbourhood',[60] and a Carlow shopkeeper who had been boycotted for refusing to close on the day of Terence MacSwiney's funeral. He and his solicitor, whom he had instructed to act against the boycotters, were both shot when out walking together.[61]

At a time when political passions were running high and the old regime was finding it difficult to maintain itself, the lot of the Southern unionist or loyalist, who attracted public opprobrium by his opinions or actions, could be a hard one. Loyalist professional men discovered their clients or patients were being intimidated. A veterinary surgeon in County Roscommon, an ex-serviceman, remarked that his practice had greatly diminished as 'a result of wearing the King's uniform'.[62] Loyalist businessmen, especially those who supplied the Crown forces or stocked Belfast goods, or kept their accounts in Belfast-based banks, were often boycotted. A large grocer in Sligo wrote that he was 'infested by pickets',[63] and another large grocer in Roscrea, whose son, a wartime cavalry officer, refused to stand up when 'the republican anthem' was played, discovered coffins and crosses painted on his walls. In Cork a well-established confectionery firm, managed by Protestant unionists, was severely boycotted because it sold Belfast goods. Another Cork firm, coal and iron merchants, whose head, Sir Harley Scott, was a leading unionist, lost a number of contracts for supplying local bodies. In Waterford the proprietor of 'a very large and progressive' motor car business, an avowed unionist, with relations in the forces during the war and who had served as a juryman on several occasions, was severely boycotted. His business was wiped out and he left Waterford to take a post in a large Belfast firm. He had, his wife wrote, 'the heart-break of seeing a business built up by twenty-five years of hard work doomed'.[64] In Cavan the owner of a drapery concern, the wife of a JP, with two sons ex-servicemen, was boycotted. She survived but in 1926 had only three assistants instead of the eight she had once employed. In

---

60 WO35/157A FS.
61 WO35/157A WK, M.O'D.
62 CO762/62EAR.
63 CO762/75JRMcK.
64 CO762/32JD, CO762/111LDH, CO762/112D, O and Co., CO762/66HS, CO762/139WJC.

Leitrim an Orangeman with two shops suffered so severely from raids and looting that he left for Belfast.[65] A shopkeeper in Kerry, an ex-RIC man, after being raided had 'to close our little shop for a year' and a Cork butcher, who had refused to supply the IRA and remained on friendly terms with the police, found 'customers gone, trade gone'.[66] It is impossible to estimate how many loyalist firms, retail or wholesale, were targeted and how many of those systematically boycotted were driven out of business. Probably most survived, helped through difficult times by faithful customers and an overdraft.

Loyalist professionals and businessmen, though they might be subjected to boycotting and threats, usually worked in urban centres where the police were able to function and where they could count on the support of the local loyalist community and on the goodwill of clients and customers, reluctant to sever long-established ties. Rural loyalists were in a much more vulnerable position. Whether in a 'big house', a farm house or a labourer's cottage, they were comparatively isolated, landed property was more difficult to protect and agricultural operations were easily disrupted. Loyalist houses were frequently raided, the raiders often looking for arms. The raids by armed and masked men tended to be at night and the raiders were sometimes rough and aggressive. There was the strain of waiting and wondering what the night sounds, the creaking of a gate, footsteps on gravel, a dog barking, might portend. An elderly lady in Tipperary, the widow of a colonel, after being raided did not go to bed at night for six months. On occasion the occupants of a house were ordered out on short notice and the house – 'a big house' or a farm house – burned. The reasons for burning a house varied. Sometimes it was a reprisal, sometimes it was to penalize the owner for his political opinions – an IRA local leader spoke of burning the houses of 'loyalists, imperialists, D.L.s and such like'[67] – sometimes it may have been to lessen his attachment to his land. There may too have been a primeval urge to sweep away the symbols of an arrogant, alien culture and of a

65 CO762/168JE, CO762/29EB.
66 CO762/27JO'D, CO762/77JC.
67 CO762/72SGT.

defeated feudalism – which may explain the incidents of sheer vandalism that occurred.

Between 1920 and 1923 at least 210 mansions and country houses were deliberately burned in the twenty-six counties.[68] Admittedly this represented only a very small proportion of the total number in the south and west of Ireland but the 'mania of house burning'[69] marked luridly (literally) the end of a long era in Irish history and brought home poignantly, to those who instinctively sympathized with the *ancien régime*, the transitory nature of things and how easily civilized living, *les doucers de la vie*, could be swept away by crude violence.

> The boast of heraldry, the pomp of pow'r,
> And all that beauty, all that wealth e'er gave,
> Awaits alike th' inevitable hour,
> The paths of glory lead but to the grave.

However an Irish poet saw the disappearance of 'big houses' in different terms:

> The little farms have left the hungry hills,
> Their strength with the usurper's power to pit,
> And crept up to the manor's crumbling walls,
> Their heritage retrieving bit by bit.[70]

From early in 1918 many rural loyalists were not only liable to be involved in the political conflict but were targets for direct agrarian action. Landlord, and large farmers, especially those with stretches of grazing land, were frequently under pressure to sell out either to the Land Commission or to a local committee. Loyalist farmers with smaller holdings were occasionally forced to give up part of their holdings or clear out. A County Leitrim farmer, a member of the Unionist Alliance who, having lost the goodwill of his neighbours, decided to emigrate with his family to

---

68 This figure is based on newspaper reports, material in CO762, a list of 'Castles and mansions burned' in Unionist Alliance papers D989/C/2/18, and M. Bence-Jones, *A Guide to Irish Country Houses*, 2nd ed., 1988. The total may be affected by errors of omission or inclusion but it probably provides a reasonable indication of the extent of the destruction.

69 *Irish Times*, 30 June 1921.

70 M. Farlay in *The Bell*, v, no. 1, pp. 4-5.

England, sadly wrote, 'we were neither landlords, graziers holding a ranch, or even eleven-months men, but just tenant farmers, paying rent to the Land Commission'.[71] The assailants, usually relied on two well-tried weapons: boycotting, that 'deadly weapon',[72] and cattle-driving. The former deprived the owner of labour (and even a small farmer would require help at harvest time) and made it difficult for him to sell at fairs and markets. The latter was often two-directional – the victim's stock being driven off his land to wander through the countryside and being replaced by stock belonging to his neighbours. Other coercive devices were smashing gates and fences, knocking down walls, spiking fields, damaging outbuildings, cutting down trees, driving cattle into corn and smashing machinery.

To what extent the drive against a particular landowner was inspired by political, religious or purely agrarian motives it would be hard to say. Victims seem to have believed it was a compound of the three. A King's County heiress explained that 'the idea was to make [the loyalists'] places no use to them with a view to getting hold of their land as aliens in the country'. A Clare landlord, a deputy lieutenant (DL), thought that he aroused hostility 'partly as a Protestant, partly as belonging to the landlord class and partly [owing to] land hunger'. A Waterford landowner referred to 'the violent and ancestral enmity which the mass of the people had to his class'.[73]

Agrarian warfare was one of the factors, the other being urban industrial unrest, that convinced unionists that the country had been infected by the revolutionary communism that had swept through Eastern Europe. In June 1920 the government published the captured draft of a treaty between the Irish Republic and Bolshevik Russia, in which both parties pledged themselves to strive against 'imperialistic exploitation' and develop commercial relations. But as might be expected, nothing was said about promoting communism – a point that might be missed by apprehensive conservatives.[74] The *Irish Times* referred to Bolshevism as the

---

71 CO762/180 ADV.
72 CO762/194JS.
73 CO762/71EHB, CO762/193MK, CO762/94GF.
74 *Intercourse between Bolshevism and Sinn Féin* (Cmd 1326), H.C. 1921, xxix.

sinister camp-follower of Sinn Féin,[75] and the secretary of the London branch of the Irish Unionist Alliance, Richard Dawson, in his *Red Terror and Green*, a book packed with detail, elaborated the theory that there was an alliance, partly dictated by expediency, between Sinn Féin, seeking political independence, and the Labour Party, which sought political independence as a prelude to the establishment of a Workers' Republic. Moderate Sinn Féiners, he thought, might view with aversion the new revolutionary economic tendencies but would be powerless to halt them, and there were Sinn Féin publicists – De Blacam and Figgis – who suggested that the old Irish world was based on soviets. The apprehensive unionist could see more concrete evidence that communism was in the air. Robert Sanders, sometime high sheriff of County Cork, described how a mob that seized the sawmill on his Tipperary property marched under the red flag, and in County Limerick the factories of a well-known butter firm, owned by a unionist family, were seized by communists (i.e. employees) who, it was said, tried to manage them on Soviet principles.[76]

The Southern unionists were mistaken in assuming that Irish labour was revolutionary and that Sinn Féin and Labour were closely connected. Certainly in the immediate aftermath of the war there was in Ireland (as elsewhere) widespread labour unrest. In many urban centres there were strikes, some well co-ordinated and for the moment alarming, and in country areas agricultural labourers organized themselves and went on strike. But, though revolutionary sentiments may have been aired, the strikes were basically over wage claims. Again, the Sinn Féin leaders, concentrating on the struggle against Crown authority, did not want to see their movement divided by agrarian quarrels; and the Sinn Féin courts, functioning as arbitration courts or as courts belonging to the legal system authorized by Dáil Éireann, often displayed sufficient respect for property rights to win the confidence of some unionists. However, between 1919 and 1923, a time when *silent enim leges inter arma*, agrarian agitators could advocate and

75 R. Dawson, *Red Terror and Green* (1920); *Irish Times*, 13 April 1920.
76 *Dáil Éireann, Minutes of Proceedings ... 1919-21*, pp. 178-9; *The Times*, 31 July, 2 Nov. 1922.

republicans condone attacks on landed property held by unionists as patriotism in action, combining the excision of obnoxious elements from Irish society with economic self-interest. 'I never was convinced', a fair-minded Church of Ireland clergyman wrote some years later, 'that the Irish republican organization was out to seize land, but what I certainly believe is that persons who were certainly of some type of anti-British seized the opportunity in the troubled times to gain their own private ends.'[77]

For about eighteen months after the beginning of the conflict between the Crown forces and the IRA, loyalists in the south and west looked forward to the restoration of law and order. As an RIC pensioner in Kerry frequently remarked, 'Never mind King George's arm is long and we will get our own back yet.' And the daughter of a well-known landowner and JP in King's County told a mob that came to the house brandishing sticks, 'Never mind, the King and the British government are behind me.'[78] On a more sophisticated level, the editor of the *Irish Times* blamed Sinn Féin for creating an atmosphere in which ill-balanced minds might be tempted to shake off all restraints. Crime, he pointed out, once tolerated in a country, 'could not be confined behind the flimsy barriers of politics'. When on a Sunday morning a number of army officers were surprised and shot in their Dublin lodgings, he passionately declared that with 'these brutal and cowardly murders' the country had reached 'the nadir of political and moral degradation'. He repeatedly called on his fellow-countrymen to co-operate with the government in restoring order and it was unfortunate, he thought, that the Catholic bishops in their 1919 pastorals dwelt on Ireland's grievances rather than on its duty to the government – 'render unto Caesar'. Later he regretted that the hierarchy's denunciations of crime were weakened by political passion and lack of sympathy with the government.[79]

The *Cork Constitution*, which strongly supported the Unionist

---

77 CO762/143RGEE. Monteagle in House of Lords (*Parl. Debates (Lords)*, 5 series, xl, 1118); M. Kotsonouris, *Retreat from Revolution: the Dáil Courts 1920-24* (Dublin 1994); J.A. Gaughan, *Austin Stack: Portrait of a Separatist* (Naas 1977), pp. 103-15.

78 CO762/32JH, CO762/74HWS.

79 *Irish Times*, 2 Jan., 3 March, 10 April, 22 Nov. 1919, 28 Jan., 17, 22 Nov. 1920.

Alliance, also deplored the campaign of crime, the vendetta against the police and the lack of public backing for the Crown forces, resulting from sympathy with Sinn Féin along with the instinct of self-preservation. It called for firm measures, suggesting that martial law might be extended and reprisals regularized – in October 1920 it approved of the government's 'reasoned and effective' reply on reprisals. Businessmen and farmers, it was confident, would support the *de jure* government when it showed itself capable of governing.[80] Two Cork unionists made practical suggestions. In May 1920 Pretyman Newman suggested that any man or woman in the three southern provinces who made a declaration of loyalty and allowed it to be put in a public place should be exempt as a rate-payer from paying for criminal injuries. A year later another Cork resident suggested that the country should be divided into military districts and all inhabitants issued with a permit having a photograph. To move from one district to another permission would have to be obtained. This would restrict 'the perambulating murders'.[81] In May 1920 Midleton in the House of Lords both pressed the government to adopt a policy which would be supported by a considerable section of Irish opinion and to take measures for the restoration of order – there should be better co-operation between the army and the RIC, the military mounting motorized patrols and sending detachments to assist the police in holding small barracks. Two months later, along with Desart and (surprisingly) Jellett, he had an interview with the Chief Secretary, Long and Churchill. The Irish unionists urged that there should be better co-operation between the military and the police and Jellett grumbled about Castle apathy. A few days later the two peers pressed the Irish committee of the Cabinet to suppress the republican courts and introduce martial law if it was a necessary prelude to effective military action. But Midleton admitted that many of his friends feared the consequences of coercion.[82] About

---

80 *Cork Constitution*, 6 Jan., 4 March, 3 May, 4, 23 June, 21 Oct., 25 Nov. 1920, 5 Jan. 1921.

81 *Parl. Debates*, 5 series, cxxxiv, 759; *Spectator*, 21 May 1921.

82 *Parl. Debates (Lords)*, 5 series, xl, 201-7. For the meetings of the Southern unionists with a group of ministers and with the Irish committee of the cabinet, see Notes on meetings, 15, 22 July, 5 Aug. in Midleton papers (PRO30/67/43).

the same time Frank Brooke, a railway director and a sometime unionist candidate who was in close touch with the Lord Lieutenant, wrote to a Cabinet minister complaining that the 'so called' government of Ireland was permitting Sinn Féin to assume control of the country. It was no use, he declared, fighting with gloves on. 'Either give Sinn Féin everything (which God forbid) or have it out with them. Don't let us go into another winter with our lives, if we are not killed, not worth living.' A few weeks later, on 30 July, a gang of armed men shot him in his office in central Dublin.[83]

By the summer of 1920 political uncertainty, violence, threats, disruption of communications, destruction of property and boy-cotting had led to a slump of morale amongst loyalists in Southern Ireland. Guerrilla warfare was beginning to wear down the resis-tance of the respectable, compelling many comfortably off, conser-vatively minded people to seek, if not peace at any price, an agreed settlement, a solution that would pave the way for a return to nor-mality. Bereft of protection, with the RIC confined to barracks, republican police patrolling the countryside and republican courts being held regularly, 'we loyalists', a Leitrim man wrote, 'cannot venture to speak or act. We have only our thoughts left to us'.[84]

Moreover, with a Home Rule bill moving towards the statute book it was obvious to many unionists that the legislative union of 1800 in its integrity was doomed. A very understandable reac-tion to the situation was expressed in July by Godfrey Featherstonhaugh, a leading member of the Connaught bar, who had been an Irish unionist MP until compelled to retire by ill-health. Southern unionists, he wrote, should be prepared to sacrifice a lot 'to bring peace to old Ireland and end a condition of chronic war-fare'. Let Ireland, he stated, 'have independence in the fullest sense' with Ulster remaining in the United Kingdom. Self-govern-ment had already brought peace and loyalty to the dominions, Ulster would soon seek reunion with the rest of Ireland and 'we unionists would soon recover our legitimate influence in the coun-cils of our country'. A week later, Woods, one of the Trinity MPs, privately stated that he thought the time for repression was past

83 F. Brooke to W. Long, 1 July 1920 (Long papers, 163).
84 *Spectator*, 31 July 1920. And see *Spectator*, 22, 29 May, 31 July, 18, 25 Oct. 1920.

and that a dominion policy would be supported by the hierarchy and Sinn Féin (except the 'gunmen', who might at first give trouble).[85] About this time the *Irish Times* began to change its stance. Early in 1919 the editor was sure an agreed settlement was impossible until 'a right national temper' had been fostered in the country by security and economic progress.[86] But by the summer of 1920 he declared the time had come for sobriety and wisdom to assert themselves. Irish unionists, he wrote, recognized 'the innate sanity as well as the unrestrained idealism' of their fellow-countrymen, and all parties in Ireland, unionists and nationalists, and perhaps even Sinn Féin, desired a generous settlement. The editor himself thought some adjustment of constitutional relations between Great Britain and Ireland was necessary, and though vague on details – he said nothing about reserved subjects or representation at Westminster – he agreed Ireland should have full control of its own taxation. Irish nationalists, he hoped, would rise to the height of a great opportunity and cultivate the advantages of full self-government 'in a Commonwealth of the greatest empire in the world'.[87]

About the middle of 1920 a deputation from the Unionist Anti-Partition League (Andrew Jameson, R.G. Leonard, a promising young barrister, and Captain R.N. Thompson, its secretary) told some London-based members of the league (Midleton, Barrymore, Donoughmore and Walter Guinness) that unionists in the South were no longer confident that the government could defeat Sinn Féin and were afraid that while it was trying to do so the 'resident unionists' would suffer terribly. The deputation suggested that the government might substitute Dominion Home Rule for the 1920 bill. This might satisfy Sinn Féin, which would, it was thought, agree to a voluntary imperial contribution and permit Ulster to contract out' (i.e. remain in the United Kingdom). Donoughmore remarked that the deputation's proposals were neither anti-partitionist nor unionist and Midleton argued that it would be impossible to rush the government into a change of policy,

85 *The Times*, 30 July 1920; R. Woods to J.H. Bernard, 6 Aug. 1920 (Bernard papers, Add. MS 52783).
86 *Irish Times*, 1 April 1919.
87 *Irish Times*, 4 July, 6 Aug., 8, 14 Sept. 1920.

though he thought that the government might be persuaded to bring forward a more generous measure once order was restored. 'What', one of the Dublin deputation asked, 'is to become of us while the law is being restored?'[88]

At the close of July 1920 the Dublin Chamber of Commerce, said to be a largely unionist body, announced that it viewed with horror the crimes and reprisals 'which are making life intolerable' and gravely imperilling their industrial and commercial interests. The policy the Chamber favoured was complete self-government for Ireland within the empire with no coercion of Ulster. A few days later a gathering of commercial and professional men in Cork called for dominion status and sent a deputation to London which had an interview with the Prime Minister. According to the strongly unionist *Cork Constitution*, the deputation was composed of 'neutrals in politics', successful businessmen who had given undivided attention to commercial affairs, but it did include an undoubted unionist, Andrew Jameson from Dublin.[89] A Queen's County meeting of deputy lieutenants and justices of the peace called on the government to offer 'the fullest measure of Dominion Home Rule that might be compatible with the integrity of the United Kingdom'.[90] The lieutenant and deputy lieutenants of County Louth, deploring the desperate situation of the country, urged that the lieutenants and deputy lieutenants of all the Irish counties should meet in Dublin, with the aim of supporting 'a generous measure of self-government which should include fiscal autonomy within the empire'.[91] In Wexford a small group of JPs met in White's Hotel. According to the RM, who attended, when he proposed that in the absence of Lord Courtown the meeting should adjourn, 'a fierce, bitter element exposed itself, anything but loyal and practicable'. With some difficulty he reduced 'wild and outrageous resolutions' into 'respectful and orderly ones', but realizing the magistrates were 'panic stricken by threats', he decided he would not attend any future meeting of JPs. A week later a meeting of Wexford JPs with Lord Courtown in the chair passed

88 Undated memorandum in Midleton papers (PRO30/67/43).
89 *The Times*, 30 July, 4, 5 Aug. 1920; *Cork Constitution*, 5 Aug. 1920.
90 *The Times*, 9 Aug. 1920.
91 Printed circular, 18 Oct. 1920 (Courtown papers, 150/4/147).

comparatively innocuous resolutions deploring the state of the country and asking for a measure of self-government.[92] The deputy lieutenants of the City and County of Cork asked for Irish self-government within the empire with safeguards for British security. Joseph Pike, who had contested Cork city as a conservative against Parnell in 1885, immediately wrote a letter to the press stating that if he had known that the resolution was going to be proposed he would have returned from Harrogate to oppose it. A week later his house was burned by a gang of armed men.[93]

At the end of August the Irish Peace Conference, a movement under the leadership of a number of constitutional nationalists and a few mild unionists or ex-unionists, suggested that the government should offer Ireland full self-government within the empire and that a gathering of representative Irishmen should adopt a constitution that would meet the special requirements of any part of the country.[94] The Peace Conference's programme was somewhat similar to that of Sir Horace Plunkett's Irish Dominion League, which attracted the support of a number of people who, if they had never voted unionist in the past, would certainly ten years later have been regarded as ex-unionists.[95] Dominion Home Rule was much favoured by *bien-pensants*. There was an agreeable vagueness as to what exactly it implied and if it obviously meant a greater degree of autonomy than Home Rule the term Dominion had an imperial resonance likely to appeal to unionists. Finally, early in 1921 a Businessman Committee, which included Jameson and Goulding, pressed for a meeting between representatives of the cabinet and the Irish people.[96]

The suggestion that an agreed settlement could be arrived at was contemptuously dismissed by Jellett, an unyielding unionist. With severe logic he pointed out that negotiations would have to

92 J.J. Roche to Courtown, 20 Aug. 1920, meeting of JPs, 1 Sept. 1920, H. Crosby to Courtown, 3 Sept. 1920, note on meeting of JPs (Courtown papers, P50/4/137, 139, 140, 151).
93 *Cork Constitution*, 23, 26, 30 Aug. 1920.
94 *The Times*, 26 Aug. 1920.
95 *Original Manifesto of Irish Dominion League* (1921) (British Library, 8146e 187).
96 See Memorandum in Midleton papers, PRO30/67/44.

be carried on with either those who had no power to stop murder or with those who were in a position to do so. In the former case negotiations would be futile. In the latter they would have to be conducted with assassins, the law-abiding and stable elements in the community being ignored – an unthinkable course of action. But another able unionist lawyer, J.B. Powell, soon to be placed on the bench, was more conciliatory. 'There is in reality', he wrote early in 1921, 'so little between what would be conceded and what would be accepted, that it seems to be appalling that the terms of peace cannot be arranged.'[97] By the spring of 1921 many Southern unionists were perforce – very much perforce – wearily prepared to accept a change in Ireland's constitutional status, a sign of the times being the decision of the Royal Dublin Society (a very unionist body) to rescind the 1917 expulsion of Count Plunkett and to increase the representation of the farming community on its council.

In the summer of 1921 the Southern unionists had the melancholy satisfaction of seeing their leaders playing for a moment a conspicuous role in Irish history – albeit in helping to arrange a surrender. In July de Valera, having been invited to meet the Prime Minister, asked Sir James Craig, Lord Midleton, Jameson, Dockrell and Sir Robert Woods to meet him in Dublin so that, 'as spokesman of the Irish nation', he might learn 'the views of a certain section of our people of whom you are the representatives'. The four Southern unionists accepted his invitation and on 4 July met de Valera at the Mansion House. De Valera, in Midleton's opinion 'a man with his head in the clouds', explained at some length that he did not want to appear to be suing for peace and that he could meet Lloyd George only as head of the Irish nation. Midleton talked about constitutional possibilities and drew de Valera's attention to violations of the laws of war, giving as an instance the murder of policemen. De Valera admitted that in war 'it is not always certain that the guilty would be the victim'. In the end de Valera agreed to go to London and Midleton immediately left for England to give an account of the conference to the Prime

---

97 *The Times*, 8 March 1921; Powell to Midleton, 9 Feb. 1921 (Midleton papers, PRO30/67/44).

Minister. On 8 July there was a second meeting, which the commander of the forces in Ireland attended, at which a truce was arranged. This came into force on 11 July.[98]

'After the great force of Southern unionism has come again into action', the *Irish Times* was sure that the Southern unionists would be 'a vital factor in any Irish settlement'. The Archbishop of Dublin, Dr Gregg, wrote to Midleton emphasizing that they should be represented at the coming conference (he did not propose names, being clearly handicapped by the fact that his senior colleague, the Archbishop of Armagh, was a staunch Ulster unionist). Gregg's predecessor, Bernard, suggested to Oranmore and Browne that the Southern unionist delegation should consist of Midleton, Jameson and Bernard himself. Bernard also wrote to *The Times* a few days before the negotiations began, eulogizing 'the loyalists of southern Ireland', who had been 'in peace and war consistently loyal to the King and empire as well as to their own country', and asking 'are they to be ignored?'[99] The answer was – almost completely.

Early in October Midleton, 'profoundly troubled about the position of the Southern unionists', managed to have a talk with Austen Chamberlain (one of the British delegation at the Downing Street negotiations). Midleton was surprised to hear that dominion status was being discussed and he urged strongly that Ireland should not be permitted to have its own army, that there should be a senate (chosen on conservative lines), that religious freedom should be guaranteed, that there should be a provision forbidding class or religious discrimination in legislation, that Irish income tax should only be on income arising in Ireland, and that land purchase should be completed.[100] On 15 November, a month after the negotiations had started, Midleton, Bernard and Jameson met the Prime Minister and four of his colleagues. Lloyd George gave a lively account of how the conference was progressing; Midleton

---

98 Midleton, memoranda on meetings, 4, 8 July 1921; Midleton to Prime Minister, 9 July 1921 (Midleton papers, PRO30/67/45).

99 *Irish Times*, 9 July 1921; Archbishop Gregg to Midleton, 13 Oct. 1921; Oranmore and Browne to Midleton, 13 Oct. 1921 (Midleton papers, PRO30/67/46); *The Times*, 5 Oct. 1921.

100 Midleton, memorandum, 7-10 Oct. 1921 (Midleton papers, PRO30/67/46); T. Jones, *Whitehall Diary*, iii (1971), p. 118.

insisted that Ireland should not be permitted to raise an army and Bernard expressed concern about safeguards for ecclesiastical property and educational institutions. In the end it was thought desirable that the Southern unionist representatives should have a meeting with Griffith, whom they saw on 17 November. Griffith agreed that land purchase should be completed before the Irish parliament was set up, declared himself to be in favour of a second chamber and promised that before any agreement on taxation was concluded the Southern unionists should be consulted and expressed his willingness to retain in the new Irish constitution the guarantees for ecclesiastical property and Trinity College embodied in the 1920 Government of Ireland Act.[101] A fortnight later, on 6 December, Midleton was summoned to Downing Street and informed that the Treaty had been signed. The next day along with his two colleagues he met the Prime Minister, the Lord Chancellor and Austen Chamberlain. When Midleton remarked that there were no safeguards in the Treaty in regard to taxation the Lord Chancellor stressed that there was a guarantee against any form of injustice in the right of appeal from the Irish courts to the Privy Council, implicit in Article II of the Treaty. Then the Prime Minister stated emphatically that the Treaty would have to be presented to parliament as a whole and could not be amended at any stage. However, in the hour of defeat the Southern unionist leaders received from Griffith a written assurance that a scheme would be devised to give them full representation in both houses of the Irish Free State legislature and that they would be consulted on the constitution of the upper house, in which their interests would be represented.[102]

The reactions of Southern unionists to the Treaty were varied – relief, shocked surprise, pessimistic acquiescence and the intention of making the best of a *fait accompli*, all being expressed. Sir Henry Robinson, who had long surveyed the Irish scene with ironic good humour, was taken aback. He had 'visualised a peace achieved by compelling the rebels to lay down their arms ... and

---

101 Memoranda dated 16, 17 Nov. 1921 (Bernard papers, Add. MS 52783), T. Jones, *Whitehall Diary*, iii, p. 165.

102 Memorandum (Midleton papers, PRO30/67/53); T. Jones, *Whitehall Diary*, iii, p. 184, Memorandum dated 7 Dec. 1921 (Add MS 52783); *Irish Times*, 28 Sept. 1922.

never thought the government contemplated a different form of peace, namely the British surrender to the forces of disorder when the rebels were believed to be on the point of collapse'.[103] Some simple men, life-long loyalists, had 'a rude awakening' and felt a sense of betrayal. Unionist farmers in County Galway, it was said, 'discovered their trust had been misplaced – it is not every man that can balance the niceties of political necessities when, having stood his ground for law and order, he finds himself in the air'.[104]

Two Trinity dons – unionist intellectuals, it might be said – gave considered views on the situation. Alison Phillips, a professor of history, who had in earlier days been on the staff of *The Times*, believed that 'the great majority of Southern unionists, accepted the Treaty 'without *arrière pensée*', as the best chance of restoring peace and prosperity to the country, because the Sinn Féin leaders knew the methods by which their fellow-countrymen could be governed, which were not precisely 'those of self-government as the term is understood in England'. He could not forbear to remark that the victory of Sinn Féin, obtained by violence, had dealt a blow to constitutional government and might well mark the beginning of the break-up of the British empire by demonstrating that 'British democracy would always yield to force'.[105] His colleague Edward Gwynn, a scholar, deeply interested in Irish affairs (he was the grandson of William Smith O'Brien, the Young Irelander), reflected between the Truce and the Treaty that

this last year has made me feel for the first time that I am essentially English and not Irish in spite of certain sympathies and antipathies. A man is what he inherits and what he draws in from his surroundings and for most of us Protestants these things are ninety per cent English or Scotch, traditions, beliefs, customs, mental furniture, all that. And why I mainly fear and draw back from the new order, which I suppose will flood us sooner or later, is not so much material loss and annoyance as

---

103 CO762/32HAR. According to a senior civil servant, during the last days of the old regime, Sir Henry Robinson, 'whose political views were strong', sanctioned pensions to loyalist local government officials that were 'far higher than were reasonable' (G.G. Whiskard to unknown, 8 Oct. 1928) (CO762/133WJH).

104 CO762/155W, CO762/187JMcK.

105 *Edinburgh Review*, ccxxxv, pp. 220-45.

the tendency to cut us away from our roots, our civilization, which is bone of our bone and flesh of our flesh. Perhaps we ought not to blame the other side for wishing to assert their separate nationality at all points, but it is hard for a man who has children to come after him ... and the College, it has got to remain.

However, he thought 'some of the other side' were friendly and might be convinced that 'we as well as they have our ideas and traditions'.[106] He expressed with depressing clarity the feelings of many of those who were soon to be termed 'ex-unionists'.

The two organizations that spoke for Southern unionism reacted in different ways. The Executive of the Unionist Anti-Partition League, meeting a week after the Treaty was signed, decided 'we have to make the best we can of the situation'. They still believed in the union, but it had failed because of distrust between Great Britain and Ireland and between creeds and classes in Ireland. Now it was to be hoped the establishment of the Irish Free State would enable Irishmen to serve Ireland and the empire.[107] This attitude was adopted by 'a small but representative' gathering of unionists from the south and west, meeting in the Engineers' Hall in Dawson Street under the chairmanship of Lord Mayo, who said they should not remain in the country only 'to hunt, fish and course'. The meeting agreed to support the Provisional Government and (taking up a suggestion made by the *Irish Times*) to encourage the formation of local committees, which might influence the organizations choosing pro-Treaty candidates in the next general election. The League, having changed its name to the Constitutional Anti-Partition League, dissolved itself in February 1923, after 'partition had been given legislative sanction'.[108]

The Irish Unionist Alliance was, as might be expected, despondent. In January 1922 its Executive Committee was apprehensive that once the Crown forces were withdrawn there would be no security for life or property. Some months later it reaffirmed its belief in the value of the union to Ireland and advised Southern unionists to abstain from voting in the coming general

---

106 E. Gwynn to J.H. Bernard, 6 Sept. 1921 (Bernard papers, Add MS 52783).
107 R.G. Leonard to Midleton, 12 Dec. 1921 (Midleton papers, PRO30/67/48).
108 *Irish Times*, 10, 12, 13 Jan. 1922; *The Times*, 20 Feb. 1923.

election because the republicans and those who supported the Free State differed only over the means of attaining the same end.[109] With the Alliance's *raison d'être* gone, the executive decided to turn itself into a relief organization, the Dublin advisory committee of the London-based Southern Irish Loyalists Relief Association. However, the London branch of the Alliance continued in being, renaming itself in 1933 the Irish Loyalists Imperial Federation, with the support of Carson and some conservative MPs. Its aim was to defend the rights of British subjects in Ireland. The Federation became moribund in the early forties and in 1943 handed over its funds (£95) to the Southern Irish Loyalists Relief Association.[110]

In parliament Walter Guinness pronounced that the only alternative to the Treaty was chaos. In accepting it they might be embarking on a slippery slope, leading to separation, but a slippery slope was preferable to a precipice. Sir Maurice Dockrell, who believed a wise man knew when he was defeated, was confident that the Sinn Féin leaders, with whom he had sat for some days, meant 'to give us good government', and he was sure the best elements in Irish life would come to the front (two of his sons were to sit in the Dáil).[111] Woods, a Trinity MP, declared in the debate on the Treaty that the country now had an opportunity of pursuing the paths of peace and progress, and he read a message from the College board, optimistically stating that it looked forward to 'the building up of happier conditions in Ireland'. But a few months later Woods's colleague, Jellett, took a very different line, passionately denouncing the government's policy as 'the ruin of Ireland and a danger of the greatest magnitude to the empire'. 'There is one crime in Ireland', he declared, 'which is the impardonable sin … . and that crime is loyalty. If you want in Ireland to have a chance to be recognised by a British government of modern days, what ever you do do not be loyal. You will never have a dog's chance if you are loyal.' In the Lords, Farnham characterized

109 26 Jan., 26 May 1922.
110 *The Times*, 7 May, 15 Nov., 6 Dec. 1934; D1507/A/47; D989/A/8/2/65; D989/B/1/3.
111 *Parl. Debates*, 5 series, cxlix, 209-11, clii, 1229, cl, 1297.

the Treaty as a cowardly surrender and a shameful betrayal, and Oranmore and Browne remarked that he did not 'relish descending from being an integral portion of the United Kingdom to finding ourselves colonials in this imperial city'. But most unionist peers unenthusiastically accepted the Treaty as a *fait accompli*, and Midleton, while pointing out that the settlement carried 'us far beyond what was regarded a year ago as a forward policy', hoped that the Irish unionists would endeavour to serve the new state, 'making firmer the ties with this country'.

Similar sentiments were expressed by the *Irish Times* in two leaders published immediately after the Treaty was signed. Irish loyalists, embarking on uncharted seas, trusting to 'the good will of a majority with which in the past they have shared little save a common love of Ireland', should, the editor stated, welcome the new regime, provided it reflected 'a broad-minded patriotism'. But, he emphasized, Ireland did not exist, and never could exist, 'apart from the empire which the blood of their sires had cemented'.[112] The *Church of Ireland Gazette* echoed the *Irish Times*. 'Though the passing of the old system has many pangs', it declared, Protestants were an integral part of the state and now had an opportunity of getting into the mainstream of Irish life. Nevertheless they had principles which no change of government could banish – they were good Irishmen but they were also good Britons, loyal to the throne and to glorious British traditions. It may be added that the Church of Ireland Archbishop of Dublin, John Gregg, declared he would accept the settlement 'as a constitutionalist', because it was imposed by lawful authority and as an Irishman would thank God for it if it really settled the Irish question. But, his daughter wrote, 'he felt as if he had been banished from the garden of Eden' (he returned to the United Kingdom in 1939 when translated to Armagh).[113]

The editor of the *Irish Times* was most anxious that ex-unionists, with 'their special contribution of character, education and experience', should do all they could to help in laying the foundations of the new state. He even hoped in January 1922 that a

112 *Irish Times*, 7, 10 Dec. 1921.
113 *Church of Ireland Gazette*, 6, 13 Jan. 1922; G. Seaver, *John Allen Fitzgerald Gregg* (1963), p. 126.

member of the minority (a term that was beginning to replace unionist) might be included in the Provisional Government,[114] and early in June he reminded his readers that the general election was being fought between 'Imperial Free State and Independent Republic' – an antithesis that would not have been altogether agreeable to the members of the Provisional Government. The *Irish Times*'s faith in the new regime received a few jolts. Commenting on the steps taken in 1922 to make Irish compulsory in the primary schools, the editor regretted that honest enthusiasts might turn the language into an instrument of oppression. The minority had no grudge against Gaelic but would resent an attempt to force it down their throats or make it a condition of their right to citizenship.[115] He was annoyed when Cosgrave in the debate on the Courts of Justice bill referred to 'an alien government'. British institutions may have been alien in the past but they had ceased to be so when the Free State took its place at the imperial conference and it should be realized that the British legal system was 'the most perfect of their common possessions'. He also deplored the disbandment of six Irish regiments. Their fame had given Ireland a special status and they might in time have been taken over by the Irish Free State. Incidentally an *Irish Times* reviewer about this time hoped that the history of the second battalion of the Royal Dublin Fusiliers would soon be in the hands of every Irish school boy.[116]

On one major issue the *Irish Times*, probably mirroring ex-unionist opinion in general, was out of line with the feelings of most people in the Irish Free State. Though in 1922 it still deplored partition, it continued to display a sympathetic under-standing of the Ulster unionist attitude. The editor looked forward to the eventual reunion of Ireland – 'the presence of Sir James Craig in an Irish parliament would be a rallying point for all the elements of sanity and conservatism' – but he insisted it could only be obtained through peaceful co-operation. Any attempt to force the pace of reconciliation by a compound of 'half overture and half obloquy' would only arouse 'the old war cry,

114 *Irish Times*, 10, 13 Jan., 12 June 1922.
115 *Irish Times*, 1 Feb., 7 March 1922, 12 Oct. 1923.
116 *Irish Times*, 20 Feb. 1922, 20 Jan., 28 Sept. 1923.

"No surrender"'.[117] The *Church of Ireland Gazette* also looked forward to the North 'taking her place with the rest of us in an Irish parliament' if it saw 'the Free State governed as a modern community should be governed', but it too stressed that the pace of unity must not be forced. 'Let Ulster alone for a few years' should be the motto of the South.[118]

While the Southern unionists were endeavouring to adjust themselves to the new regime their leaders were seriously perturbed over constitutional issues. Once the treaty had been approved by Parliament and Dáil Éireann, a series of steps were taken to legalize the transformation of twenty-six United Kingdom counties into a Dominion, the Irish Free State. In the middle of January 1922 the Dáil appointed a Provisional Government, which, when installed in office by the Lord Lieutenant, took control of the Irish administration. In March an act was passed at Westminster confirming the treaty and empowering the King by orders in council to transfer governmental functions in Ireland to the Provisional Government. At the end of May the Lord Lieutenant dissolved the parliament of Southern Ireland (i.e. the Second Dáil), summoning a new Dáil which met in September. Before polling day the Irish Free State constitution, drafted under the auspices of the Provisional Government and agreed to, with some modifications, by the British government, was published. When the new Dáil met it enacted the constitution and towards the close of the year the Free State was constituted by two acts of parliament (the Irish Free State constitution being printed as a schedule to the first of them), which received the royal assent on 5 December, and on 6 December T.M. Healy was appointed Governor-General and the Free State legislature provided with its second house, the Senate.

While the Free State constitution was being shaped the Southern unionist leaders hovered on the margin of politics. In accordance with Griffith's pledges, the draft constitution provided that elections to the Dáil should be by proportional representation (which, when employed in the recent Irish municipal elections,

117 *Irish Times*, 28 Jan., 12 Oct. 1922.
118 *Church of Ireland Gazette*, 2 Dec. 1921, 27 Jan., 27 Oct. 1922.

seemed to have caught the public fancy) and that there should be a second chamber, the senate. It may be added that when the constitution was being debated by the Dáil, the university members, including the three Trinity College representatives, were seated in the Dáil; the Irish government, Bernard reflected, 'is sensible of the advantage of having some educated men in the house'.[119] The first senate, with a membership of sixty, was to be composed of thirty members elected by the Dáil and thirty nominated by the executive, it being understood that a number of ex-unionists would be among those nominated. Subsequently the senate was to be elected, the whole country forming a single constituency, a scheme that, in Midleton's opinion, would exclude the most prominent men in industry and commerce and the larger landowners. As regards its powers the senate could hold up a bill for nine months, the Dáil having exclusive authority over finance bills.[120]

About the middle of June, after the conclusion of strenuous discussions between the British and Irish ministers on the draft constitution, Midleton, Donoughmore, Jameson and the Provost (Bernard) had meetings with Griffith, Kevin O'Higgins and Hugh Kennedy, with Churchill in the chair. Bernard in his diary sums up the result of the meetings as 'not wholly satisfactory' and he signed the dignified, pained statement issued by the ex-unionist representatives. They complained that though they had been given an opportunity of 'seeing and discussing' the articles in the constitution affecting the composition of the senate and the relations of the two houses, the other articles had not been submitted to them. They appreciated the efforts that had been made to meet their wishes but regretted that in forming the senate the 1920 Government of Ireland Act had not been followed, and they expressed the view that the senate would not afford a genuine protection to the minority.[121]

When in November Midleton, Donoughmore and Desart met

119 J.H. Bernard to Midleton, 6 Oct. 1922 (Midleton papers, PRO30/67/51).

120 Midleton considered the Senate's proposed powers too limited (Memoranda of interviews with D. Figgis, 28, 29 April 1922 [Midleton papers, PRO30/67/50]).

121 *The Times*, 13, 17 June 1922; Bernard diary; memorandum of meetings, 12, 13 June 1922 (Bernard papers, Add. MS 52783).

Cosgrave (who Desart considered 'an educated man, of good appearance and manner, very quick and intelligent'), they told him that the senate's powers were too limited. Cosgrave in reply 'spoke much of the psychology of Ireland and the necessity of relying on persuasion rather than power'. Midleton, supported by Oranmore and Browne and Lansdowne, wanted to attempt in the Lords to amend the provisions in the Free State constitution bill relating to the senate. However, Iveagh, Bernard, Jameson and Desart were against taking action. Desart considered the amendment would injure the very people they wished to help. Bernard, admitting that 'it was hard for a man to judge his own motives' believed that it was not from cowardice that he and Jameson refused to back Midleton's proposal, but rather 'because of our conviction of the futility of trying to amend the constitution at the eleventh hour'. Jameson tried to console Midleton by assuring him that 'you are quite right as to Irish politics being a source of endless trouble to anyone foolish enough to meddle with them'.[122]

When the Free State constitution was being debated by the Dáil, the Provisional Government insisted that the clauses relating to the senate were to be taken unamended since they had been drafted in consultation with the Southern unionist representatives. Kevin O'Higgins, the Minister for Justice, argued that the Dáil should go 'a little beyond the line' in meeting the Southern unionists, 'when the thing they looked on and felt was a buttress had been swept away and they found themselves in the awful position of being at the mercy of their fellow countrymen![123] In the first senate of the thirty nominated members, a dozen were unionists (or more correctly ex-unionists) and about ten others (including Lord Grenard, Sir John Keane, Lady Desart and W.B. Yeats) might be considered to have a unionist background and certainly tended to act with the ex-unionists. As time went on the number of ex-unionists in the Senate dropped and the Senate itself, a body with limited powers, attracted far less public attention than the Dáil.[124]

122 Memoranda of meetings, 18 Oct., 6, 9 Nov. 1922; Desart to Midleton, 26 Nov. 1922, J.H. Bernard to Midleton, 2 Dec. 1922, A. Jameson to Midleton, 6 Dec. 1922 (Midleton papers, PRO30/67/50, 53).

123 *Dáil Debates*, i, 482.

124 D.O'Sullivan, *The Irish Free State and its Senate* (1940), pp. 89-95.

The first chairman of the Senate was Lord Glenavy, whose political evolution illustrates the political adaptability which perforce many Southern unionists displayed. As James Campbell he had been for fifteen years a unionist MP before being appointed Lord Chief Justice (in 1916) and subsequently Lord Chancellor. He had been a very active supporter of the Ulster resistance to Home Rule, but during the war he made a fresh examination of his approach to Irish problems and by 1917 he favoured Home Rule for the whole of Ireland with no coercion of Ulster. In 1920 he was said 'to have completely lost his nerve'. In fact he wanted to go on living in the South of Ireland (his critic, another leading unionist lawyer, retired to County Tyrone after the Treaty). As chairman he dominated the Senate by a combination of *fortiter in re* with, for most of the time, *'suaviter in modo'*. He even made a bold bid to reunite the North and South and end the civil war. He explained to Sir James Craig that if Northern Ireland and the Irish Free State were reunited, the Irregulars, feeling they had attained what they were fighting for, would lay down their arms. He proposed that in a united Ireland the North would continue to have its own parliament, judiciary and administration and would possess a veto on all Irish legislation applying to Northern Ireland. Craig simply pointed out that at the last general election Northern Ireland had voted to remain outside the jurisdiction of the Dublin parliament.[125]

125 *Dublin Express*, 21 Aug. 1918; J. Ross to W. Long, 30 Jan. 1920 (Long papers, 947/334); G. French, *Life of Sir John French* (1931), p. 367; Glenavy to J. Craig, 4 Jan. 1923, J. Craig to Glenavy, 29 Jan. 1923 (PRONI Cabinet 8V/1).

William Edward Hartpole Lecky (1838–1903), *Vanity Fair*, 27 May 1882.

Right:
Professor Edward
Dowden.

Below, left:
Arthur Warren Samuels.

Below, right:
William Morgan Jellett.

*Courtesy the Board of
Trinity College, Dublin*

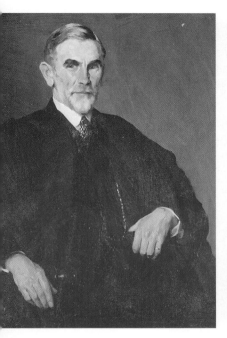

Above, left:
Edward Gwynn,
Provost of Trinity
College, Dublin,
1927–37.

Above, right:
James Henry Mussen
Campbell, 1st Lord
Glenavy.

Right:
John Henry Bernard,
Archbishop of
Dublin 1915–19,
Provost of Trinity
College, Dublin,
1919–27.

*Courtesy the Board
of Trinity College,
Dublin*

Crown infantry departing from the
North Wall, Dublin, from *Graphic*,
23 December 1922 (*The Board of
Trinity College, Dublin*).

Lord Midleton, from *Graphic*, 16 July 1921
(*The Board of Trinity College, Dublin*).

A sombre cartoon from *Punch*, 10 May 1922, illustrating the plight of the RIC after the Treaty (*The Board of Trinity College, Dublin*).

Three burnt-out houses: (*left*) Palmerstown, Co. Kildare, from *Illustrated London News*, February 1923; (*above*) Castle Boro, Co. Wexford, photo by George Gossip; (*right*) Desart Court, Co. Kilkenny, burned in 1922, photo by Maurice Craig (*Irish Architectural Archive*).

Robert Smyllie, editor of *The Irish Times* 1934–54 (*The Irish Times*).

VI Travail

FROM THE TRUCE (July 1921) to the end of the Civil War (about May 1923) was a period of confusion and conflict. For almost six months between the Truce and the Treaty (December 1921), over much of the south and west, the republican courts and police functioned simultaneously with courts acting under royal authority and the RIC. For instance, when an agricultural show was held in County Kilkenny the RIC directed the traffic and the republican police patrolled the grounds, and in Castlerea, County Roscommon, the republican court, having taken over the court - house, allowed the County Court judge to hold quarter sessions in an upstairs room.[1] With the Crown forces disheartened and cautious and the republican civil and military machinery rather rudimentary, the law-abiding were often uncertain from whom to seek protection. Then, once the Treaty was signed, the RIC was concentrated in the Dublin area as a preliminary to disbandment and the withdrawal of the army began – the departure of the last units from Dublin, long a garrison town, in December 1922, bringing home to people the vast change that had taken place.[2] But it was some time before the Irish Free State government was able to exercise undisputed authority throughout the country. The rift in the republican ranks, revealed by the acrimonious Dáil debates on the Treaty, rapidly widened, and a number of IRA units defied the Provisional Government. There were in the IRA fervent idealists who felt committed to a strict interpretation of the republican creed and who believed that the IRA, a citizens' army, had the duty not only to defend the country but to preserve its political

---

1 Desart to Midleton, 25 Sept 1921 (Midleton papers PRO30/67/46); *The Times*, 7 April 1922.
2 *The Times*, 19 Dec. 1922.

integrity. Many IRA men must have been irritated by seeing, once the struggle with Crown authority was over, the quiet, respectable and comfortably off, who had been fairly passive in insurrectionary times, resuming their customary predominance in Irish public life; men who had for about two years been living a hazardous and hardening existence must often have found it difficult to return to humdrum routine. In April 1922 the anti-Treaty forces, already in control of much of the south and west, occupied the Four Courts and other buildings in Dublin. After prolonged negotiations the Provisional Government, which from the beginning of the year had been forming a regular army, went vigorously on the offensive. By the end of the first week in July it had captured all the posts occupied by its opponents in Dublin, and during July and August the well-equipped Free State forces in a series of co-ordinated advances captured the urban centres held by the republicans (the Irregulars) – Limerick, Waterford, Kilkenny, Cork, Sligo, Tralee. Though there was a prodigal expenditure of ammunition, the casualty lists were not long; the Irregulars tried to halt the advance of the Free State columns by destroying railways, bridges and telephone wires. They also destroyed public buildings and business premises and country houses belonging to ex-unionists or Treaty supporters. Devastation and dislocation could be regarded as a form of economic warfare that would compel the community in despair to put pressure on the government to make concessions to the anti-Treaty party. Also a campaign of destruction offered opportunities for inflicting injuries on obnoxious persons, for paying off old scores and for widespread looting. Though by September 1922 the Provisional Government forces were victorious in the field, and the new police (the Civic Guard) was taking up duty all over the country, determined if diminishing bands of Irregulars continued to carry on a guerrilla war until May 1923.

During the almost two years that elapsed between the Truce and the end of the Civil War loyalists in the south and west were despondent and often apprehensive. It was a shock to the supporters of the old regime to see the familiar legal and political framework – the RM, the RIC, the garrison, the lord lieutenant and symbolically the Castle – being swiftly swept away. To make matters worse, at a time when the normal restraints on violence had been weakened, loyalists, the disheartened adherents of a defeated cause, found themselves the targets of intense popular hostility, being often subjected to 'petty tyrannies and illegal exactions' and sometimes to even more severe forms of harassment.[3] The bitter antagonisms nourished by their attitude and actions during the struggle against the Crown forces still festered, and to the opponents of the Treaty they were the discredited and discreditable allies of the pro-Treaty party.

Loyalists also suffered from the repercussions in the South of events in Northern Ireland, where there were outbreaks of political and sectarian violence. In Belfast especially, there was rioting and sniping and a number of murders were committed. The nationalists, though by no means passive, suffered severely and the IRA intervened with the aim of protecting the Catholic minority and in the hope of destablizing the Northern Ireland administration. The Southern Catholics sympathized intensely with their co-religionists in the North, whom they saw as victims of one-sided violence – a pogrom. In the autumn of 1920 a boycott of Belfast goods and Ulster-based banks had begun in the south and west. From January 1921 it was organized by Dáil Éireann and in January 1922 it was discontinued by the Provisional Government. In March it was reimposed by an IRA convention, meeting in the Mansion House, Dublin.[4] The Irregulars not only tried to enforce the renewed boycott – a policy that hit loyalist businessmen with Northern connections hard – but took steps to secure accommodation for Catholic refugees from Belfast at the expense of Southern loyalists. In Dublin for about six weeks a Belfast boycott committee billeted refugees in the houses of well-known unionists and for some days refugees were to be seen sitting 'fearfully' in club armchairs in the Kildare Street Club.[5] In Galway Lord Ashtown received a notice headed 'Oglaig na h-Éireann' – 'As a result of the treatment of the Catholic population of Belfast and

---

3 *Parl. Debates*, 5 series, cliv, 2137.
4 *The Times*, 6 Sept. 1920; *Dáil Éireann Debates*, p. 19; National Archives, Cab. minutes DEI/4; *The Times*, 23 Jan. 1922; *Irish Times*, 24, 27 March 1922.
5 *The Times*, 6 May 1922; *Parl. Debates*, 5 series, clv, 527, 1530, E. O'Malley, *The Singing Flame* (1978), p. 75.

other northern towns by the Orange gunmen there', it said,

thousands of men, women and children are homeless and starving and their immediate needs must be supplied. ... The executive committee of the IRA have decided that the unionists and freemasons of the south and west be compelled to supply their needs. You are ordered to leave your residence at Woodlaw which with your entire property is confiscated.[6]

In a number of other instances the harassing of Protestant loyalists was justified by referring to the sufferings of the Northern Catholics – 'remember Belfast and the way the poor Catholics were driven out of it'.[7]

Public meetings having called on the Southern Protestants to condemn the behaviour of their Northern co-religionists, Protestant groups in various localities in the South condemned the outrages in the North. In Dublin a gathering representing the Protestants of the south and west deplored the murders and outrages that had occurred in Ulster and other parts of Ireland.[8] Two leading organs of Southern unionist opinion, the *Irish Times* and the *Church of Ireland Gazette*, when commenting severely on the violence in the North blamed lawless elements on both sides, and the *Irish Times* pointed out that unionist Ulster was being goaded to fury by the murder of policemen and the destruction of property. The *Gazette*, which had attributed the boycott to envy of Belfast's commercial success, pointed out that Protestants had often been the victims of violence in the North. Clearly the Southern unionist reaction to events in the North was significantly different to that of the great majority of the inhabitants of the twenty-six counties.[9]

It is easy to see why the loyalists aroused animosity, and after the Truce, with the normal machinery of government suspended over most of the country, many of them were victimized by passionate republicans and agrarian agitators. One large, easily identifiable category of loyalist was singled out for attack: the RIC.

---

6 CO762/15A.
7 For instance, CO762/110DEB, CO762/112DO, CO762/40MD, CO762/42MG.
8 *Irish Times*, 12 May 1922.
9 *Irish Times*, 22, 24 March 1922; *Church of Ireland Gazette*, 3 June 1921, 10 March, 2 June 1922.

According to Cope, the assistant under-secretary, there was 'a concerted movement' to expel members of the RIC, pensioners and their families from the country.[10] 'The people', Austin Stack wrote, 'in various parts of the country naturally look upon men who served in the British force up to the last moment as having been our enemies during the war.' He admitted, however, that there may have been exceptional instances in which a member of the RIC afforded assistance to the IRA.[11] The possibility that a member of the RIC might have assisted the republican cause was indicated in a communication addressed to a former head constable in Cork. He was told he could only stay in the 'brigade area' if he could produce a letter of recommendation from the IRA in the district where he had served during the war. Since he had 'no intention of seeking any favour from the rebels', he left at once for England.[12] Another former head constable in Cork, who was working in a land agent's office, received a notice: 'You have been serving the British all your life and now you are serving the landlords. Fly.' As a result he was 'spending the remaining years of my blighted life, a fugitive from my native land'.[13] An ex-sergeant, with two sons in the force, after his house was burned in June 1922, had with his younger children to travel from Galway to Kildare 'without boots on our feet in tramps garb'. An ex-RIC man left Limerick after being 'assaulted, beaten, booed and boycotted'. In Roscommon, when the wife of a sergeant and their children were ordered to clear out, 'a large crowd mocked and jeered'.[14] In Tipperary an RIC man was told to leave or he 'would be plugged'. An ex-sergeant in Carlow was notified, 'the flying column for the extermination of ex-RIC pensioners, spies and informers is expected in a few days'. He left immediately for Belfast.[15] These were not idle threats. Between the Treaty and May 1922 thirty-four members or ex-members of the RIC were shot. As a result about two thousand disbanded members of the RIC

---

10 A. Cope to ____, 22 June 1922 (Department of Taoiseach, S 1842).
11 CO762/126TD.
12 CO762/118PC.
13 CO762/35JPD.
14 CO762/39MR, CO762/126PC, CO762/58BG.
15 CO762/4JB, CO762/92FT.

and a number of pensioners took refuge in Britain. In spite of being harassed an ex-sergeant in Kilkenny displayed the spirit that had animated the force in the past when he wrote, 'I served the government until the last and would serve it again as required.'[16]

Another category of loyalist who suffered, sometimes severely, between the Truce and the end of the Civil War were landowners, large and small. A number of landlords or 'ranchers' found themselves under intensifying pressure to sell out. Loyalist (usually Protestant) farmers from the summer of 1921 were to an increasing extent harried, being raided – one strongly unionist large farmer in County Tipperary was raided eighty-three times in the post-Treaty period[17] – forced to subscribe to republican funds or compelled to accept Irregulars as billetees. The billetees, often in the later stages of the civil war 'weak and scabby and sore, not a penny in their pockets not a pipeful to smoke, nothing to do from one weekend to another',[18] could be exacting and alarming guests. Sometimes they insisted on the best of food. A Protestant farmer in Queen's County said that his billetees demanded bacon and eggs for breakfast, meat for dinner, eggs for tea. A King's County loyalist complained they demanded meat three times a day and occupied all the bedrooms, compelling him and his family to sleep on the pantry floor. Another loyalist farmer complained that when they wanted milk they milked his cows. As for payment, the Irregulars told a Bundoran hotel-keeper, an ex-serviceman and a strong unionist, he should send the bill for the food they consumed to his friend King George. A Galway farmer and his family were kept in a constant state of terror owing to the carelessness with which his billetees threw bombs and firearms about – it may be added that the Irregulars also burned a couple of Union Jacks which they found in the house.[19]

In addition to billeting, loyalist farmers were subjected to boycotting, which often meant the withdrawal of labour, cattle-driving, the destruction of crops (which might necessitate the prema-

---

16 *Parl. Debates*, 5 series, cliv, 1717, clvi, 171, CO762/6L.
17 CO762/90RH.
18 *The Stories of Sean O'Faolain* (1958), p. 71.
19 CO762/187GK, CO762/155GT, CO762/109TN, CO762/179NCHI, CO762/142RDF.

ture sale of stock, and the commandeering of motor cars, carts and horses. Sometimes pressure was put on a loyalist to give up his farm or at least some of his land.[20] The interruption of normal farm work could have severe financial consequences – a Cork farmer spoke of himself as 'pauperised'[21] – so that the dread of debt was added to the strain of dealing with the Irregulars or hostile neighbours.[22] 'Life was made a misery',[23] a County Cork farmer declared, and a Kildare rector remarked that a loyalist farmer whose house had been raided and ransacked reminded him of men in France 'who had gone to bits after a bad bout with the Boche'.[24]

In some areas the pressure on loyalists seems to have been particularly severe. In east Donegal 'a ferocious lot' of Irregulars established a camp at Convoy from which they descended on Raphoe. Loyalists were boycotted, their motor cars were commandeered and their shops plundered. 'We lived in a state of constant fear and dread', wrote a Protestant solicitor, whose house was occupied by fifty billetees who would return at night after making raids.[25] In Monaghan a number of Protestant businessmen were driven out. Those with larger businesses tended to return when things became normal, but others, the proprietors of small concerns, stayed away, probably migrating to the North.[26] In Cavan loyalist and Protestant businessmen were boycotted and looted and farmers harassed, sometimes being turned out of their farms. Once the police and military left, a Protestant solicitor wrote, 'how we escaped the mob element I don't know'. He himself was turned out of his office by 'three lads'. The daughter of a landed gentleman, a

20 For instance CO762/63JP, CO762/113RB, CO762/196MMcM.
21 CO762/150AJ.
22 CO762/5F, CO762/150AJ.
23 CO762/113JB.
24 CO762/196WFH.
25 CO762/175RMB, CO762/81DW, CO762/102RW, CO762/54RM, CO762/173RMB.
26 E. Michean, 'Sectarian Conflict in Monaghan' in *Revolutionary Ireland, 1917-22*, ed. D. Fitzpatrick (1990), pp. 16, 107-17, and T. Dooley, 'Monaghan Politics in a Time of Crisis' in *Religion, Conflict and Co-existence in Ireland*, ed. R. Comerford, M. Cullen and J.R. Hill (1990), pp. 235-51.

sometime high sheriff, had a decidedly unpleasant experience. An energetic unionist, friendly with the RIC, who worked for the Red Cross and always hoisted the Union Jack for a British victory, she was boycotted and then arrested on 'a trumped-up charge' of attempting to shoot a Free State soldier. After a week's imprisonment she was released.[27] To the south, in Westmeath, attacks on Protestant business firms were reported. For instance, a Protestant grocer who had built up a good business and who had supplied the RIC was taken into the country by armed men who threatened to shoot him. He immediately left for Belfast.[28] To the west, around Carrick-on-Shannon, a small colony of Protestant farmers were subjected to 'continuous persecution' and a number left for Northern Ireland.[29] In Longford in May 1922 eighteen young men, seemingly Orangemen, were arrested and charged with drilling. The local rector, who was Dean of Ardagh, saw General MacEoin, whom, he wrote, 'I have known from boyhood', and they were soon released. The Dean thought that the reason the men had been arrested was to force them to leave the area, as many other Protestants had done.[30] To the west, in Ballina, a number of Protestant businessmen were notified by an IRA brigade commandant that because of the continued massacre of Irish citizens in the north-east they were to be deported and their property confiscated. A group of Ballina Catholics wrote on their behalf to Griffith, asking him to take steps to prevent the expulsion of 'decent, inoffensive' men, who have 'no sympathy with their brothers in the north'.[31] In County Galway some Ballinasloe Protestants, including a Guinness agent, the manager of a boot shop and a stationmaster, were ordered to leave the town.[32] In Queen's County, the mountains to the west were, according to a Protestant farmer, occupied during 1922 by 'roving bands of Irregulars' who 'often demanded food and left us hungry'. There was also at this time in Queen's County, it was reported, a well-organized land agitation, influenced

27 CO762/144GF; CO762/137EJWA.
28 *Irish Times*, 13 June, *The Times*, 14 June 1922, CO762/135HC.
29 CO762/151S, CO762/152F.
30 CO762/39GL, CO762/40AMcV, CO762/41JC.
31 Unknown to A. Griffith, 4 May 1922 (Department of Taoiseach, S565).
32 *Irish Times*, 16 June 1922.

by sectarian feeling and in some places managed by local land committees. The leaders of these committees, according to an evicted Protestant farmer, got 'young fellows ... who were no mark for damages' to do their work. A few Protestant farmers were evicted in the Stadbally area and another Protestant, 'a steady, hard-working man', was forced to surrender forty-eight acres he had bought in the Timahoe area.[33] In nearby Luggancurran there had been in the 1880s a prolonged struggle between Lord Lansdowne and many of his tenants, leading to evictions, the Protestant tenants siding with their landlord.[34] By 1914 all the evicted, whom the Land Commission thought should be reinstated, had been granted holdings, but bitter memories still lingered and in 1922 a number of Protestant farmers, boycotted and threatened, had to leave their holdings in 'a general exodus'. The cry, according to one of the evicted, was 'Grabbers out, owners in'. The evicted seem usually to have returned to their farms after a short interval but they often had to sell stock and found the land had deteriorated in their absence. Some miles to the north-east of Luggancurran, around Ballyfin, 'all the loyalists were boycotted' – one of them had recently proclaimed his politics by flying the Union Jack on Empire Day 1920.[35]

In north Tipperary, near Nenagh, according to the Bishop of Killaloe, 'scarcely a Protestant family escaped molestation', with predators coming down from the hills – though he added that things were very different elsewhere in his diocese.[36] Loyalists in Cork and Kerry, areas where the Irregulars were strong and for a time in control, not only suffered from 'humiliations, injuries and losses'[37] – billeting, exactions, commandeering, raiding and boycotting – but in the spring of 1922 were panic-stricken when armed bands shot a dozen Protestants, several of them well-known loyalists, in their homes. A particularly gruesome episode

---

33 CO762/144SB, CO762/70DE, CO762/93WS, Department of Taoiseach, files S 566, *Parl. Debates*, 5 series, lix, 571, CO762/71JK, CO762/74MEAM.
34 *Parl. Debates*, 3 series, cccxxxvi, 1148, 1161.
35 CO762/125SW, CO762/155HB.
36 T.S. Berry to the Minister for Justice, 10 June 1922 (Ministry for Justice, files H5/372).
37 CO762/88TGB.

occurred near Clonakilty when the house of a JP, a strong unionist, was burned down. The owner and his son were compelled to
dig their own graves and then shot; the JP's nephew, an ex-officer
who fired on the raiders, was hanged. Other loyalists, believing
themselves threatened, fled, there being, according to the *Irish
Times*, 'an exodus' to England, a hundred refugees from the
Dunmanaway and Bandon areas leaving by boat, some without a
handbag or overcoat. One prominent supporter of the British government, when his home was visited by armed men escaped and
went 'bare-headed and in his slippers' through the fields to temporary safety. Later he arrived in England, and another loyalist meeting him in London described him as a good example of a strong
man who had got 'a bad dose of shock'.[38]

The rough treatment meted out to loyalists in the twenty-six
counties at the beginning of the 1920s contrasts strikingly with
the peace, placidity and good-neighbourliness associated with the
Irish countryside. But insurrection and civil war had hardened
men's tempers and weakened the legal and social restraints on violence. As an experienced county court judge said in 1924, 'in the
revolution Ireland had passed through, many of the inhabitants of
the country saw red and did things which in their saner moments
they would not do'.[39] Then, Sinn Féin ceaselessly and emphatically
reiterated that the Irish nation was entitled to the whole-hearted
allegiance of every Irishman. Intelligent Sinn Féiners seem to have
hoped that unionists, at least in the South, influenced by changing
circumstances and their inherent 'Irishness', would unite with
their fellow-countrymen and be absorbed into the Irish people.[40]
At the grass-roots level, fervent, unsophisticated men sought to
enforce conformity to the national ideal by quick, crude techniques, bullying or clearing out the dissentients. In Donegal
raiders said they 'would clear all the Protestants out of the county'. In Mayo a Church of Ireland clergyman, a sometime chaplain
to the forces, said he was told by the men who raided his rectory,

38 CO762/133WGW; *Irish Times*, 1 May 1922, CO762/64DGW.
39 CO762/9RMDS; *Cork Examiner*, 29 July 1924.
40 For an exposition of this point of view see M. Collins, *The Path to Freedom*
   (1922), p. 42.

'they would bomb the whole b—y lot of us to H—l'. In
Roscommon Protestant farmers were ordered 'to clear out and
leave the place to the Roman Catholics'. In one district in
Waterford, according to a Protestant, all Protestant houses were
burned; a Protestant farmer in Kerry stated that Protestants there
were referred to as 'the English garrison'; and a Church of Ireland
farmer in Cork was called 'a Sassenach' – 'the Irish term for a fol-
lower of the British'.[41]

It would be unfair to imply that the anti-loyalist campaign was
mainly inspired by *odium theologicum*. Catholic loyalists were
assailed as well as Protestants. A widow in County Leitrim, with
two sons in the army and a son-in-law in the RIC not only suffered from cattle-driving but was debarred by the republicans
from the family pew in the local Catholic church. Even an ultra-
unionist Church of Ireland clergyman admitted that the 'IRA
always maintained that they did not interfere with people because
of their religion' and he advised a Cork farmer, whose horse had
been taken because he was a Protestant, to report this to the IRA.
He did so and the horse was returned. Protestants were singled
out for harassment because religion was the easiest way of identifying a person's politics. After all, a Church of Ireland clergyman
in County Cork wrote, 'I am glad to say to be a Protestant spells
loyalty.'[42]

It is perhaps unnecessary to add that in a time of widespread
political violence there was bound to be plenty of ordinary crime,
the line between the two being not always precise. For instance in
1922 the rector of Listowel, a sometime chaplain to the forces, was
knocked down when he tried to stop some men demolishing part
of his glebe wall. This may appear to have been a bad case of political and sectarian violence – the rector himself referred to it as
'Bolshevikism'. But apparently the reason for breaking down the
wall was not ideological; it was to open a route for out-of-hours
drinkers to the back doors of nearby public houses.[43]

41 CO762/34RJG, CO762/171AF, CO762/36RB, CO762/100ABR, CO762/85AH,
    CO762/196HMcM, CO762/142VJA, CO762/137SM.
42 CO762/178WW, CO76/145MPMcK, CO762/107AMB.
43 R.A. Adderley to unknown, 12 June 1922 (Ministry of Justice, files H5/371).

As conditions in the south and west deteriorated a number of loyalists sought refuge in Britain and Northern Ireland. In May and June a number (probably some hundreds) of Protestants from east Donegal, mainly farmers, threatened by the Irregulars, took refuge in County Londonderry and it was said that during 1922 a large number of loyalists, 'hundreds of families', from all the border counties, and some even from as far afield as Kerry entered Northern Ireland from the Irish Free State.[44]

It may be assumed that loyalist refugees in the North would receive assistance from friends or fellow members of a Church or some other organization. But refugees in Britain often presented a problem. At the beginning of May 1922 the Chief Secretary admitted that a number of 'terrorised' British subjects from the South of Ireland had fled to Great Britain. In the middle of May the government set up a committee, the Irish Distress Committee (renamed the Irish Grants Committee in March 1923) to investigate applications from persons normally resident in Ireland who had been compelled to leave their homes, to relieve their immediate necessities and to furnish the Irish Office with details so that it could press the Provisional Government to take steps to enable the refugees to return.[45] At the same time the British government in a communication to the Provisional Government expressed the hope that the latter would accept financial responsibility for these 'homeless and destitute refugees'. The secretary to the Provisional Government replied that his government would accept liability in the cases of 'a certain number of law-abiding citizens' who had fled. But he added there is 'an organized movement amongst certain elements in both countries to discredit both governments ... [and] that it was a matter of common knowledge that a considerable number of persons have left Ireland on the plea of compulsion without any justification'. He concluded by devoting the remainder (about 40 per cent) of his letter to the sufferings of the northern Catholics.[46]

44 Parl. Debates, Northern Ireland, 1 series, ii, 1172; Derry Sentinel, May, June 1922.

45 Parl. Debates, 5 series, cliii, 1520, cliv, 534; Irish Grants Committee; Second Interim Report, Cmd 2032, H.C. 1924 xi.

46 Relief of Irish Refugees: Correspondence between H.M. Government and the

The refugees from Northern Ireland in the Irish Free State by April 1923 apparently numbered sixteen hundred,[47] and were accommodated in three workhouses. In November 1922 Cosgrave told the Dáil that a large proportion of the refugees were young men who had joined gangs of Irregulars, but the Department of Local Government, which was responsible for their welfare, thought the number of impostors negligible. Nevertheless the Department put pressure on the refugees to return home as soon as circumstances permitted. The cost of maintaining these refugees amounted to £17,651, a debt honoured by the Colonial Office. On the other hand, the Free State government met in March 1923 a bill presented by the British government for £11,587 expended by the Irish Distress Committee on relieving refugees from Southern Ireland.

The Irish Distress (or Grants) committee, under the chairmanship successively of Sir Samuel Hoare, Lord Eustace Percy and William Ormsby-Gore, was composed of a few MPs, Sir Henry Wynne, who had been chief Crown solicitor in Ireland, and Ernest Crutchley, who had worked in Dublin Castle. Its secretary was Reid Jamieson of the Colonial Office, and representatives of the Ministry of Labour and the War Office were added to its secretariat. In June, shortly after the committee was constituted, Hoare complained that with the sum at its disposal 'all we can do is to give the refugees small doles to keep them from starvation'. A few days later the Colonial Secretary announced that 'the treasury had given the committee 'carte blanche with certain limitations'.[48] The committee kept in close touch with the Southern Irish Loyalists Relief Association (a voluntary organization to be described later), and rather than turn applicants into pensioners it preferred to give an applicant a lump sum which would enable him to start a new career. Up to 1924 it handled 7500 applications, of which 5600 were for immediate assistance. It approved of 4300 applications, not only making grants and loans but also making advances

---

Provisional Government of Ireland relating to the Liability for the Relief of Irish Refugees, Cmd 1634, H.C. 1922, xvii.

47 *Dáil Debates*, i, 588; Ministry of Finance files, F287.
48 *Parl. Debates*, 5 series, clv, 1755, 1821.

amounting to £52,000 on compensation decrees and on arrears of rent. From the end of 1924 the committee was busy winding up its business transferring its responsibilities to the Southern Irish Loyalists Relief Association or to the Irish Grants Committee set up in 1926, and it seems to have held its last meeting in September 1926.[49]

Official relief was preceded and generously supplemented by private charity. As early as May 1920 the Irish Loyalists Defence Fund was established with the aims of providing information about conditions in the south and west of Ireland and assisting loyalists who had suffered from oppression. Supported by Carson, Richard Dawson, the London secretary of the Unionist Alliance and two MPs, Duncannon and Foxcroft, among others, in the following two years it relieved about 4400 loyalists and also assisted many RIC men. In 1922 it merged with the newly formed Southern Irish Loyalists Relief Association.[50] The Association was founded in July 1922 with Lord Linlithgow, a rising young Conservative politician, as chairman and an imposing list of peers and MPs, drawn largely from the right wing of the party, as supporters. After it had been functioning for about eighteen months it had interviewed 9400 refugees, provided clothing for about 2400, found accommodation for 1380 and posts for 2036. It also made loans 'which had been very fairly repaid'. The Association, Carson stressed, was just as keen to help loyal Roman Catholics as Protestants – the former 'had often upheld the flag with greater danger to themselves than the Protestants'.[51] Shortly after its foundation the Association was provided with a very useful Dublin branch, when the executive of the Irish Unionist Alliance, realizing that its political activities had 'necessarily been suspended', decided to turn itself into an advisory committee for the Association. Harry Franks, J.E. Walsh and the Rev Robert Weir, with the help of a very efficient secretary, Miss D.M. Murray, and

49 *Parl. Debates*, 5 series, clvi, 1726, clxvi, 1572. *Irish Grants Committee, Second Interim Report*, Cmd 2032, H.C. 1924, xi. For the minutes of the committee see CO762/207, 208.
50 *The Times*, 6 May 1920, 3, 14 July 1922; *Morning Post*, 15 June, 5 July 1922; *Spectator*, 19 March 1921.
51 *The Times*, 29 Jan. 1925, SILRA minutes in 989/B/3/27.

some useful local informants, threw themselves into the task of investigating claims, and either affording immediate relief or sending details to the London office of the Association. Weir was particularly active. A fervent evangelical (he had started his clerical career in the Irish Church Missions, which carried on missionary work amongst Irish Catholics), he was a curate and then rector in a very disturbed part of Queen's County.[52]

For years the Association issued appeals and fund-raising entertainments were organized on its behalf – a concert in Carlton House Terrace (tickets from the Dowager Marchioness of Duffrin and Ava and Mrs Ernest Guinness), a ball in the Hyde Park hotel, and matinee performance at the Chelsea Palace.[53] In a grimmer form the Association's work was encouraged by the Truth about Ireland League, founded by Mrs Stuart-Menzies and supported by Colonel Sir Alexander Sprot MP, Brigadier-General Prescott-Decie and Lady Bathurst, the owner of the *Morning Post*, who, though she did 'not lay claim to any first-hand knowledge' about the sufferings endured by the Irish loyalists, was very sympathetic. The League held meetings which were addressed by loyalist refugees, 'the Irish martyrs', some in deep black; one meeting was for women only; 'decency forbids', it was explained, 'the terrible truth being told before a mixed audience'.[54]

The Association seems to have been very active until the close of the 1920s. In 1938 its president, Lord Salisbury, having drawn attention to two significant developments – that it was becoming harder to secure subscriptions and that the Association's work in Ireland was now mainly amongst ex-servicemen who had become the responsibility of the British Legion – suggested that the Dublin office, which was receiving a subsidy from London, should be closed. The Dublin committee, resenting dictation from London, remonstrated vigorously. It handled cases that could not be dealt with by the British Legion, and by disregarding red tape it was often able to tide people over their difficulties until they could receive help from another source. In the end the Association, now

52 Irish Unionist Alliance papers, A109, D989A/8/2/65; D989/B/1/10.
53 *The Times*, 20 May 1924, 9, 15 May, 4, 13 July 1925, 24 Feb., 20 Sept. 1926.
54 *Morning Post*, 10 June, 26 July, 17 Aug. 1922; *The Times*, 10 June 1922.

apparently a small body dominated by ex-unionist exiles from Ireland, decided to continue subsidizing the Dublin office. Salisbury resigned and a small devoted group kept the Association going, the Dublin office continuing to help distressed loyalists (often ex-servicemen) with clothing, boots and food vouchers. In 1956 the Association moved its London office to Dublin and six years later in 1962, the committee, having exhausted its capital and having a very small subscription income decided it could no longer carry on.[55]

About the time when the Southern Irish Loyalists Relief Association began work, a more aggressive organization, concerned not with relief but compensation, was formed. The Irish Compensation Claims Committee was headed by a 'number of representative men amongst the sufferers', with Robert Sanders of County Cork as chairman. In a statement issued shortly after its formation it asserted that there was a co-ordinated movement (partly controlled by the Third International) 'to expel from Ireland those that have at any time shown British sympathies' – including many Roman Catholics who had sons in the British army or who had been active in recruiting.[56] In the general election of 1922 the committee arranged for candidates to be asked would they do everything possible to protect the interests of Irish loyalists and support their claims to compensation, and until the end of the 1920s it assisted loyalists in preparing their claims for submission to the Irish courts or to the British government committees set up to afford them financial help.[57]

Inevitably politics and charity were interfused. 'Die-hards' could scarcely avoid a touch of *schadenfreude* when drawing attention to a conspicuous consequence of the coalition's tendency to prefer expediency to honour – the plight of the betrayed Irish loyalists. But it would be a mistake to assume cynically that the distressed Irish loyalists were regarded by conservatives as simply

---

55 Salisbury to E. Walsh, 29 July, 8 Nov. 1938, E. Walsh to Salisbury, 3 Aug. 1938 (Unionist Alliance papers, D989/B/3/1, 27), and D/989/A/8/2/65, D/989/B/I/2, 3, 10, D989/B/2/12.

56 *Irish Times*, 2 June 1922.

57 *The Times*, 2 June 1922, 2 Nov. 1923; *Morning Post*, 16 Aug. 1922; CO762/153TM, CO762/I/I.

a card in the political game. To many it was profoundly disturbing to see decent people, who had done their best to maintain British ideals, harassed and reduced to penury, and charity was actuated by deep and genuine pity.

With the ending of the Civil War the position of those loyalists who had been under pressure rapidly improved. The Provisional Government and the first Irish Free State government were composed of pragmatic nationalists, eager to get on with constructive work and resolute upholders of law and order. In the middle of May 1922 when a small Church of Ireland deputation (the Archbishop of Dublin, the Bishop of Cashel and Sir William Goulding) drew Michael Collins's attention to the ill-treatment experienced by Protestants in some areas, he assured them that the government would maintain civil and religious liberty, adding (perhaps revealing some ambivalence in his outlook) it was obvious that 'the murders in Belfast had an effect on the present situation but that the Belfast massacres could not be considered any justification for the outrages to which the deputation had alluded'.[58] Shortly afterwards the Provisional Government issued a proclamation expressing regret that 'a small number of law-abiding persons' had been compelled to leave Ireland and accepting responsibility for relieving their pecuniary distress, adding that a number of people had left the country with the aim of discrediting the Provisional Government.[59] Early in the new year (1923), with the Irregulars dissolving in defeat, the new police force and the new courts assured the protection of persons and property throughout the country, and the government took steps to provide compensation for those who had suffered in the Civil War and to complete land purchase, substituting a regulated price for illegal expropriation.

Compared with the thorough methods for dealing with unpopular minorities developed during the twentieth century in eastern and central Europe and elsewhere, the harassment of the Southern loyalists was not noticeably severe. Perhaps about sixty (including members of the RIC and Protestants in Cork) were killed after the Truce and a number were menaced, boycotted, bullied, frightened, plundered or deprived of their land. But the campaign against them was ill co-ordinated and sporadic. A number of those expelled returned after an interval, and most loyalists in Dublin, Cork city and the less disturbed parts of the countryside escaped unscathed. If it was easy for a landlord or sometime landlord (with a portfolio of investments, including land stock) to leave Ireland – Lady Gregory in 1921 heard that 'furniture vans engaged for nine months ahead are taking goods from the country to England'[60] – the loyalist professional or businessman, the shopkeeper or farmer would find it difficult to contemplate uprooting themselves, abandoning what they had built up and starting afresh in a strange environment. After all it was possible to avoid hostile pressure, as the case of an harassed Protestant farmer in Tipperary illustrates in reverse. Having, it was reported, 'a hot and abrupt manner, he was unable to pass himself with the republicans as well as some other loyalists'. Indeed some loyalists may even have found the stress and strain they went through a challenge – a Kildare farmer, a strong unionist, declared 'the reason why I am staying here is I know they are doing their best to get us all out'.[61] Others, however, were dismayed by the disintegration of the local loyalist community. For instance a grocer in Nenagh, an ex-serviceman, wrote that 'nearly all the county families who were the backbone of our business' had been forced to leave, and on a lower level, a Galway game-keeper pointed out that 'the gentlemen of the county who supported the Game Protection Association having left owing to terror', he was unemployed.[62] So, though the majority of loyalists in the event remained in the Irish Free State, a fair number left for good and there must have been those who discouraged the next generation from staying on. It is safe to say, then, that the pressure exercised on unionists between 1919 and 1923 partly accounts for the striking fall in the Protestant population of the twenty-six counties between 1911 and 1926, from 327,000 to 221,000.

60 *Lady Gregory's Journals*, ed. D.J. Murphy, i (1978), p. 648.
61 CO762/186JAS, CO762/139HSL.
62 CO762/57CHB and also CO762/108WR; CO762/62MS.

VII Compensation

ONCE THE TREATY was confirmed and the Provisional Government (to be succeeded at the close of 1922 by the government of the Irish Free State) installed in office, a number of important 'winding up' issues – the future of civil servants in the Irish Free State, the disbandment of the RIC, compensation for losses in the 1919-21 conflict and the completion of land purchase – all of which affected loyalists, had to be tackled. The first two issues can be disposed of quickly. Article x of the Treaty stipulated that public servants who wished to retire should receive fair compensation on terms not less favourable than those accorded in the Government of Ireland Act of 1920. About 2400 civil servants seem to have wished to exercise their rights under the article, and all would have gone smoothly enough but for a technical dispute – how far was a treasury minute of March 1922 to be taken into account when the pensionable incomes of a number of civil servants was being calculated. Discontented civil servants took the matter to the courts and after five years of litigation, which incidentally revealed the reluctance of the Free State government to accept the right of appeal to the judicial committee of the Privy Council, they secured a judgment in their favour from the committee. The British government ended the matter, which obviously was beginning to damage Anglo-Irish relations, by agreeing to pay the difference between the two levels of pension – a solution very satisfactory to the civil servants concerned and to the Irish taxpayer.[1]

An act passed in the summer of 1922 provided for the disbandment of the RIC, 'that great and historic force', on terms which, it can be said, were not ungenerous. These terms, the Chief Secretary explained, had to be settled with regard to 'the state of

[1] *Dáil Debates*, xxix, 1687.

the public purse', but he added that the government 'was not going to quibble over a shilling'. For the purpose of calculating the pension to be paid to a member of the force, ten or twelve years were to be added to his actual service. He could apply to commute all or part of his pension or to augment it in its early years, receiving a lesser pension in later years. Members of the RIC who were compelled to leave home could claim a disturbance allowance. To settle questions arising under the act, a tribunal was appointed, consisting of a retired Home Office permanent under-secretary, a senior RIC officer and a senior Treasury official. The tribunal granted 6941 disturbance allowances together with 1261 grants to men who had lost household effects on being compelled to leave home. The tribunal agreed to 1600 commutations of pension for the purpose of emigrating and permitted 1269 applicants to commute for the purpose of buying a small business or a farm, usually in Ulster.[2]

An urgent problem faced by the British and Provisional governments in the immediate post-Treaty period was compensation for injuries to persons and property sustained between the beginning of 1919 and the Truce (July 1921). A number of persons had secured decrees under the Malicious Injuries Acts but in the south and west the defendants, the county councils, did not enter an appearance, so that awards made on *ex parte* evidence tended to be high. However, the county councils refused to pay the sums decreed, and though it was legally possible for a successful claimant to seek and secure a garnishee order, in the prevailing conditions he would have found it hard to execute it – Dáil Éireann issued a warning that action would be taken against any person or his legal representative attempting to execute a garnishee order. The government's response was to secure power to deduct the amount payable under malicious injury awards from the loans and grants the county councils were entitled to receive from the imperial exchequer. As a result, by July 1921 most of the personal

---

2 12 & 13 Geo. V, c. 55; *Royal Irish Constabulary: Terms of Disbandment*, Cmd 1618A, *Royal Irish Constabulary: Revised Terms of Disbandment*, Cmd 1673, HC 1922 xvii; RIC tribunal report, 26 Feb. 1922 (CO762/1/16); *Parl. Debates*, cliii, 2244, 2283–6; K. Fedorowich, 'The Problems of Disbandment: the RIC and Imperial Migration, 1919–29' in *IHS*, xxx, pp. 88–110.

injury claims by government servants or supporters of Crown authority had been met.[3]

At the beginning of 1922 representatives of the British and Provisional governments agreed on the lines that a settlement of the compensation question should follow. Regarding personal injuries, 'each side would look after its own injured' (the comparatively few 'border line cases' would be dealt with by agreement. As regards damage to property, in the pre-Truce period each side was to pay for the losses it had inflicted. Unpaid, undefended decrees were suspended – it was felt that many claims were inflated, litigants 'erring on the side of generosity' in estimating their losses – and all claims for malicious damage to property, including the destruction inflicted by the military authorities under martial law, were to be heard and determined by a commission composed of three members, one nominated by each government and a chairman appointed by agreement. This commission was to decide what compensation in 'reason and justice' should be awarded for malicious damage to person and property inflicted between 1 January 1919 and 11 July 1921 in cases where no decree had been obtained or where the case had been undefended.[4] Empowering the commission to rehear undefended cases, a conservative MP with an Irish background asserted, implied cancelling the statutory rights of British subjects to awards made before the Treaty. But Churchill had already explained that though 'the existing machinery for assessing compensation' had not been suspended, it was inoperative and a more effectual mode of redress was offered by the commission.[5] A year or so later the Irish Free State Compensation for Damages Act annulled the undefended decrees.

The commission consisted of three members, C.H.J. Thomas, deputy chief valuator to the Inland Revenue, nominated by the British government; J.C. Dowdall a prominent Cork businessman, nominated by the Provisional Government; and a chairman, Lord

---

3 10 & 11 Geo V c.66; *Parl. Debates*, 5 series, cxxxviii, 1121; cxlvii, 622; cl, 640.

4 *Parl. Debates*, 5 series, cl, 2249-56; *Compensation (Ireland) Commission: Warrant of Appointment*, Cmd 1654 HC 1022 xvii; *Compensation for Malicious Injuries: Letters to the Provisional Government*, Cmd 173, HC 1922 xvii.

5 *Parl. Debates*, 5 series, clv, 1661.

Shaw, a Scottish lawyer, the subject of an exceptionally candid notice in the *DNB*, appointed by agreement. Shortly after his appointment Shaw left for a visit to the United States, the House of Commons being assured that in his absence the commission would continue to work with 'undiminished powers'. But in September Sir Samuel Hoare, a Conservative MP destined in two months' time to be a Cabinet minister, visiting Dublin, was shocked by how slowly the commission was working. He stressed that with thousands of unheard claimants, the English critics of the Treaty, whose views were expressed by the *Morning Post*, would be reinforced by an 'army of influential Irishmen', and he 'threw a bomb-shell into the commission' by urging it should immediately revise its methods and greatly increase its staff.⁶ As a result his ally in Ireland, Cope, the bustling assistant under-secretary, was soon able to inform him that the commission was 'getting more like the hive of industry it should be'. Cope understood that Shaw, who apparently proposed to hand over the hearing of claims to the heavily burdened county courts, resented that he had 'butted into something that was not my business'.⁷ Cope was unperturbed.

In November Shaw resigned, having expressed the opinion that the work of the commission would probably take many years and was replaced by Sir Alexander Wood-Renton, a sometime chief justice of Ceylon and the author of several legal works.⁸ Shortly after Shaw's resignation, to speed up the work of the commission a number of 'investigators' (experienced valuators), two for each county, were appointed to assess claims, with claimants having the right of appeal to the commissioners.⁹ As a result by February 1923 the commission, in spite of 'the condition of roads and railways', was dealing with claims at the rate of four hundred a week.

---

6 S. Hoare to W.S. Churchill, 20 Sept. 1922, S. Hoare to J. Butcher, 13 Oct. 1922 (Templewood papers, file 13).

7 A. Cope to S. Hoare, 12 Oct. 1922, L. Curtis to S. Hoare, 12 Oct. 1922 (Templewood papers, file 13).

8 *Parl. Debates*, 5 series, cliii, 1775, clv, 1488, clv, 1428, clix, 309, clx, 315, 350.

9 *Parl. Debates*, 5 series, clx, 1647-56.

By the time the commission concluded its work in March 1926 it had made awards in 17,792 cases of the 40,674 that came before it, and awards totalling £7,048,152 against £19,107,282 claimed. It should be added that many of the claims were for trivial amounts.[10] The commission's smooth functioning was only once disturbed by a serious inter-governmental dispute. It arose in 1924 over the clause in the commission's terms of reference relating to destruction inflicted by the military under martial law. The Treasury contended that it could only make awards for 'official reprisals' in the proclaimed area; the Free State government argued that martial law was a state of affairs independent of a proclamation, that the British interpretation of the terms of reference was in 'a narrow and niggardly spirit' and that the commission should consider injuries inflicted by the Crown forces on persons associated with the national movement anywhere within the twenty-six counties. For good measure the Free State government also complained that the Treasury and the Colonial office were corresponding with the commission and demanding to see its files. In the event the Irish Free State view was, practically speaking, accepted, and when the commission completed its work Amery, the Colonial Secretary, felt able to assure Cosgrave that the Shaw commission had been 'strongly influential in promoting better feeling'.[11] A quick comparison between the amount claimed and the total awarded naturally suggests that the commission could not have given universal or profound satisfaction. But almost certainly many claims were inflated – possibly to allow for scaling down – and a number of claimants, frustrated by delays, must have been thankful to receive something in the end.

While the Shaw commission was working through pre-Truce compensation claims, conditions in the south and west were rapidly producing a large crop of post-Truce injuries and losses. As early as July 1922 the Provisional Government appointed a strong committee to consider its general policy on compensation

---

10 Department of Finance files, F19/2/26; CO905/1-2, CO762/212.
11 T. Healy to J.H. Thomas, 3 July 1924, H. Kennedy to W. Cosgrave, 15 May 1924 (Department of Finance files F19/40/24); L. Amery to W. Cosgrave, 1 April 1926 (F 19/2/26). For supposed inflation of claims see *Parl. Debates*, cliv, 1388 and F10/2/26.

and in 1923 the Oireachtas enacted the Damage to Property (Compensation) Act. The act annulled unpaid awards granted under undefended decrees between 21 January 1919 and 11 July 1921 (though the holders of such decrees could of course make a fresh claim for compensation in the Free State courts). It provided that compensation should be limited to direct damage and should not extend to cover consequential loss; and that there should be no compensation for the loss of money or jewellery nor for the loss of chattels, if it could not be proved they had been taken by the members of an unlawful association. Compensation for buildings should be based on market value. When making an award for the destruction of a building the judge could attach a full or partial reinstatement condition, and he could grant permission for a reinstatement award to be used to erect a residential building or buildings in any part of the Irish Free State (it had been pointed out in the Senate that a person whose house had been destroyed, in some cases under circumstances of 'considerable indignity', might not want to rebuild in the same neighbourhood).[12]

When defending the bill Cosgrave emphasized that 'we have endeavoured to arrive at as fair a distribution of what we can afford to pay in the circumstances'. With a comparatively poor community having to foot the bill for an enormous amount of destruction and damage, the government was bound to be anxious to limit the amount that might be claimed, and it was pointed out by the Department of Finance that owing to the magnitude of the total sum involved a detail in the bill 'of apparently slight importance' might result in the expenditure of thousands if not a million pounds'.[13] The exclusion of money and jewellery was justified on the grounds that such losses were hard to verify and that the loss of jewellery involved little practical hardship. As regards looting, the Court of Appeal had decided that larceny *simpliciter* should not be a subject for compensation under the Malicious Damages Acts – it was not prepared 'to make the rate-payers liable for every theft'.[14] At a time when houses in the south and

---

12 *Senate Debates*, i, 915.
13 *Dáil Debates*, ii, 1746; J. B[rennan] memorandum (F316/10).
14 In Lyburn v Armagh County Council (see A.D. Bolton, *Criminal Injuries (Ireland) Acts* (5th edn 1922), p. 35, Ministry of Finance F363/10).

west were, according to the Minister for Justice, crammed full of loot, one house being 'more like Tutankhamun's tomb than anything else',[15] this was a hard ruling for the victims, who would often find it difficult to prove that the plunderers belonged to an illegal organization. On the question of consequential damages the law was uncertain. In 1920 the Lord Chancellor, Sir James Campbell, had decided that a claimant under the Malicious Damages Acts was entitled to receive damages as he would in a civil action. Shortly afterwards his successor, Sir John Ross, ruled that a county was only liable for losses arising from 'primary acts'. He added that though everybody would agree that innocent persons should be adequately compensated, nothing would be 'more unjust than the imposition of that intolerable burden on the rate payers'. Obviously if consequential damages were not to be taken into account many claims arising from the disturbed condition of the country between 1921 and 1923 would be ruled out or greatly reduced. For instance, if farm buildings were destroyed the owner's farming profits would be greatly diminished or if business premises were destroyed the owner would lose his trading profits – but in each case the only admissible claim was for loss of buildings. On the other side it was argued that the results of taking consequential damages into consideration would be far-reaching. If consequential losses were admitted, Ernest Blythe, the Minister for Finance, declared, everybody would be claiming consequential losses and 'you would find the country trying to live by taking in one another's washing'.[16]

Later Cosgrave admitted that the 1923 act had been 'very tightly drawn', and as part of the 1925 agreement with the United Kingdom the Free State government increased awards under the act by an *ex gratia* payment of 10 per cent. In 1927 the Fianna Fáil opposition, hinting that the government had yielded to British pressure, asked if the increase had been made 'purely and simply' on the initiative of the Irish government. 'Not purely', Cosgrave replied, rather 'practically entirely but not exclusively'. Later Cosgrave admitted that there had been widespread complaints

---

15 *Dáil Debates*, ii, 2086.
16 *Dáil Debates*, ii, 1386.

about the unsatisfactory sums awarded under the 1923 act. Our supporters, he explained, complained but not as loudly as the ex-unionists – 'minorities', he remarked, 'suffer most in times of political strain'.[17]

Simultaneously with introducing the 1923 Damage to Property Act, the Free State government set up a commission to determine what compensation should be awarded for personal injuries sustained since the Treaty. The commission handled 6616 cases. Of these 1876 were dismissed as outside its terms of reference or because the application forms were not completed. The 4740 awards were meant to cover medical expenses and pecuniary losses but did not allow for 'suffering'.[18]

Those Southern Irish landlords who at the time of the Treaty had not sold out were unlucky. In 1918 the convention, estimating that 600,000 acres remained unsold, approved a land purchase scheme which, broadly speaking, provided that the remaining landlords should be bought out, the purchase price of an estate being fixed at approximately fifteen years rental, paid in 5 per cent stock, the landlord also receiving a cash bonus. Lloyd George indicated his approval of the scheme as part of a general settlement of the Irish question and in 1920 Lloyd George, Bonar Law and the Chief Secretary all stated that the Government of Ireland Act would be accompanied by a land purchase act on the lines of the convention's scheme.[19] In the event a land purchase bill was not introduced in 1920 until almost the end of the session and it only received a first reading. However, Irish landlords must have been reassured to see that in the Home Rule bill of 1920 land purchase was a subject reserved to the imperial parliament. During the following session (1921) Austen Chamberlain, the leader of the House of Commons, announced that the government regretted that owing to pressure on parliamentary time it was impossible to bring in an Irish land purchase bill. During the same session in the Lords, Oranmore and Browne (who himself had sold out in 1912),[20] backed by other Irish peers, pressed the government to

---

17 *Dáil Debates*, i, 728-9, xv, 75-6, xxi, 1497-9, xiii, 1307-13.
18 Department of Finance files, F20/70/24; CO762/212.
19 *Parl. Debates*, 5 series, cxxvi, 432, cvii, 933, cxxix, 620.
20 *Parl. Debates* (Lords), 5 series, lxiii, 84.

fulfil its pledges on land purchase, and Birkenhead stated that 'as part of the general scheme for dealing with the Irish situation this [land purchase] is one of the questions that must be dealt with, and dealt with upon the lines which the government has already indicated.' But he later remarked that any promise regarding the land question 'must be construed in relation to the circumstances as they existed then' (the implication of these words may not have been grasped by all his listeners). Before the end of the year changing circumstances – the need to reach agreement with the Dáil Éireann delegation in the Downing Street talks – 'put it out of our power', Birkenhead explained, to introduce Irish land legislation.[21]

In February 1922 two representatives of the Irish Landowners Convention, F.S. Stewart and William Alexander, had a meeting with Patrick Hogan, the Minister of Agriculture in the Provisional Government. Hogan agreed that land purchase, which he made clear was a matter for his government, should be completed, and he cheerfully assured the delegates that Irish credit would stand at least as high as British.[22] About the same time the Chief Secretary informed the House of Commons that land purchase would be a matter for consultation between the two governments. But shortly afterwards a deputation from the landowners' convention who had come over to London were bluntly told by Churchill, the Colonial Secretary, that they should get in touch with the Provisional Government – though he hinted that Great Britain might help to finance a settlement of the Irish land question.[23]

Shortly after taking office the Free State government boldly tackled the land question, and its land purchase act of 1923, the last major Irish land measure, had two aims – the completion of land purchase and the acquiring of land, either by agreement or compulsory purchase, for congests (those on uneconomic holdings) and landless men. It provided for the compulsory purchase of the remaining estates, the landlord being granted approximately fifteen years' purchase after a substantial reduction in rents together with 75 per cent of the arrears of rent due to him, the

21 *Parl. Debates* (Lords), 5 series, xl, 420, xlv, 1069-70, liv, 1240.
22 Memorandum, 14 Feb. 1922 (Midleton papers PRO30/67/49).
23 *Parl. Debates*, 5 series, cli, 1460, Memorandum, Midleton papers, PRO30/67/51.

price being paid in land bonds guaranteed by the United Kingdom government. The immediate reaction of the more vocal Irish landlords was that the effects of the measure would be 'little short of disastrous'; to concede 25 per cent of arrears to the tenants, at a time when they had enormous bank deposits, put 'a premium on dishonesty'[24] (insult was added to injury when the remaining Northern Ireland landlords were bought out on much better terms). On the other hand, it was said in the Dáil that the behaviour of Irish landlords in the past 'put them completely out of court with regard to any claim they could make on our consideration'.[25] The Free State Minister for Agriculture said the act did 'rough justice', and a balanced observer, sympathetic to the Irish landlords, pronounced that though the terms of the 1923 act were not generous or even just, given the circumstances they were merciful; the government had done its best to be just to 'a powerless and unpopular minority'.[26] If some ex-unionists suffered considerable pain during the final stages of the liquidation of the Irish landlords, from 1923 all Irish landowners with a substantial holding – large farmers, the possessors of demesne land or grazing land (and a hundred acres could be regarded with envy as a ranch) – were for many years apprehensive that the Land Commission, 'that great two-handed engine at the door', might descend on them and acquire a substantial part of their property for distribution. Many Irish politicians believed that the Irish people were animated by 'the virile and healthy desire to till the soil',[27] and between 1923 and 1971 the Land Commission acquired about three million acres for redistribution.[28] Though not discriminated against, ex-unionists were likely to suffer disproportionately from the Commission's activities – in 1926 when Protestants mounted to a little over 7 per cent of the population of the Irish Free State they comprised 17 per cent of the farmers with holdings over two hundred acres.

When the land purchase act of 1923 was being considered in

24 *The Times*, 19 June 1923.
25 *Dáil Debates*, ii, 1152.
26 *Senate Debates*, viii, 1014; *The Times*, 17 Sept. 1923.
27 *Dáil Debates*, xlviii, 2379.
28 *Land Commission Report*, 1971-2.

the Senate, Sir John Keane suggested that the British government's honour might be redeemed 'if the purchase price to be paid to the Irish landlord was increased by a British grant'. The *Irish Times* reinforced this view by an ingenious argument. Though the Irish landlords might have ceased to be 'the backbone of the British garrison in Ireland', they had not ceased enriching their country by their inherent gifts of loyalty, leadership and the capacity for public service. Now, since the Free State was 'a Dominion of the empire', the British government had a direct interest in maintaining the quality of its people.[29] In July 1923 Midleton raised the question of Irish land purchase in the Lords, arguing that it was incumbent on the government to carry out the pledges that had been given. He pointed out that under the 1920 act the landlords would have received a bonus estimated as amounting to £6,000,000 and that 'to redeem the honour and credit of this country', this should be paid by the United Kingdom. He was supported by Oranmore and Browne, who, accepting that the Free State act of 1923 gave the best terms that could be expected from an Irish government about to face a general election, called on the British Government to make good the losses suffered by 'those who have upheld your flag for nearly eight centuries'. Birkenhead made a pungent speech in which he ridiculed Midleton's obsession with the Convention and his belief that its land purchase scheme had 'verbal sanctity'. He argued that the Free State act was 'an equitable settlement' on the lines of the 1920 bill and met the pledges given by the coalition ministers. Speaking for the government, the Colonial Secretary said that it would consider the position of those affected by the Free State land purchase scheme but that he could hold out 'no hopes at present nor possibly at any time'.

Three years later Oranmore and Browne, who asserted that paying the bonus, which he believed the landlords were entitled to, would be a matter of £300,000 a year, pressed the House of Lords to appoint a select committee to consider the pledges on Irish land purchase given by ministers between 1920 and 1923. He was supported by Midleton and Carson, the latter being more

29 *Senate Debates*, ii, 1475, *Irish Times*, 23 July 1923.

than thankful to say that he had no personal interest in any pledge of any kind made by the British government. The motion was carried by 35 to 33, the majority including twenty peers closely associated with Ireland. The government did not offer any evidence to the committee, which reported that the pledges had not yet been fulfilled, and in May 1927 Oranmore and Browne asked the house to resolve that it relied on the government to take such measures as it deemed right to ensure their fulfilment. The debate followed predictable lines. Carson spoke of the treachery of the British government to those who were once their friends in Ireland, Midleton referred to those who were left in the lurch, Peel for the government contended that the pledges referred to in the debate, were conditional promises, depending for their fulfilment on circumstances; and Haldane said that 'statesmanship' forbade the fulfilment of an obligation which had devolved on the Irish government by taking six million from the British taxpayer. Oranmore and Browne's motion was carried by 54 to 36 and that ended the matter.

The workings of the Shaw commission, the land act of 1923 and the Damage to Property (Compensation) Act, 1923, left loyalists in the twenty-six counties disappointed and with a strong sense they had been badly treated. Acting 'under the mantle' of the Shaw commission the sub-commissioners had reduced the judges' awards on average by 40 per cent. Surely all dissatisfied persons were entitled to a hearing before the commissioners? The terms offered by the 1923 land act were certainly poorer than those proposed by the convention, and the Southern landlord, when he received fifteen years' purchase, could sadly contrast his lot with his equivalent in Northern Ireland who received twenty years' purchase. The defects of the Damage to Property (Compensation) Act were only too obvious. The exclusion, to a great extent, of looting and of consequential loss, meant for instance that compensation could not be claimed for damage inflicted by a boycott or the seizure of lands, and the practice of often making a substantial proportion of a building award conditional on reinstatement penalized an owner who did not wish to live any longer in Ireland. Admittedly, to expect to receive the replacement value for a large mansion with fine woodwork and plaster work would be unrealistic and indeed might saddle the owner with a white elephant (even in England, a Labour peer pointed out, country houses were a drag on the market), but assuming that that owner was to have a house equalling in 'in point of substance, dignity and style' the one destroyed,[30] some of the awards were too low.[31] Besides relying on the general merits of their case, the claimants attached great weight to two statements. In July 1922 the cabinet sub-committee on Ireland, when stating that the responsibility for meeting post-Treaty claims to compensation, had devolved on the Irish government, nevertheless admitted that His Majesty's government 'cannot divest themselves of the duty to see that such claims were met equitably and promptly'. A few months later the same opinion was expressed by the Prime Minister, Bonar Law, in a speech at Glasgow. The people who were suffering in the South of Ireland, he said, had 'their claims naturally on the Irish government', but it would be the duty of the British government 'in communication with the government of the Irish Free State' to see that those claims were 'fairly, honourably and justly considered'.[32]

The question of compensation for the Southern loyalists was raised in the House of Lords in July 1923 and in March and July 1924. On the third occasion Carson, after displaying his forensic skill when outlining a number of hard cases, concluded by arguing that since the British government had withdrawn all protection from its loyal subjects it was its duty to provide adequate compensation for their losses. Shortly after the Conservatives returned to power at the end of 1924, a deputation headed by the Duke of Northumberland drew the new Colonial Secretary's attention to the hardships sustained by the Southern loyalists. Amery, the Colonial Secretary, was sympathetic but reflected in the privacy of his diary that 'one cannot compensate in practice against all the consequences direct and indirect of a successful revolution, as the old American example showed'.[33] Six months later in July 1925 Shelborne, 'an

30 *Senate Debates*, i, 827-30.
31 Report of Irish Claims Association [c.1925] in Unionist Alliance papers, D989/B/2/9.
32 *The Times*, 24, 27 Oct. 1922; *Compensation for Malicious Injuries: Letter to the Provisional Government of Ireland*, Cmd 1736, H.C. 1922, xvii.
33 L. Amery, *Diaries*, 1896-1929 (1980), p. 395.

elder statesman of high ideals', proposed in the Lords that the government should appoint a commission to make recommendations as to what compensation should be paid to Irish loyalists. After he had been passionately supported by Carson, who demanded that the promises repeatedly given should be kept, and by Lansdowne, who spoke from sad experience, Salisbury, the leader of the House (and Shelborne's brother-in-law) suggested that 'an informal committee' should consider the question. In July Amery appointed a committee to report on whether the British government had fulfilled all its obligations to the Irish loyalists. The committee was composed of two ministers (Clarendon and Eustace Percy), three persons who could speak for the loyalists (Northumberland, Danesfort and Sir Henry Wynne) and a Scottish lawyer, Lord Dunedin, who acted as chairman.[34] Having heard Major White, the secretary of the Southern Irish Loyalists Relief Association, and Lipsett, an Irish QC, representing the Compensation Claims Association, the committee empowered Dunedin to draft and present a report. In his report, dated July 1925, Dunedin accepted that the British government had an obligation to ensure that those in the South of Ireland who had loyally supported it in the disturbed period preceding the Truce should be compensated for the hardships they had endured 'beyond the inevitable dislocation' resulting from the change of regime. There were, Dunedin suggested, three standards that could be applied in assessing the compensation that might be paid – those embodied in the pre-1923 Malicious Injuries legislation; the criteria applied by the Shaw committee; or the terms of the Free State Compensation Act of 1923 together with the rules for assessing personal injury issued by the Free State government in the same year. Dunedin decided that all these standards should be set aside, preferring 'a broad interpretation in terms of history rather than law'. Due regard should be paid to a very wide variety of injuries sustained by loyalists, though of course compensation already paid should be taken into account. Cases should be dealt with by a small committee presided over by a lawyer.[35]

---

34 For the composition of the committee see CO905/17.
35 *Report of the Commission Presided over by Lord Dunedin*, Cmd 2748, H.C., 1926 ix, CO762/1/17.

The government accepted the Dunedin report and appointed a strong advisory committee to hear claims for losses and injuries sustained between the Truce and 12 May 1923 – the end of the period of 'acute disturbance'[36] in the Irish Free State – because the claimant had supported the government in the pre-Truce era, and to recommend awards. The committee was composed of Sir Alexander Wood-Renton (chairman), Sir James Brunyate and Sir John Oakley. Wood-Renton, after a distinguished career in the Colonial Legal Service, had carried out a number of government missions and had, as Chairman of the Compensation Claims Commission, wide experience of Irish conditions and claimants. An erudite lawyer, the author of legal textbooks, he was hard-working, fair-minded and kindly, with a Scottish sense of humour 'enhanced by the agreeable accent in which it was conveyed'.[37] Brunyate had been a member of the Indian Civil Service, serving for some years as secretary of the Finance department. Oakley (who declined any remuneration) was a past president of the Surveyors Institute. The committee's indefatigable secretary was Reid Jamieson, who had been secretary to the Irish Grants Committee. Shrewd, compassionate and alert to detect fraud or exaggeration, he was expected both to place claimants' statements before the committee and, if he thought it advisable, to contest them. Expressed more tactfully, his role was to submit a claim with all the relevant material that might support or weaken it. Jamieson was very level-headed and managed to fulfil his dual role satisfactorily, putting the applicant's case in full before the committee with his own comments. In any event the committee could, and often did, interview claimants in person or hear their legal representatives.[38] Moreover, having examined a case thoroughly, they frequently disagreed with their assiduous secretary. For instance, when a Belfast-based motor firm claimed for cars taken from their Dublin premises by the Irregulars in 1922, the secretary argued that the situation at the time was too serious for the Irregulars to indulge in spite against a loyalist firm. 'The Irish',

---

36 *Parl. Debates*, 5 series ccvi, 1660-1.
37 *The Times*, 19, 20 June 1933.
38 *Parl. Debates*, 5 series, ccix, 829.

he added, 'had always been famous as soldiers', and it was in accordance with 'their natural aptitude' for military tactics that they had seized the cars. The committee, however, on the assumption that the firm had suffered injury on account of its known loyalty, made a substantial award in its favour.[39]

Applicants were furnished with a form which asked for details about the applicant's losses and injuries, compensation already received and present financial circumstances. The applicant was required to show that his injuries and losses were due to his allegiance to the British government in the pre-Truce period and to give the names of two referees. In many cases the committee through its secretary sought for further information in the form of accounts (if possible certified), bank statements and valuers' reports. In a number of instances, however, it came up against a serious obstacle. Many Irish farmers and small businessmen were slack about keeping accounts. As a Roscommon publican said 'such bookkeeping as there was was of the most elementary kind'. A Clare grocer wrote that her practice was 'to buy and sell and keep the surplus money', and, as might be expected, farmers at fairs were paid in ready money. Even a Crown solicitor had to admit 'no regular books were kept in my office'.[40] There were of course good reasons why in some instances precise evidence for losses could not be produced. 'I have a contempt for you Englishmen', an indignant Limerick solicitor wrote, 'who button up your pockets and say "you are robbed and murdered but we cannot acknowledge that unless you have a receipt duly signed by the robber or murderer".'[41]

The committee not only scrutinized the material presented to it and the referees' reports but often took steps to obtain an opinion on the claimant's case from independent sources, a procedure that, if they had been aware of it, would have disconcerted some of the more audacious claimants. The secretary had a number of knowledgeable correspondents in Ireland, including three former Crown solicitors, well-informed, worldly-wise lawyers, a well-

---

39 CO762/131HF.
40 CO762/167EW, CO762/167PF, CO762/175WJC.
41 CO762/87ASWS.

known land agent and a number of Church of Ireland clergymen, who were prepared to make discreet inquiries into a claimant's character, conduct, reputation and financial circumstances. The secretary made a point of comparing the claims made by disbanded members of the RIC with the statements they had previously made to the RIC tribunal, sometimes discovering marked discrepancies. He also obtained from a Dublin accountant a memorandum on Irish economic conditions[42] – claimants when estimating their losses sometimes failed to allow for the fall of prices after 1920. Jamieson kept in close touch with Major White, the secretary of the Southern Irish Loyalists Relief Association, who had sources of information through the association's branch office in Dublin and who shared his anxiety to relieve genuine distress and to ensure that the available resources were not wasted on undeserving cases.

The committee's terms of reference obviously ruled out losses and injuries sustained before the Truce. However, if the loss or injury, for example a pre-Truce boycott, had been continued post-Truce, the post-Truce damage would be considered by the committee. It should be said that a number of applicants, either through carelessness or excessive optimism, made a wholly pre-Truce claim which of course was immediately ruled out. The terms of reference also ruled out losses and injuries arising from the change of regime or the general condition of the country, rather than from the claimant having been singled out because of pre-Treaty loyalty.[43] Naturally there were borderline cases, and the claims of an ex-serviceman injured by a bomb thrown by the Irregulars at Free State troops, of two country gentlemen whose houses were destroyed because they were Free State senators, and of loyalists who lost property during the fighting in Dublin in June 1922, were ruled out. Again the committee was not prepared to consider the claims of Crown solicitors for loss of office because they were removable under the old regime, but it was prepared to compensate them for loss of private practice as a result of pre-Truce support of the government.[44]

---

42 CO762/112D & Co.
43 CO762/43F, CO762/68D, CO762/WS.
44 CO762/115HEC, CO762/82JK, CO762/62JE, CO762/127.

In addition to its terms of reference the committee quickly evolved a number of guidelines. It ruled out applications from public companies – it would be impossible to assess the politics of a multitude of shareholders – but it was prepared to consider claims from private companies. In a few cases it applied the *de minimus* rule – a small loss suffered by a relatively well-off applicant was scarcely hardship and could be disregarded. But in two instances in which the secretary urged the rule should be applied – in the one case the applicant claimed for a large amount of uninsured jewellery, in the other for two Purdy guns and a quantity of wine – the committee made awards.[45] On the other hand, small claims from poor applicants sometimes received generous treatment – a small farmer was granted £15 for, *inter alia*, his good overcoat.[46] Considering applications from disbanded members of the RIC, the committee took into 'serious account' how the claimant had been dealt with by the RIC tribunal.[47] Often it decided that the tribunal's award sufficed but in some cases it recommended a grant – for instance where the claimant or his wife had suffered harassment after the tribunal award had been made. In a large number of cases in which a claimant's injuries and losses resulted from agrarian violence, the committee, apparently working on the assumption that agrarian animosity had been greatly inflamed by political hostility, viewed the claim sympathetically and made an award, sometimes overriding the secretary who argued that they were instances of purely agrarian trouble. Too low a price (in the eyes of the landlord) offered under the land act of 1923 was not, the committee ruled, an injury within its terms of reference, but the reduction in the capital value of an estate shortly before it was purchased, as a result of agrarian violence, was treated as a loss. Naturally, when dealing with damage to person or property the committee took into account compensation already paid by the Free State and it considered it was not a court of appeal from the Free State courts. Nevertheless, it was prepared to revise Free State awards in exceptional cases, for example when a judicial report was altered by

45 CO762/1, CO762/35C, CO762/53C, CO762/133Lady M.
46 CO762/154CH.
47 CO762/65WD.

administrative action (i.e. by the Minister for Finance) or when a claim for personal effects was excluded under the 1923 act. When an award for the destruction of a house was 'clogged' with a reinstatement condition the committee felt it was not debarred from considering it and it was prepared to take in account the pleasures of ownership and latent potentialities. Most important of all, the committee took into account losses arising from a boycott and consequential losses, for instance income lost as a result of seizure of land or profits lost from the destruction of plant or premises (including farm buildings). It also considered claims for losses incurred by temporary or permanent removal from Ireland under duress – cost of travel and accommodation and loss of earnings until the claimant returned to Ireland or settled in England.[48]

In its final report the committee reported that it had received 4032 applications and had recommended 2237 awards, ranging from £10 (compensation for a commandeered bicycle) to £53,700, granted to a Dublin businessman who had been in constant touch with the Chief Secretary. After being taken from his car and forced to face a firing party, he immediately left Ireland, had a breakdown and stayed away for some years. During his absence his property deteriorated and his company sustained disastrous losses. The claimants comprised all classes in Irish society – peers, policemen, publicans, professional men, businessmen, shopkeepers, landlords, farmers, shop assistants, labourers. Many claims were rejected because they fell outside the committee's terms of reference or the guidelines it adopted. Some claimants failed to complete a form or supply adequate evidence. A good many RIC claims were dismissed on the grounds that the claimant's case had been satisfactorily dealt with by the RIC tribunal. About half a score of claimants could be ruled out because they had been neutral in the pre-Truce period – for instance a Dublin businessman who frankly stated that he 'never associated or mixed myself in politics, my entire interest being concerned with the proper conduct of my business'.[49] A number of claimants who probably believed they had a genuine

---

48 For the principles on which the committee acted, see its Report (CO762/212) and Committee minutes, especially 3 Nov. 1926 (CO762/209).
49 CO762/203MC.

case failed to convince the committee they deserved compensation. There was, for instance, the financially distressed proprietor of a poultry farm who fervently emphasized her loyalty and her membership of the Church of Ireland but, according to Major White, 'her troubles were caused by non-payment of rent to several landlords'.[50] One area in west Clare produced a large crop of petitions – 'claims from Ennistymon', the secretary wrote, 'are regarded with the utmost suspicion'. The claimants, for the most part possibly vaguely loyalist in sentiment, were often desperately poor and frequently expressed themselves with considerable fluency. An investigator in the area was probably correct in saying that many people felt that 'any yarn was good enough if there is money to be got from England'.[51] A case that involved prolonged investigation and two hearings by the committee was that of the owner of fishing boats based on Howth who claimed that because of his loyalty his nets were seized by the IRA. It was concluded by the committee that he had over-stretched himself financially and that his nets had been seized by his creditors. Living in impoverished circumstances in London, and claiming to be a distressed loyalist, he strove to mobilize English public opinion in his support, writing to the Prince of Wales, the Prime Minister and the Colonial Secretary and securing petitions from sympathizers, including trade unionists.[52]

Then there were the claimants – about seventy or eighty – who were downright dishonest. These included half a dozen applicants, who, enquiry revealed, were republicans – one had had three sons 'on the run'; another, a woman shopkeeper in Kerry, was going about in tailor-made clothes and furs, being 'the good friend' of one of the IRA 'boy generals'. A third was a dentist who had been a JP. He had failed to perform his duties as a magistrate, had avoided even greeting the police in the street and, it was reported, 'was always on the lookout for money'.[53] Finally, there were applicants who might be loyalists but whose claims were highly dubious. There was the Tipperary merchant who 'drank, gambled and

50 CO762/189MB.
51 CO762/26TC, CO762/92PM, CO762/33TJB, CO762/26TC.
52 CO762/52.
53 CO762/190TB, CO762/196SBO'N, CO762/172PAO'R.

never suffered as a loyalist'; there was a Cork publican, 'a rank outsider and never-do-well', and there was a Cork auctioneer, 'a great rascal' who employed a solicitor who would 'get the harness off a nightmare'. A Clare man's support of the British government was, it was reported, confined to carrying golf clubs for English gentlemen, and a small shopkeeper in Cavan was said to have manifested her loyalty by ordering goods from Belfast – using the boycott as an excuse for not paying for them.[54] A Kerry grocer and provision merchant, who submitted his bank book as evidence for his losses, was summoned before the committee and severely censured when it was discovered that business payments had been made into his wife's undisclosed account.[55]

In striking contrast to the audacious dishonesty displayed by a comparatively small number of claimants, was the attitude of a small farmer in County Leitrim, a widow, a Protestant loyalist, who was desperately poor. With a keen sense of honesty,[56] it was pointed out, she was afraid of exaggerating the losses she had suffered during a raid and claimed only £12.19.0. The committee awarded her £25. There were also two successful claimants, the widow of a JP living near Ballinasloe and a Donegal farmer, a leading local unionist, who informed the committee that they did not wish to take their grants if by doing so they deprived a poorer claimant of an award.[57]

In their final report the committee stated that 'investigation alone could disclose the depth of the misery that has been caused and the extent of the mischief that has been done'. Certainly a wide and melancholy variety of injuries and losses are reflected in the applications that came before the committee. Some claims arose from a major tragedy, the death of a close relation, a breakdown in health, or, in the material sphere, the ruin of a business, the destruction of an historic mansion, the devastation of a carefully tended estate – a Limerick landowner under local pressure had, after fighting hard, to relinquish the ownership of a property

54 CO762/82RB, CO762/15C, CO762/48DTL, CO762/96McN, CO762/54R.
55 CO762/162JFC.
56 CO762/174S.
57 CO762/189MDW, CO762/182/FGA.

that had been in his family since 1174 and in which he had invested £25,000, planting and building; the owner of Derryquin Castle in County Kerry, after continuous raiding, the burning of the castle and the destruction of its garden and greenhouse and the loss of his pedigree herd, declared 'one of the fairest spots on earth is now a waste'.[58]

But in a vast number of instances the sufferings involved were in a lower key. For instance, a Westmeath landowner, a DL, had lived pleasantly, employing a large outdoor and indoor staff, until 'the anarchy, trouble and terror arose against England's loyal Irish subjects'. Then, after being boycotted and intimidated and seeing his house vandalized (an Adams ceiling perforated), he and his wife had to live in London on £2 a week lent by relations. An elderly landowner, a sometime high sheriff of Leitrim, boycotted and without servants, was compelled to cook for himself. A County Meath JP after being raided had to leave for England, where he 'could not afford to hunt or keep a man to look after his car'. A clergyman who defended the authority of the Crown, lost in a raid the manuscript of his work on the growth of toleration – if it had been published, he believed, he 'would be in a much better position than that of a country rector'. The ex-editor of the defunct *Cork Constitution*, who had in his day been an influential unionist, 'an extremely proud, sensitive man', living in distressed circumstances, found himself exposed to 'the derision of those who through armed rebellion had secured victory'. A Mayo landlord who, having been raided, was forced to live in England, deeply regretted he could not send his children to boarding schools (this problem seems to have been ultimately solved), and a Presbyterian farmer in the same county was also worried that he could not give his children an adequate education.[59]

An ex-army officer had started an agricultural course in Longford, intending to farm there but, getting into trouble with the local 'Shiners', he decided to join the auxiliaries and on disbandment had to live on his capital. Another ex-officer, a Clongowan, who on demobilization had hoped to become a solicitor in

---

58 CO762/37HB, CO762/58CWW, *The Times*, 3 Oct. 1922.
59 CO762/5ARHT, CO762/13JOL, CO762/9WHB, CO762/8RHM, CO762/94WJL, CO762/105VATSC, CO762/48JP.

Kerry, was kidnapped and threatened. He joined the auxiliaries, and on disbandment, not being able to return home, had to take a post in London. A Protestant farmer in Cork, an ex-soldier, said that 'a dead set was made at me' and he was not permitted to take part in the activities of the Gaelic Athletic Association, though in the past he had won championships. A Dublin woman and her two daughters who had worked in Dublin Castle, being threatened, had to leave Drumcondra for Battersea 'where we know practically no one'. The two daughters of a badly boycotted County Kildare landowner were reduced to playing in a London jazz band. A County Cork draper, a refugee in London, 'fretted himself away owing to the loss of a comfortable home and living'. A colonel's wife was saddened at being forced by raids to leave their nice house in Tipperary, 'with its wood, garden, trout and salmon fishing and rough shooting ... it was an ideal house for good birth but small means'; and Lord Killanin was deeply depressed not only at the destruction of his property but by the intensity of the hostility directed against him as a conspicuous loyalist; having given his whole life to serving his county and country, 'all his old affections and associations were broken and outraged'.[60]

It may be said, of course, that the hardships sustained by the Southern loyalists were on the whole not excessively severe nor long-lasting. It may also be asserted that their sufferings were consequent on failing to comprehend or on defying the inevitable. Revolution – or, if that is too formidable a term to characterize what occurred in Ireland during the early 1920s, major changes involving demolition and reconstruction – is bound to leave debris. But this would be poor consolation for those who felt that history took a wrong turning and that the better cause was defeated. In any event the contemplation of historical trends does little to mitigate the pain resulting from loss and injury.

When the Irish Grants Committee was set up the government could not know what was the extent of the hardship the committee was expected to deal with, but it had in mind that the expenditure involved should not exceed £400,000, a figure that was privately

---

60 CO762/63BAR, CO762/168JTM, CO762/148WB, CO762/120MM, CO762/19AB, CO762/10JLP, CO762/127MT, CO762/55K.

communicated to the committee. After the committee had been at work for about a year it was clear that its recommendations would considerably exceed the sum mentioned, so in December 1927 the government decided to extend the limit on the committee's expenditure to £625,000. About the middle of December Wood-Renton met the Chancellor of the Exchequer, Winston Churchill, whom he 'unhesitatingly' told that 'within the limits of our terms of reference fair and reasonable compensation could not be afforded by any such sum' as £625,000. The Chancellor expressed his appreciation of the work of the committee 'apart from its financial aspects',[61] and ten days later he informed the House of Commons that the government would meet in full awards up to £250 and would pay 50 per cent on awards between £250 and £1 000 and 30 per cent on awards above £1,000.[62] This decision was challenged by a well-organized protest movement. The Southern Irish Loyalists Relief Association published a number of cases and arranged for some of the sufferers to meet the press. The association stressed that much of the suffering had been caused by the British government's swift withdrawal of the army and the police, 'leaving the countryside at the mercy of rough bands'. A long statement in *The Times*, signed by four peers (Carson, Danesfort, Northumberland and Selborne) and three MPs (Davison, Gretton and Somerville) declared that if the government reduced the awards it would be treating its fellow subjects with meanness and ingratitude as well as committing a breach of faith. A well-attended meeting of MPs urged the cabinet to implement the pledges given by successive governments[63] and Carson in the Lords threatened 'seriously to discuss [distressing cases] one day after another'.

In February 1928 Churchill announced important modifications in the payment scheme adumbrated in December. All awards up to £1000 were to be paid in full and on awards above that figure 60 per cent was to be paid immediately. The government had decided to raise the limit on the amount to be expended to £1,000,000, and

61 Account of Wood-Renton's interview with the Chancellor of the Exchequer, 12 Oct. 1927 (CO762/1/23).

62 *Parl. Debates*, 5 series, ccxii, 574-5.

63 *The Times*, 6, 10, 15 Feb. 1928.

Amery was confident that when the committee had finished its task it would be possible within this figure to pay all awards in full, thus ensuring 'a fair and honest fulfilment of our pledges'. The Conservative MPs who had been strongly urging the Irish loyalists' claims were for the moment placated, and after a bitter speech from a Labour ex-minister, born in Waterford, John Wheatley, attacking comfortably-off people in the South of Ireland who realized they had a chance of getting their hands into the pocket of the British taxpayer, the vote was passed without a division.[64]

But Amery's calculations were completely upset by the postponement of the final date by which a claim had to be made. About a thousand new claims arrived and the Dominion Office thought that £1,400,000 would be required. At this point Churchill dug in his heels. 'Unfortunately,' he remarked, 'the Treasury has to defend a good many positions that cannot be reconciled with generosity or gentlemanlike largess', and he considered that the Exchequer had been 'treated very badly in regard to the whole matter' by the Dominion Office. The furthest he was prepared to go was to raise the limit to £1,070,000 so that all claims could be paid in full on the February 1928 scale,[65] and on 17 December 1928 Amery informed the House of Commons that the government's decision to pay only 60 per cent on awards above £1000 was final. This provoked Howard Bury (who still prided himself on being a County Westmeath JP and DL) to refer to the government 'quibbling' over the small amount involved.

In the new year the supporters of the distressed Southern unionists again went into action. A letter signed by three peers (Northumberland, Danesfort and Carson) and four MPs (Gretton, Howard Bury, Davison and Somerville) drawing attention to the grave injustices inflicted on the Southern unionists appeared in *The Times*. The Southern Irish Refugees Relief Association arranged for a number of Southern loyalists to address a public meeting, at which it was pointed out that withholding 40 per cent meant ruin to a man 'struggling to keep together his little property', and steps were taken to brief a group of conservative MPs.

64 *Parl. Debates*, 5 series, ccxiii, 1904-35; L. Amery, *Diaries 1896-1929*, p. 536.
65 M. Gilbert, *Winston S. Churchill*, v, *Companion*, Pt. 1, pp. 1207, 1390-1.

When on 19 February Amery attempted to defend the government's decision on the awards he ran into a sustained parliamentary storm. A number of Conservative backbenchers called on the government to meet an honourable obligation. Churchill made, in Amery's opinion, a thoroughly intransigent speech, stressing that it was dangerous for the house 'to wear down the constitutional guardians of the public purse'. He was answered by Hugh Cecil, who in 'a blast of bitter analysis', asserted that economy did not mean failing to pay a debt of honour and that 'you could not value an obligation of honour on a principle of percentages'. It was clear that most of the Conservatives in the House would probably vote against the government and that they would have Labour and Liberal support. The government whips scurried to and fro, Churchill and Amery hurried to see the Prime Minister and Baldwin came down to the chamber and moved to report progress. The next day Amery told the Cabinet that the only way out of the impasse was to pay in full. His colleagues agreed but at the same time were anxious to ease things for Churchill, who was full of fight and hinting at resignation if not supported. Baldwin tactfully postponed a decision to give the Chancellor of the Exchequer a chance to find a feasible solution.[66] Ten days later, on 1 March, Amery announced that payment in full would be made on the recommendations. The total required he thought, would work out at £1,627,000, giving £100,000 either way. This was a trifle optimistic. When in March 1930 the committee's work was complete, the sum required to meet its recommendations amounted to £2,188,549.[67]

66 Parl. Debates, 5 series, ccxxiii, 2593-5, ccxxv, 967-1020; The Times, 7, 20 Feb. 1929; L. Amery, Diaries 1896-1929, pp. 574, 587-9.
67 Parl. Debates, ccxxxvi, 810.

VIII Staying On

FROM 1922, WITH THE IRISH FREE STATE established by legislation passed at Westminster and in Dublin, it was clear even to the most defiant die-hard that so far as three-quarters of Ireland was concerned, the Union was gone beyond recall. This was brought home by the flying of the Tricolour, the playing of 'The Soldier's Song', the renaming of streets, the lavish use of Gaelic in official nomenclature, postal stamps without the monarch's head, a new coinage, new police and military uniforms, and the predominance in public life of men with a Sinn Féin background. Still, Free State residents who had been unionists could not abandon overnight the convictions and attitudes of a lifetime, and for years 'ex-unionists' formed a distinctive element in Southern Ireland. Indeed some of those whom the 'plain people' of Ireland would probably have labelled 'ex-unionist' had in the past been constitutional nationalists, who, far out-distanced by Sinn Féin, shocked by republican tactics and out of sympathy with the new nationalism of the twenties, found themselves more at home with many of their former unionist antagonists. For instance Sir John Keane, widely regarded as the quintessence of intelligent ex-unionism, had been a mild Home ruler,[1] and Frank MacDermot, a strong advocate of the Commonwealth connection, had been a Nationalist candidate in West Belfast.

Since considering oneself an ex-unionist constituted an attitude of mind rather than membership of a political party, it is naturally impossible to estimate with any degree of precision the numerical strength of ex-unionism. Its core of course was still the Protestant section of the community, 10 per cent of the population of the twenty-six counties in 1911. By 1926 it had fallen to just over 7

---

1 *Nineteenth Century and After*, lxxv, 488.

per cent of the population, from 327,000 in 1911 to 221,000 in 1926, a fall of 32.5 per cent (the Catholic population fell during the same period by 2.2 per cent). The decline continued and by 1981 the members of the three major Protestant denominations – Church of Ireland, Presbyterian, Methodist – numbered only 115,000, forming 3.47 per cent of the population (Catholics amounting to 95 per cent). Also, as might be expected, the proportion of Protestants in the professions and amongst the large farmers steadily declined.[2]

A number of reasons have been suggested for the fall in the Protestant population of the twenty-six counties. A factor accounting for about a quarter of the fall between 1911 and 1926 would have been the withdrawal of the army and the disbandment of the RIC. Undoubtedly too in the early 1920s a number of unionists in the south and west of Ireland lost heart and uprooted themselves. Then there were long-term demographical factors. The Protestant marriage rate in the twenty-six counties was comparatively low (many of the young having emigrated), their fertility rate was also comparatively low and the children of mixed marriages, because of the rules of the Catholic Church and the absorptive power of a larger group, tended to be brought up as Catholics.[3] Finally, at a time when emigration was 'the predominant demographic feature of this country', Protestant emigration was disproportionately high. There had long been a tendency for young Irishmen of an adventurous disposition to seek good openings in Great Britain or the empire, and in the 1920s for those with an ex-unionist background there was a disincentive to staying at home: the requirement to have a knowledge of Irish for entry into the civil service or the legal profession. Also, for many ex-unionists emigration meant leaving what they had been brought up to regard as a somewhat parochial environment to play a part on a wider stage. On emigrating, an ex-unionist ceased

---

2 For statistics relating to Protestants in the professions and in agriculture see K. Bowen, *Protestants in a Catholic State: Ireland's Privileged Minority* (1983), pp. 85-7.

3 *Commission on Emigration 1948-54*, p. 115; B.M. Walsh, *Religion and demographic behaviour in Ireland* (Institute of Economic and Social Research Papers, no. 55, 1970).

to be one of a small minority out of sympathy with many of the ideals countenanced by the new regime, and therefore liable to be discriminated against. As it had once been said by a Liberal Cabinet minister, 'all minorities must suffer. It is the badge of their tribe.'⁴ Many Protestants (and some Catholic ex-unionists) thought they might easily become the victims of discrimination. In the forties W.B. Stanford, a young Trinity don, a keen member of the Church of Ireland who wanted his co-religionists to be 'loyal to Ireland before all other countries', wrote about the pressures to which Protestants in the Irish Free State were subject – exclusion from some public appointments and from some forms of philanthropic work, sometimes unfair treatment in business (most evident in the provinces) and having to put up with the assumption that the only true Irishman was a Roman Catholic. Stanford was not alone in recognizing these pressures. About the same time two Church of Ireland bishops expressed themselves cautiously on similar lines⁵ and some members of the laity were despondent. A boarding-house-keeper from King's County, the daughter of an Orangeman, wrote 'no Protestant will ever get fair play in the Irish Free State'; a small farmer in Cork was sure no Protestant would ever get a job in competition with a Roman Catholic – 'it is all priests and the Irish language'; and another farmer in Westmeath, an ex-serviceman, wrote in 1927, 'Thank God things are better now but a Protestant remains more or less in anxiety because only Protestants will admit themselves to be loyalists.'⁶

It should be said at once that successive governments in the twenty-six counties were emphatically and genuinely against discrimination on religious grounds. They were determined to be fair and could afford to be generous to a small and declining minority. Protestants received a disproportionately large number of legal appointments, and Blythe, the first Free State Minister of Finance and Douglas Hyde, the first President of Éire, were both Protestants. Of course Blythe, a Gaelic enthusiast and Sinn Féiner,

---

4 *Parl. Debates*, 4 series, clv, 1033.
5 W.B. Stanford, *A Recognized Church: The Church of Ireland in Éire* (1944), pp. 17-18; W.B. Stanford, *Faith and Faction in Ireland Now* (1948), pp. 20-4; *The Bell*, viii, no. 3, p. 226-7; iii, no.5, pp. 392-4.
6 Co762/166FAB, Co762/193JA, CO762/42WGMcK.

and Hyde, the founder of the Gaelic League, could scarcely be regarded as typical Protestants, let alone ex-unionists. Moreover, the success of Protestants in professional and business life – a number of well-known Protestant firms continued to flourish – demonstrates that the majority in the Irish Free State set a high value on toleration or refused to allow denominationalism to affect to their own detriment their behaviour in practical life. Nevertheless there is 'kindly discrimination', offering a helping hand to friends, old schoolfellows and the children of friends, and so far as this form of discrimination was concerned a member of the minority might easily find that he had fewer useful connections and fewer strings he could pull than a competitor from the majority – though it should be added that members of the minority in the Irish Free State were remarkably good at looking after their own. Moreover, a belief in discrimination can become an *idée fixe*, providing the unsuccessful with a more satisfactory explanation for failure than mere lack of merit.

But for the ex-unionist life in post-Treaty Ireland was not all decline and despair. He might frequently indulge in *Laudator temporis acti*, seeing pre-1914 Ireland through a golden haze, and he regarded with distaste the methods by which the new state had been brought into being (speaking privately of 'gunmen' and dismissing with contemptuous disgust the achievements of the republican 'army'). But he soon realized that though the Treaty had involved a revolutionary transfer of political power there were remarkably few drastic changes in his own environment. The Oireachtas and the civil service were shaped on lines familiar to those bred in the British tradition, showing few traces of the romantic return to Gaelic ways foreshadowed in some Sinn Féin writings of the revolutionary era.[7] More important to an ex-unionist, many of the institutions to which he was especially attached remained unaltered or changed very slowly. The new legal system – its courts, the content of the law, legal principles and the organization of the profession – was closely modelled on

---

7 For instance Darrell Figgis had asserted that everything that had been introduced by England into Ireland was destined for rejection (D. Figgis, *The Gaelic State in the Past and the Future* [1917], p. 56).

the old. The barristers even retained their wigs.[8] The Church of Ireland and Trinity College continued to function as before. The *Irish Times* published a substantial amount of United Kingdom news and its editorials strove to adopt unionist principles to new conditions, rebuking Free State personalities and parties with detached superiority. The membership of the well-established clubs changed slowly. The Royal Irish Academy, whose founder was George III, in 1936 sent an address of condolence to Edward VIII on the death of his father. Sometime landlords exercised considerable influence in the councils of the Royal Dublin Society, and Horse Show crowds always greeted a British or Swiss victory in the jumping ring with a vigorous rendering of 'God Save the King'. As late as 1956 the membership of the Turf Club (in which ex-army officers loomed large) was, in the opinion of the Minister for Finance, 'for the most part out of touch with Irish affairs'.[9] The mail boat still ran, every term a number of boys left the Free State for schools in Great Britain and Northern Ireland, young Irishmen continued to join the army and the civil services, English touring companies came regularly to the Gaiety and ex-unionists, who scorned Gaelic games, could enjoy playing or watching rugby, cricket and hockey. In practice an ex-unionist could live for most of the time, especially in his hours of ease, with like-minded people, ignoring to a remarkable extent those aspects of the new regime which he found repugnant – slipping out of the theatre before 'The Soldier's Song' was played and punctiliously referring to Kingstown and Sackville Street. (I was once rebuked by an elderly don for referring to O'Connell Bridge after speaking of Sackville Street. 'It is Carlisle Bridge', he forcibly enunciated, 'only the nationalists call it O'Connell Bridge.')

But though ex-unionists were a definite section of the community with distinctive views and attitudes, they did not inhabit a compound: they had innumerable contacts, economic, social, benevolent and sporting, with their fellow-countrymen. Some ex-

8 The ultra-unionist W.M. Jellett, withdrawing from politics after 1922, built up a very large practice at the Irish Free State bar (*The Times*, 28 Oct. 1936).
9 F. D'Arcy, *Horses, Lords and Racing: The Turf Club 1790-1990* (1991), pp. 301-2, 320-1.

unionists probably felt completely at ease only with those who shared their opinions on the change of regime. But there were others who happily shared common interests of profit or pleasure with people who belonged to a very different political tradition. In a sorely divided society, Irishmen had learned how to avoid contentious issues when in the congenial company of adherents of a different faith, religious or political. So though old, deep-seated loyalties persisted, most of the time they were dormant and did not interfere with the daily round.

The Southern unionists, though defeated politically and to a considerable extent excluded (or self-excluded) from the exercise of political power, were very conscious that they could make a contribution of inestimable value to Irish life. They had in their ranks a disproportionate number of the pedigreed, the propertied and the professionally successful, of prosperous businessmen and large farmers. So even those ex-unionists who were very ordinary people felt they belonged to a *corps d'élite*. Ex-unionists – including those who were not very bookish – were proud of the Anglo-Irish literary heritage. They also (even those who were Catholics) prided themselves on possessing what were regarded as the Protestant virtues, a stern sense of duty, industry and integrity together with the ability to enjoy gracefully and whole-heartedly the good things of life. The *esprit de corps* that inspired the ex-unionists was voiced with vibrant force by Yeats in his famous and thunderous intervention in a Senate debate in 1925. Speaking for the minority, he declaimed, 'we are no petty people. We are one of the great stocks of Europe. We are the people of Berkeley; we are the people of Swift; we are the people of Parnell.' Ex-unionists, with a good conceit of themselves, would certainly have agreed with Yeats, though some of them might have thought him to be over-flamboyant. However, the same attitude was expressed in more matter-of-fact language some years later by another senator, Sir John Keane. 'The loyal minority', he said, 'may not be large in numbers ... but they do contribute largely to the well-being of the state. Even in material matters, matters of taxation, they pay out of all proportion of their numbers. In country life they are the only centres of civilization. They are large employers of labour, they are responsible for the poor all round them. Their names adorn the pages of Irish history. Swift, Goldsmith, Burke, Wellington, Roberts, Berkeley.'[10] The Southern unionists, the editor of the *Irish Times* told his readers (largely ex-unionists), have 'kept British ideals – old fashioned we admit – of justice and service alive. In all Britain's wars they led their fellow Irishmen – and Englishmen too – to victory. In peace they have been good citizens, leaders of trade and commerce, foremost in science, literature and the arts.' Ten years later he emphasized that 'their brains and their money' have been spent freely in the service of the Irish Free State. About the same time a chance remark in an editorial revealed the gap between Healy and the bulk of his fellow-countrymen. Exhorting all sections in the country to co-operate in 'the noble and holy task' of nation-building, he called on them 'to play up, play up and play the game' (Newbolt did not figure in the nationalist literary canon).[11]

Even Lennox Robinson (a son of the rector), though a mild nationalist, in his play *The Big House*, first produced in 1926, permits his heroine, Kate Alcock, an Alcock of Ballydonal, to proclaim defiantly the value of the tradition to which she belongs. 'We are formidable', she said, 'if we care to make ourselves so, if we give up our poor attempt to pretend we are not so different. We must glory in our difference, be as proud of it as they are of theirs.' Her parents, burned out by the Irregulars, leave Ireland, half in relief, half in despair, for England. But Kate, their only surviving child, is determined to stay on, rebuild, and do her best to participate in local activities. 'It is my life', she affirms, 'it is my country.' Robinson takes for granted that Ireland would sustain a severe loss if it rejected her – so indeed would all his ex-unionist friends. In a rather lighter vein, another fictional young woman from a similar background asks, 'Don't you think we the ex-unionists represent something they might be poorer for losing – a sort of oasis of culture, a little reserve of leisure. They might have a kind of unionist national park where we could live unmolested in our natural surroundings.'[12]

---

10 *Senate Debates*, xv, 928.
11 *Irish Times*, 9 March 1920, 7 Nov. 1930, 25 Jan. 1926.
12 B. Fitzgerald, *We are Besieged* (1946), p. 30.

Membership of the Commonwealth, even in the very attenuated form it assumed after 1936, enabled ex-unionists to continue to manifest their deep-rooted convictions – loyalty to the Crown, enthusiasm for the British connection, pride in the Irish contribution to the empire – in time-honoured ways, by flying the Union Jack, drinking the loyal toast, singing what they still termed the national anthem, 'God Save the King'. They could of course claim that these gestures not only expressed pent-up emotion but displayed a strict respect for constitutional forms. After all the King was head of the Commonwealth of which the Free State, later Éire, was a member. Something of the intensity of feeling that could be expressed by joining in singing the national anthem is conveyed by an *Irish Times* report on 12 November 1931 of an Armistice Day commemoration in Phoenix Park – 'then came an item that was not on the programme, one of those incidents that are all the more impressive because of their spontaneity. From somewhere in the crowd came the sound of women's voices, singing something that was too faint to be recognized at first, but gradually swelling until everyone caught the notes of the National Anthem. All over the crowd it spread, caught up by fresh voices.'

Some years earlier, on a much less serious occasion, feminine loyalty asserted itself. The *Irish Times*, describing 'A viceregal garden party' given by T.M. Healy as Governor General, remarked that a majority of the women folk had 'not forgotten their manners and curtseyed as they were presented to His Majesty's representative'. Some years later the acerbic Beatrice Webb, visiting Healy's successor, James McNeill, noticed that 'the smart folk curtsey, somewhat derisively ... aristocracy patronizing "the King's representative" and "the humble do not curtsey"'. Mrs Webb was probably maliciously mistaken about 'derisively'. Bernard reflected the mixed feelings of ex-unionists when, after dinner at the Viceregal Lodge, he noted in his diary that he found Healy 'a hospitable old fellow but what a change from viceregal days'. Nevertheless his wife made 'profound curtsies' to the Governor General.[13]

One of the strands that held ex-unionists together was educa-

---

13 *Irish Times*, 12 Nov. 1931, 15 June 1925; J.H. Bernard's diary, 18 May 1923, 7 May 1924; *Beatrice Webb's Diaries*, 1924-32, ed. M. Cole (1956), p. 250.

tion – the Protestant schools, to some extent Clongowes, the English public schools and above all Trinity College. With three centuries of tradition behind it, Trinity College was undoubtedly a venerable institution, and its customs, traditions and roll of distinguished alumni gave it a unique position in Ireland – even if, as its critics suggested, it was living on its past. But though its *fin de siècle* golden age was over and competition from the newer universities was increasing, the Trinity teaching staff still comprised a number of talented and vigorous personalities (six of those working in College in 1930 received notices in the *DNB*), including some whose marked idiosyncrasies added to the store of legend that constitutes an important element in institutional *esprit de corps*. Most of the dons had entered middle age before the Treaty – the vice-provost in the early 1930s, Westropp Roberts, had been a Fellow of two years' standing when the first Home Rule bill was introduced, and Trinity College was, by ex-unionist standards, noticeably politically correct. Until 1939 Commencements concluded with the playing of 'God Save the King', which on occasion those assembled in the hall sang enthusiastically; until 1945 the King's health was drunk at College dinners and for years on public occasions the College flew the College flag, flanked by the Tricolour and the Union Jack. The last time the Union Jack was flown was in 1935 for the jubilee. Early in 1936 on the King's death, the College, in defiance of rule and custom, flew the Royal Standard – at half-mast. In 1929 the committee managing the College Races (an athletic and social function) decided that if the Governor General came 'God Save the King' should be played. On hearing this the government advised the Governor General not to attend the Races. The Races committee offered a compromise, suggesting that both 'God Save the King' and 'The Soldier's Song' should be played, but this was rejected. The affair was gravely discussed by the Free State government and the Colonial Office and was commented on by the King himself. If the undergraduates had known about these repercussions they would have been thrilled.[14]

Cosgrave defended his government's point of view by arguing that the Commonwealth conception implied the separate national

14 B. Sexton, *Ireland and the Crown 1922-36* (1989), pp. 118-19.

identity of each member. 'If this state is to be saved for the commonwealth', he wrote, 'we must safeguard the lives of the citizens of this state from extremists on the one side and the life of the nation itself from extremists on the other.' To him, some ex-unionists at least were dangerously hostile to the ideals, political and cultural, to which he and his party were committed. Indeed, Cosgrave and his supporters must have been often irritated and sometimes embarrassed by the frank, aggressive determination of ex-unionists to emphasize those aspects of the constitution which they preferred to play down. Desmond FitzGerald was driven to remark that some of 'the people who had been unionist' argued on the assumption that the Treaty was either the Act of Union or the Home Rule bill of 1912.[15]

Trinity's easy-going – and in hostile eyes arrogant – aloofness from much of contemporary Irish life was an irritant, a cause of regret and a challenge to nationalists. In 1934 de Valera, speaking with intransigent courtesy for 'the historic Irish nation', warned a Trinity audience that the Irishmen who had done so much for the British empire and whom they admired, were men 'whose spiritual home was not here at all'. If 'you want to be part of the Irish nation', he declared, 'the basis of your pride must be achievements for the Irish nation. The Irish nation wants you today as those who thought with Thomas Davis wanted you a century ago. We want Trinity men not to have their hearts and their minds centred upon another country.'[16]

The Trinity men he addressed may have wryly appreciated de Valera's well-intentioned sincerity, but he had been answered eight years earlier by a loyal Trinity graduate. Trinity's duty, the *Irish Times* had declared, was 'to serve learning, to serve Ireland and in serving Ireland to serve the empire'. Though it should be generous to the claims of a national culture, it must refuse to harbour 'a narrow and parochial patriotism' and must defend 'the spiritual independence and vigorous sanity' common to Berkeley, Burke, Mahaffy, Salmon and Tyrrell. 'When', the editorial concluded,

---

15 W. Cosgrave to unknown, 19 June 1929 (Department of Taoiseach, file S3262A); *Dáil Debates*, xi, 1414.
16 *Irish Times*, 8 Nov. 1934.

'the petty tyrannies of these days have vanished and their petty authors are forgotten, Ireland once clothed and in her right mind, will thank the steadfast champion of her intellectual liberties.' A few years after de Valera's speech in Trinity, a vigorous *Irish Times* editorial by another fervent Trinity man asserted that Trinity, though it may have gone against what is called the will of the people, though it may have represented a class of society opposed in many respects to the rank and file, and though it may have contributed more than the rest of Ireland to the honour and glory of the British empire, was nevertheless 'a microcosm of Ireland, one of the chief forces operating for Irish unity, and at the same time well aware that Ireland's destiny is bound up with that of the British Commonwealth of nations'.[17]

The undergraduate body, about fifteen hundred strong, comprised southern Protestants, Catholics whose families were prepared to ignore the Hierarchy's attitude to Trinity, or, more likely, who possessed the *savoir faire* to make a successful request for permission to enter College, and Ulster Protestants, energetic in work and play, if, in the eyes of fastidious southerners, often deficient in polish. The overwhelming majority of the undergraduates were ex-unionists or, if from Northern Ireland, unionists. Loyalty to the Crown was instinctive and they were proud to be British subjects and Commonwealth citizens. Since a high proportion of the graduates sought careers in Great Britain or abroad and almost all of those who remained in Southern Ireland moved into the private sector, the professions, their fathers' firms or farms, they could stay to a remarkable extent outside the mainstream of Free State politics. Youthful radicalism often expressed itself in cynical and would be witty comments on the new Irish establishment. The antics and exuberant oratorical infelicities of local politicians and the more extravagant denunciations of Trinity provided endless amusement – when it was suggested that the College Historical Society no longer take the *Catholic Bulletin*, fervently nationalist and vehemently Catholic, robustious and vitriolic, a counter-resolution received an overwhelming number of signatures. But if post-Treaty Trinity was somewhat detached from its

---

17 *Irish Times*, 14 Dec. 1926, 8 July 1937.

Irish surroundings, it would be a mistake to see the College, dons or undergraduates, retreating into inglorious isolation. Rather, it was extremely anxious to be in touch with the world *extra muros* and *extra Hibernia*. The principal college societies took a fair range of English newspapers and magazines. A steady stream of English men of affairs and men of letters addressed meetings in Trinity and many bright undergraduates had their eyes fixed on the Home, Indian and Colonial civil services.

Naturally, the College was not monolithic. There were mavericks amongst the dons: Edmund Curtis, the historian, of Donegal Protestant stock brought up in England, was a mild nationalist; Jock Beaumont, a lecturer in Irish, was a somewhat disillusioned republican; Rudmose Brown, the Professor of French, was a natural anti-authoritarian. Amongst undergraduates, with their propensity for unorthodox attitudes, there were a few Gaelic enthusiasts and fewer strong republicans. Some conscientious intellectuals tended to draw apart from what seemed to them the unthinking and anachronistic unionism of their contemporaries. But a diet of the *New Statesman* and the *Criterion*, an appreciation of Yeats, James Joyce and T.S. Eliot, with visits to the Gate, academic detachment, pacifism or socialism and the Left Book Club, created a gulf between the progressive Trinity man and the typical Irish nationalist as least as wide as that between a fervent nationalist and a committed Ulster unionist.[18]

By the 1940s a Trinity College undergraduate from the South of Ireland might be described as a very moderate nationalist, accepting what his parents regarded as 'the new' regime, fond of Ireland but glad that it was in the Commonwealth, partly out of hereditary sentiment, partly because it placed his country in a wider context, partly because the Commonwealth was a force for good in the world and partly for the important practical reason that it was not unlikely he would earn his living abroad. For the intelligent undergraduate and even more for the senior members of the College, Trinity's future at this time seemed distressingly uncertain. With straitened finances the College was moving into an era of university expansion. But in 1947 the Éire government

18 For TCD c.1940 see J. White in *The Bell*, x, no. 2, pp. 63-75.

began to make an annual grant to Trinity (by preserving a useful Irish institution the government made what in the long term proved to be a good investment). By an eccentric coincidence, just before the government subsidy was inaugurated an influx began of English-educated undergraduates into Trinity and for about quarter of a century the College was more anglicized than ever before. But by the close of the 1960s a period of gentle *Gleichschaltung* set in and Trinity, with the overwhelming majority of its undergraduate population coming from the Republic, to a great extent conformed to local patterns.

The *Irish Times* was to some extent an emanation of Trinity, its two outstanding editors during the first half of the twentieth century, John Healy (from 1907 to 1934) and Robert Smyllie (1934-54), both being devoted sons of the house. In some other ways they were strikingly different. Healy graduated in Classics and Modern Literature before being called to the bar. Smyllie's academic career ended abruptly in 1914 when, while travelling in Germany, he was interned in Ruhleben, near Berlin, at the outbreak of the First World War – a hard but stimulating experience, the camp having a lively intellectual life. Healy was dignified, austere and rather reclusive. Smyllie was genial and gregarious. Both were men of principle and purpose, to whom journalism was a high calling. Healy's ideal, once the union was gone, was a united, liberal-minded, prosperous Ireland, an enthusiastic member of the Commonwealth, cherishing its links with Great Britain and the empire. He clung jealously to the few links that still bound Ireland and the United Kingdom together, 'watching with sadness their gradual loosening by Mr Cosgrave's government and their virtual destruction under the presidency of Mr de Valera', conducting a close and continuous rear-guard action with every weapon at his disposal from cool logic to ridicule. Smyllie, a younger man by twenty years, realized that the old unionism was dead beyond recall and that Éire was now an independent state. But he earnestly desired that Éire should keep in close touch with the United Kingdom and be a whole-hearted member of the Commonwealth which stood for freedom of thought and action, individual liberty, stability, tolerance and peace – not least because he believed those external contacts might do something to correct the narrow, self-righteous, petty-minded and parochial nationalism which he abhorred.

Both Healy and Smyllie were stylists, keen on the *mot juste* and the apposite quotation (in Healy's case frequently a Latin one) and their well-considered editorials were characterized by clarity, coherence and force. They also strove to produce a balanced paper in which Irish, British and foreign news, literary criticism, the theatre, sport and social life, all received due attention. It may be added that on Saturdays Smyllie indulged himself by writing under a *nom de plume* a causerie dealing largely with the doings of casually met old friends. It was very popular with his simpler readers and was impossible to parody. Independent, informative, outspoken and ready, with the assurance of the old Southern unionist world, to rebuke, commend and criticize Irish trends and personalities, the *Irish Times* enjoyed considerable prestige in Ireland. Indeed when Dubliners spoke of the *Times* they usually meant the *Irish Times* (though there was a minority within the minority who felt that their day was incomplete without *The Times*). Strangely enough in the decades following the Treaty the Dublin newspaper which commanded the highest degree of intellectual respect was the sometime unionist *Irish Times*.[19]

Many ex-unionists, as might be expected, remained politically unassimilated. As late as the 1940s it was reported that there were a number of voters, excellent citizens in many ways, who remained 'sulking as it were in their tents and living on their memories of the irrecoverable past when Ireland was under British rule'.[20] One of them was Lennox Robinson's brother, Tom, who summed up his feelings by remarking 'the union is a *cause juge* therefore I no longer fash myself with politics, finding it impossible to work up any interest in the bickerings of the Dáil'.[21] Needless to say the unassimilated remained quite alive to the absurdities of Irish political life. The story of the TD, highly indignant at hearing himself referred to in debate as a Bulgarian and

---

19 *The Times*, 31 May 1934; *Irish Times*, 30 May 1934, 13 Sept. 1954, 12 May 1937.
20 *The Times*, 21 June 1943.
21 E.S.L. Robinson, *Three Homes* (1938), p. 144.

completely placated when told that the term applied to him was in fact vulgarian, was repeated with gusto by ex-unionists.

But there were ex-unionists who were anxious to take part in public life, and ex-unionists as a whole (even those who had gone into internal exile) were prepared to exercise the franchise in those constituencies in which there was the possibility that a candidate more or less of their own way of thinking might be returned. Bryan Cooper, 'that great lonely gentleman, lonely as some banished Roman in a land where the eagles had departed', eager to serve his county 'even though it had chosen a destiny very different from that of his earlier ideals', was returned to the Dáil for South County Dublin, an area he had represented as a unionist in 1910;[22] Dublin townships returned Good and Benson, pre-Treaty unionists, Good, who had been a unionist candidate in 1918, standing now 'as a businessman, not in any sense a politician';[23] Donegal for many years returned Major Spoule Myles, who had won an M.C. in the war; Alexander Haslett, a Protestant and an Orangeman, sat for some years for County Monaghan; J.H. Beamish, who had been a member of the Unionist Alliance, standing as 'a Progressive', was one of the Cork city TDs for five years; and John Cole, a solicitor, who sat for Cavan, in a Dáil debate spoke of himself as representing 'the ex-unionist, Protestant minority'.[24] Then until 1935 there were three Trinity College representatives in the Dáil. One of them, William Thrift, an unpretentious man of affairs who became a vice-chairman of the Dáil, once explained his political outlook. Until the Treaty he had been a unionist, but when he found the views he held had become impracticable, he 'turned over the page completely'.[25] His colleagues were Alton, a good-humoured classical scholar who had won an MC when defending Trinity during the 1916 insurrection, and Sir James Craig, a medical man, primarily interested in public health, who was replaced in 1933 by R.J. Rowlette, another medical professor.

22 *Letters of W.B. Yeats*, ed. R.J. Fenner (1977), ii, p. 512.
23 *Irish Times*, 11 Feb. 1932.
24 *The Times*, 23 July 1937.
25 *Dáil Debates*, i, 570.

Naturally ex-unionists tended to criticize the new Ireland for being too inward-looking and too ready to condemn England for being selfish, arrogant, immoral and materialistic. To them, aggressive, self-satisfied, smug, bitter, narrow Irish nationalism was most persistently and consistently expressed by the drive to restore Irish as the main or sole medium of communication. For fervent supporters of the Gaelic movement 1922 seemed to mark the beginning of a new golden age. In the new Irish state power was in the hands of men who believed that the Irish language, 'waylaid, beaten, robbed and left for dead',[26] should be a central feature of the nation's cultural life and a guarantee of the country's political independence. The Free State constitution declared Irish to be the national language (English being equally recognized as an official language) and steps were immediately taken to make the country at least bilingual in the foreseeable future. As a highly intelligent advocate of the language policy explained, it might be expected that soon Irish would become the language of the home and of literature with English remaining as the language of science, instruction in some branches of higher education and 'to a large degree the language of commerce'.[27] Fervent enthusiasts looked forward to seeing Ireland an Irish-speaking nation. From 1922 a knowledge of Irish was a requirement for entrance to the civil service – according to the *Irish Times* 'an economic and educational folly'[28] – and it was hoped that the work of the civil servants would soon be carried on in Irish (in fact it had to be admitted in the early 1920s that owing to the attitude of the outside public the system was still geared to working in English).[29] In 1929 it was enacted that persons born after 1 October 1914 seeking admission to either branch of the legal profession had to possess a competent knowledge of Irish. In 1922 Irish became a compulsory subject in primary schools and soon a pass in Irish was required at the intermediate and leaving certificate examinations, on the results of which grants to secondary schools were based.[30]

---

26 *Coimisiún na Gaeltachta: Report* (1925).
27 *Studies*, xvi, pp. 8 ff.
28 *Irish Times*, 3 Dec. 1930.
29 *Commission on the Restoration of the Irish language, Summary in English of the Final Report* (1963).
30 *Report of the Department of Education 1933-4*, p. 54.

Ex-unionists were sceptical about the value of Irish and irritated by the methods employed to promote its use. They resented being conscripted into a cultural crusade with which they had little sympathy. Some were interested in Celtic lore and Irish archaeology but for most of them Irish did not seem to be their hereditary lost tongue, the key to their historic past. It might, it was granted, be desirable to learn a second language, but why should it be Irish? In the Senate Sir John Keane remarked that when he went about the country he did not find 'fierce enthusiasm' for the revival of the Gaelic language, and Bagwell, complaining that the speaking of Irish was being promoted by 'artificial encouragement and coercion', emphasized that it was for the Senate to ensure that idealists did not 'run away entirely from common sense'. To this another senator retorted that 'if our language does not appeal to a member there is something lacking in his patriotism and nationality'.[31] In the Dáil, during the debate on legal education, Bryan Cooper, though not hostile to Irish – he had endeavoured to learn it – came out firmly against compulsion, and Major Myles, who wanted the money expended on promoting Irish to be spent on the social services, declared that thousands of Irish speakers in Donegal could only say 'Goidé mar tá tú' in Irish.[32]

At the beginning of the new era, early in 1922, the *Church of Ireland Gazette* warned the government not to move too fast in promoting the use of Irish in primary education, pointing out that Irish would never become the language of the Irish race abroad and that its revival would drive a wedge between north and south.[33] Some years later the *Irish Times*, having made an obeisance to Gaelic – there was not a citizen, it said, which did not feel that national sentiment owed a duty to the Irish language – went on to urge that such sentiment must be subordinated to practical considerations. Young Protestants were often being prepared for professions and services which were over-stocked in Ireland and Protestant parents therefore felt that the tyranny of Irish in the schools menaced their children's prospects in life. The *Irish Times* called for 'a free trade in ideas and an honest contest of values in

31 *Senate Debates*, viii, 505, 514, xii, 372, xiii, 21.
32 *Dáil Debates*, xxvii, pp. 730, 1467.
33 *Church of Ireland Gazette*, 10 March 1922.

the field of education', emphasizing the right of the child to 'decent equipment for the adventure of life in any part of the Commonwealth'.[34]

Pupils with an ex-unionist background often avoided the burden of Irish because they went to schools in Great Britain or Northern Ireland. In 1942 it seemed that these avenues might be closed. A clause in a School Attendance bill provided that a child not attending a national (primary) school or a recognized school would not be deemed to be receiving a suitable education unless such education had been certified by the Minister of Education as suitable. To many people it seemed that this provision would empower the minister to prevent parents from sending their children outside Éire for their education. Sir John Keane bluntly declared that the minority which he represented had for generations sent their children to English public schools and fully intended to continue doing so. Did a suitable education, he asked, mean an education that included Irish and Irish history taught from a nationalist standpoint? Surely, he added, it was in the national interest that their citizens should have a broad outlook. One of the Trinity senators, Joseph Johnston, pointed out that 'some people only find their Gaelic soul when thoroughly immersed in the atmosphere of the English public schoolboy system'. The Minister, though he said that he would not use the power of certification to prevent children from being educated outside the country, did not deny that the power could be used for that purpose, and the opponents of the provision must have felt that their case was reinforced by the arguments of a strong supporter of the bill, Senator Ó Buachalla from County Galway. Ó Buachalla argued that the aim of Irish education should be to restore as far as possible 'what has been robbed and flinched from them in every department of national life', and if people of wealth were sending their children anywhere they liked, flouting the intention of the Irish people to 'get back the Irish language', then the minister was perfectly right to secure power to stop them.[35] After an interesting debate in

---

34 *Irish Times*, 12, 25 June 1924, 9, 14 Dec. 1926. See also V. Jones, 'Government Policy: The Church of Ireland and the Teaching of Irish, 1940–1950' in *Irish Educational Studies*, x, pp. 177–87.

35 *Senate Debates*, xxvii, 541-2, 875, 819.

which two principles enunciated in the constitution were frequently referred to – the right of parents to provide for the education of their children and the duty of the state to ensure a certain minimum of education for every child – the minister's power of certification was retained in the bill. But at a later stage the bill was referred by the President to the Supreme Court which pronounced it unconstitutional – the definition of 'a certain minimum of education' was a matter for legislation and should not be left to the minister's discretion. The *Irish Times* was delighted with this decision, which, it declared, showed that the rights of parents could not be set aside by those 'who would form us all in a standard Gaelic mould'.[36]

Some years later, after 'the Irish language experiment' had been functioning for twenty-five years, the *Irish Times* in a powerful editorial declared that 'all honest citizens must admit it has been a ghastly failure'. The blunt truth was that the Sinn Féin ideal of a Gaelic-speaking Ireland was 'just as far away as it ever was'. Would no political party, the *Irish Times* asked, have the honesty to say that it was prepared 'to cut the losses on compulsory Irish'? But a few years later it had to accept sadly that no politician would run the risk of being labelled an anti-idealist by urging a reversal or deceleration of the official policy on Irish.[37]

Ex-unionists were frequently exasperated by the methods employed to promote the use of Irish, by the tone of cultural superiority adopted by many supporters of the language, and by their insistence on treating the use of Irish as one of the principal civic virtues. They may, however, have noticed that by mid-century keen Gaelic enthusiasts were asking themselves why the campaign to make the country Irish-speaking or at least bilingual had made so little progress. It was hard for them to accept that the drive behind the Irish revival was bound to weaken when speaking or trying to speak Irish ceased to be a feature of the struggle for national independence. Moreover, the argument that without a national language a community would lack cohesion and fail to obtain recognition as a distinctive entity amongst the nations was

---

36 *Irish Times*, 16 April 1943.
37 *Irish Times*, 2 Feb. 1948, 12 May 1951.

contradicted by post 1922 developments. The inhabitants of the Irish Free State, Éire or the Republic, saw themselves as united by geography, common interests and, to some extent, common characteristics and saw their country playing a definite role on the international stage. Other factors were working against the spread of Irish. At the beginning of the century it was still possible to assert that Irish countrymen were living a life analogous in many respects to that of the tillers of the soil in the remote Irish past. Later in the century industrialization, urbanization and the mechanization of agriculture were creating an Ireland far removed from the world of the Táin Bó Cuailnge. Moreover, the revival was overshadowed by other issues – economic, educational, social, ecological, European – and those who were concerned over these questions had already an adequate medium of communication. As a lover of Irish with a remarkably dispassionate outlook on the language situation wrote, 'no man feels the need to speak Irish habitually if he wants to get on in Irish life'.[38] Other Gaelic enthusiasts, echoing the Gaelic League's early denunciations of Unionists and West Britons and the ruling class in general, poured scorn on 'the commercial and business elite' who 'today still tend to accept the old stratified system of ethnic symbols and identities within the Anglo-Irish world' and who, 'in spite of a patina of internationalism', were in outlook and way of life – 'housing, styles, diets, leisure activities' – thoroughly anglicized.[39] This *cri de coeur* may have sprung from a realization of the irresistibility of fashion. By the 1970s it seemed certain that Irish would not become the ordinary spoken tongue of Irishmen and even those who were convinced that the Irish language was 'one of the essential elements in preserving the individuality and distinctiveness of a people', admitted that the great majority did not want to lose proficiency in the use of English and that therefore a realistic objective would be a 20 per cent use of Gaelic (outside the Gaeltacht).[40]

---

38 S. Ó Catháin, 'The Future of the Irish Language' in *Studies*, lxii, pp. 303-22.
39 H. Tovey, D. Hannon and H. Abrahamson, *Irish Identity and the Irish Language* (1989).
40 *Implementing an Irish Policy* (1972).

There were three other issues on which many ex-unionists held, and some voiced, views differing from majority opinion in the Irish Free State – divorce, birth control and censorship. In the early 1920s the Oireachtas, by not providing a procedure for dealing with divorce bills, made it impossible to obtain an absolute divorce in the Free State, and the 1937 constitution laid down that no law should be enacted providing for the grant of a dissolution of marriage. When the Senate in 1925 was considering private bill procedure, Bagwell argued that to refuse divorce facilities was in effect making a Church law into state law, a step that would be regarded as 'tyrannical and as depriving a large number of citizens of facilities which they have hitherto enjoyed'; and W.B. Yeats, describing himself (scarcely accurately) as 'a typical man of that [Protestant] minority', defiantly deployed the reasons for permitting divorce and fervently denounced clerical intolerance. The *Irish Times* on 12 June regretted 'the manner' of Yeats's intervention. Many of his arguments were perfectly sound but the whole temper of his speech was hurtful and aggressive – *Ne poeta ultra ligram*. It judiciously observed that the 'problem of reconciling the minority's constitutional freedom with the dictates of the majority's conscience is by far the most delicate problem with which this state has been or is ever to be faced'. 'Breadth of vision and the appreciation of an unfamiliar moral outlook', it pointed out, 'are plants of slow and fragile growth on this side of the Irish sea.' Nevertheless, the existing situation, it asserted, meant that 'subjects in the Irish Free State are being deprived of a right which is guaranteed by the constitution and is inherent in citizenship of the British Empire'.

In 1929 when the clause in the Censorship of Publications bill banning books, articles and advertisements advocating birth control was being debated in the Dáil, Thrift, arguing that birth control was not a subject which could be dealt with by 'hard and fast' rules, declared he was opposed to banning books on the subject, though he disapproved of birth control propaganda produced not for sociological reasons but for profit.[41] When in 1935 section 17 of the Criminal Law bill forbidding the importation of contraceptives

---

41 *Dáil Debates*, xxvi, 635-7.

was being debated in the Senate, Bagwell, having emphasized that there were wide differences of opinion on birth control amongst good citizens, argued that 'matters of conscience are best left to the individual'. Discussing the same section in the Dáil, Rowlette issued a cautious caveat. It would be a mistake, he said, to accept section 17 without 'any consideration of the possible consequences'.[42]

When the Censorship of Publications bill of 1929 was being debated, ex-unionists, while hesitant about defining what should be the limits of censorship, were clearly anxious to restrict its scope. Bryan Cooper, who regarded censorship as 'a necessary evil', reminded the Dáil that the more stringent the penalties the greater the incitement to a 'literary bootlegger', and Haslett, though he favoured the suppression of 'the obscene and the indecent', stressed it was not the duty of the Dáil 'to travel into the realms of other kinds of immorality'. In the early 1940s the working of the Censorship Act was criticized vigorously by Sir John Keane, who argued that 'progress in all countries comes from the student and the intellectual minority', and about the same time the *Irish Times* observed that the dominant class in the country, while professing to believe that Irishmen exceeded all other races in virtue, paradoxically insisted on keeping them well apart from every occasion of sin.[43]

Over the three issues that have just been mentioned many ex-unionists were deeply aggrieved, even though the actual degree of injury sustained may have been comparatively slight. Few of them contemplated divorce (in England at this time the divorce rate compared to the marriage rate was one to seventy-five); birth control was seldom mentioned, and it was possible for residents in the twenty-six counties who were determined to obtain contraceptives to do so. As for the Censorship Board, its activities frequently aroused indignation mixed with contemptuous amusement. In its lists of banned books it frequently included amongst pornographic or semi-pornographic items works of widely acknowledged literary

---

42 *Senate Debates*, xix, 1252; *Dáil Debates*, liii, 2017.
43 *Dáil Debates*, xxvi, 668, 693, *Senate Debates*, xxx, 1052; *Irish Times*, 19 Nov. 1942.

merit. However, since the banning of books in this category tended to lag well behind publication, it is doubtful if the intellectual life of many intelligent readers, resident in the twenty-six counties, was seriously interfered with.

The debates over censorship revealed a somewhat incongruous convergence of opinion between many ex-unionists and an important section of the Irish literary world. During the struggle for independence it seemed to many Irish men of letters that moral forces released by insurrection might create a new Ireland, traditional but progressive, where authority would be benign, and men and women would realize their full potentialities in happy co-operation. But 'the green and trim Free State', 'smug, obstinate and pertinacious',[44] concerned with immediate practicalities and suspicious of the unconventional, fell far short of the ideal. Ireland, AE sourly reflected in the early 1930s, was like 'a lout who had become a hero and subsided into a lout'.[45] Disillusioned literary men, eager to experiment and to be in fruitful contact with contemporary currents of thought, and ex-unionists, who regarded a balanced broad-mindedness as part of their British inheritance, joined in detecting, deploring, and resenting the symptoms of oppressive provinciality in post-Treaty Southern Ireland.

When irritated by nationalist parochialism, ex-unionists were thankful that the Free State was part of the world-wide British Commonwealth of nations. Deeply conscious of the links, economic, cultural and social, that still connected the Irish Free State with Great Britain, 'the strands which still exist of the mighty cords which once bound the two countries together',[46] ex-unionists greatly cherished the Free State's position as a Dominion, a member of the British Commonwealth, 'an association of people with natural affinities and with the same ideals, working for peace in the world and civilization'.[47] At the time the Free State became a dominion the Commonwealth was rapidly evolving, politically

44 K. O'Brien, *Prayer for a Wanderer* (1938), p. 284.
45 *Letters of W.B. Yeats*, ed. R.J. Fenner, i, p. 531.
46 *Parl. Debates (Lords)*, 5 series, lxiii, 47.
47 Sir John Keane speaking in the Senate (*Senate Debates*, xv, 927).

and constitutionally – a process scarcely comprehended by the politically less alert. By 1914 the Dominions as regarded their domestic concerns were practically speaking independent (though relics of their old colonial status survived) and their role in international affairs was acknowledged by their place at the peace conference. Therefore the Irish Free State was part of a club whose rules were soon to be revised with the aim of bringing them into accord with imperial realities. Imperial statesmen and publicists cheerfully or wryly accepted the inevitable, believing (or striving to believe) that the Commonwealth, a bold, creative experiment, could combine autonomy and individuality with common loyalties, continuous consultation and close co-operation. *Faute de mieux* Irish ex-unionists accepted Dominion status as a substitute for the union, which enabled them to preserve their allegiance to the Crown and their status as British subjects and to feel that, if alienated politically from most of their neighbours, they could participate in the activities of the British community. But Cosgrave's government, though committed to the defence of the Treaty as the best bargain that could be obtained in 1921 and one that they expected would provide a stepping-stone to complete independence, stressed dominion autonomy and conceived the role of the Irish Free State in Commonwealth deliberations as being to hasten the process by which the dominions evolved into independent states, with all traces of subordination to the imperial parliament and the British government being swept away. For them, Ireland's membership of the Commonwealth reflected willingness to belong to a useful association which included Ireland's best customer. As one of Cosgrave's ministers put it, 'while we are in the British commonwealth of nations we are there for severely practical purposes, to gain solid advantages for our people'.[48]

At the very outset of the new regime a fairly simple matter, Medical Registration, demonstrated that the determination of the government to assert the Free State's independence might endanger career prospects – and also showed how a controversial constitutional issue could be resolved pragmatically. In May 1924 the president of the British Medical Council announced that it was no

---

48 *Dáil Debates*, liv, 393.

longer legally possible for the Council (whose jurisdiction was restricted to the United Kingdom) to place on the General Register persons qualifying in the Irish Free State. This threatened the viability of the Free State medical schools since only 35 per cent of their graduates practised in the twenty-six counties. The Irish medical profession, never languid in defence of its interests and loyalties, urged the government to take steps to ensure the continuance of the existing system of registration. Provocatively, the government adopted the attitude that it was incompatible with the Free State's constitutional status for one of the most important professions in the nation to have its centre of gravity and headquarters in another country – some members of the government, an ex-unionist wrote, had yielded to 'an over-heated instinct of political independence'.[49] What the government in fact had in mind was a form of reciprocity that would preserve both national dignity and the privileges enjoyed by Irish medical graduates, and by 1927 a solution was evolved. There would be an Irish Free State Medical Council administering an Irish Free State register, but Free State representatives would continue to sit on the GMC, persons qualified from the Free State medical schools would be entitled to place their names on the General Register, and the GMC would continue to exercise a supervisory role in Irish medical education.

This solution foreshadowed the lines on which the much wider subject of the status of Irish citizens in the United Kingdom was to be settled. Under the Irish Free State constitution persons domiciled in the twenty-six counties became Irish citizens, and in 1934 in the Dáil debates on a bill defining fully the concept of Irish citizenship de Valera emphatically stated that 'the word "subject" is abhorrent to an Irish nationalist and the word "allegiance" is equally abhorrent in so far as it is to an outside country'.[50] But though he repudiated the ideal of a common imperial or commonwealth citizenship, he readily, if less rhetorically, was prepared to extend reciprocal privileges to the citizens of those countries that gave privileges to Irish Free State citizens, and simultaneously

49 *The Times*, 28 May 1924, 17, 24 Aug. 1925; *Senate Debates*, iv, 695.
50 *Dáil Debates*, liv, 338, 1641-2.

with the Irish Nationality and Citizenship Act of 1935 becoming law, the Free State government issued an order under the Aliens Act conferring on British and Commonwealth citizens a status they already possessed in the Free State. Even more important, the British government continued until 1948 to maintain that (with a few exceptions) a person born in the King's dominions had the status of a British subject. In 1937 Great Britain and the Dominions decided that the new constitution did not effect a fundamental alteration in Éire's status in the Commonwealth. Éire's decision in 1949 to become a republic might have been expected to markedly affect the position of Irishmen in the United Kingdom and the Commonwealth but, as a result of complex legislation passed at Westminster in 1948-9, 'Irishmen may in certain circumstances claim to be British subjects, but even those who are not British subjects are to be treated as British subjects.'[51] Ex-unionists could therefore continue to regard themselves as British subjects – a matter to them of great sentimental as well as practical importance.

From the establishment of the Irish Free State in 1922, the *Irish Times*, reflecting ex-unionist opinion, never ceased to dwell on the value of the Commonwealth connection, and it continuously urged the Free State government to co-operate heartily with the other members of the Commonwealth and more especially with the United Kingdom, Ireland's nearest neighbour. Shortly before the 1923 Imperial Conference the *Irish Times*, having declared that 'the interdependency of the Anglo-Saxon peoples' was steadily becoming more obvious, and that a prosperous British empire was vital to 'the race which these islands have born', demanded that steps should be taken to co-ordinate imperial foreign policy and defence, to encourage imperial trade, to plan empire settlement and to improve imperial communications. 'The British empire', the *Irish Times* declared at the close of the 1926 Imperial Conference, was 'the most powerful progressive force in the world' – and incidentally the conference had brought Dublin nearer to both London and Belfast. The paper was constrained to regret, however, that the Irish Free State's fiscal policy

---

51 I. Jennings and C.M. Young, *Constitutional Laws of the Commonwealth* (1952), p. 376.

was creating obstacles to inter-imperial trade and that FitzGerald, the Irish minister for external affairs, 'seemed to part reluctantly with old fears and prejudices'.[52] For good measure the *Irish Times* emphasized the economic benefits of Commonwealth membership. Economically the British empire was almost a perfect unit, every commodity known to man being produced under the British flag and every Commonwealth country having a privileged position in the British market. Should the Free State become a republic, the *Irish Times* prophesied in 1926, its situation would be grim. Free State citizens would be aliens, the Empire marketing board would discourage the purchase of Free State products and the Bank of England would refuse to support its currency. Soon the leaders of the republic would be on their knees in Whitehall.[53]

In the mid-twenties ex-unionists were shaken by the government's declared intention to nullify the right of appeal to the Privy Council by reaffirming by an act of the Oireachtas any decision of the Free State Supreme Court that had been overruled by the Privy Council. The Minister for Justice, Kevin O'Higgins, asserted in the Dáil that when the Treaty was being implemented it had been assumed that the judicial committee of the Privy Council would grant leave to appeal in only a very limited number of cases. In any event, he added, the right to appeal from a Dominion court to the Privy Council was an anachronism that should be abolished. The *Irish Times* promptly pointed out that the right of appeal was regarded by many citizens as 'a very precious guarantee of their personal liberties', and it referred sadly to the government's policy of 'sap and mine'.[54] Three years later, when Ernest Blythe, the Minister for Finance, stated that the government would ignore decisions of the judicial committee of the Privy Council, the standing committee of the general synod of the Church of Ireland sent a deputation to Cosgrave. It expressed the alarm of a considerable body of 'former unionists, now loyal citizens of the Irish Free State', who they acknowledged had been treated in a 'fair and generous way', at being deprived of the right of appeal to the

---

52 *Irish Times*, 3 March, 16 Aug. 1923; 1, 14, 16 Dec. 1926.
53 *Irish Times*, 11 Jan. 1932, 7 Dec. 1934, 16, 28 Nov. 1926.
54 *Irish Times*, 4 Feb. 1926.

Privy Council. Cosgrave's reply did nothing to allay their fears. The deputation's views were reiterated in a letter to the press from the Archbishops of Armagh and Dublin. The abolition of the right of appeal, the Archbishops thought, though it might gratify Irishmen's desire for independence would weaken the sense of security enjoyed by a minority which was regarded with jealous hostility by elements of the population.[55]

At the beginning of the 1930s the *Irish Times*, deploring the 'cold and disparaging' attitude adopted by the Cosgrave government to the empire, asked, could not the Minister for External Affairs recognize the King 'not as an impersonal necessity' but as symbolizing the grandeur and fellowship of the empire? It regretted that at the 1930 imperial conference the Free State delegation was chiefly concerned with advertising an independence that no one questioned and seemed unable to realize that the full benefits of commonwealth membership could not be reaped by a member of the brotherhood that enjoyed brooding on points of isolation.[56] In the following year, with the enactment of the measure known as the Statute of Westminster, all restraints on dominion sovereignty vanished and it became only too obvious to those ex-unionists who painfully digested Berridale Keith that the Commonwealth connection would for the future rest on goodwill and a recognition of common interests. However, the *Irish Times* optimistically hoped that the Free State government would have in the future 'an enlarged vision of the Irish Free State's place and prospects in the British empire', that those 'small reserves and jealousies' which inflicted slights on England and impeded Irish unity would disappear and the Free State, with 'maturing judgement' and 'her native gift of vision', would make an increasingly valuable contribution to Commonwealth councils.[57] But about three months after the Statute of Westminster received the royal assent de Valera's first administration came into office and soon started to make crystal clear the centrifugal possibilities inherent in Dominion status, passing legislation that effectively transformed the Free State into

---

55 *Irish Times*, 25 Nov. 1931, 7 Nov. 1930.
56 *Irish Times*, 18 Nov. 1930, 18 July, 25 Nov. 1931.
57 *Irish Times*, 25 Nov. 1931.

a republic, connected with the Commonwealth simply by the King being retained as 'an instrument' to perform on the advice of the Éire government certain functions in foreign relations.

Ex-unionists despairingly protested again Mr de Valera's constitutional legislation. The removal of the oath of allegiance from the constitution in 1932 produced a political apologia from Thrift, one of the Trinity representatives in the Dáil. 'Prior to the Treaty', he said,

I was no politician. I voted unionist, I held unionist views. I took no part in political activities but with many I was sick of political strife. I was sick of things that were done on both sides, things which I abhorred and abhor still. But the Treaty came and there was a chance in it that old things might pass, that we might wipe the slate and start afresh with every section of the community bound together on one platform to work for the salvation of this unhappy land.

The Southern unionists, he declared, had accepted 'the Treaty with misgivings ... in a spirit of self-sacrifice ... prepared to do their best', and the oath was a pledge of the bargain that was made with them. The oath, he explained, meant a lot to him, implying allegiance to the state and an acceptance of the Irish Free State's voluntary membership of the British Commonwealth of nations with the Crown as a symbol of unity.[58] Three years later Thrift, speaking for 'what are called the minority in this country', declared that the abolition of the Senate was causing thousands to ask why had they lent their support to the Free State government.

In 1933 the right of appeal to the Privy Council was abolished. This aroused Carson to make his last parliamentary speech on Irish affairs. The loyalists in the Irish Free State, loyal 'as ever men were', had been abandoned and betrayed by the Conservative Party. All the safeguards had been set aside and rendered useless. Politics, he reflected, 'is about the only profession I know of in which a man may be the most false prophet or be the most false in giving promises and breaking them, and yet be liable to no penalty whatsoever'. This speech delighted old members of the Unionist Alliance in Dublin, including Jellett and Walsh, who wondered if,

58 Dáil Debates, xli, 923-4.

in the light of de Valera's conduct, the Statute of Westminster could be amended.[59] The *Irish Times* was somewhat more realistic – not expecting action by Great Britain but simply reaffirming its own faith. In the spring of 1937, the day before the draft 1937 constitution was introduced into the Dáil, having defiantly issued a coronation souvenir magazine, it published a leader with the ringing title 'Gentlemen the King',[60] asserting that the Commonwealth was by far the mightiest group of nations that had ever been known, standing for 'freedom of thought and action, individual liberty, stability, toleration and peace' in an era of 'exaggerated nationalism, parochial jealousies, of petty feuds'. The Commonwealth, an example of human endeavour in a common cause, an association of many areas in allegiance to a common king, was a concept 'the full grandeur of which has not yet been realized by mankind'. Fittingly the leader ended with the prayer, 'God Save the King'.

During the Second World War Éire exercised its sovereign independence by remaining neutral, the tenuous Commonwealth links proving to be of no significance. The older generation of ex-unionists thoroughly identified themselves in thought and feeling with their cross-channel contemporaries, making a regular and almost ritual habit of listening to the BBC news, and many of the younger generation served in the forces. In a country where 'isolation from a tortured world invested all activities with unreality', ex-unionists, it was said, 'though they accepted pragmatically the expediency of Irish neutrality, were ... ashamed of not being involved in the struggle against Nazism, ashamed of being protected by England, ashamed even of not suffering enough?'[61]

Once the war ended, the *Irish Times*, conscious that 'history on the grand scale is being made beyond our shores',[62] and reflecting the opinions of most of its readers, was extremely anxious that the Commonwealth connection should be maintained. Very thankful at the beginning of 1948 that Fine Gael openly favoured

59 *Parl. Debates (Lords)*, 5 series, xc, 332-4; J.E. Walsh to Carson, 10 Dec. 1933 (Carson papers, D1507/A/48/41).
60 *Irish Times*, 12 May 1937.
61 G.K. White, *A History of St Columba's College* (1980), p. 151.
62 *Irish Times*, 28 May 1951.

Commonwealth membership, the *Irish Times* bitterly resented the coalition's decision, announced in the autumn, to repeal the External Relations Act and declare a republic – so far as Fine Gael was concerned, 'a cynical somersault' putting 'party expediency before political honour'. Three years later the editor wrote that there were many people in the country who felt they had been tricked by Fine Gael three years earlier, and who would never put their faith in politicians again.[63] But the editor was not blinded by his genuine indignation. He explained to his readers that there had been in the recent past 'a periodic disregarding of formularies ... precious in the eyes of may Irishmen'. Yet so fast 'does the sense of values change in these days of confusion', he thought that their loss seemed to have made little real difference. Now, few people, beyond the ranks of a dwindling minority, cared a rap about the repeal of the External Relations Act. What we must strive for, he robustly declared, was to replace the link once provided by the Crown with new bonds, stronger because more realistic, between the twenty-six counties and the Commonwealth.[64]

But there were those who saw the repeal of the External Relations Act, the snapping of the last strands of the golden link, in more tragic terms. Though two of Trinity's three representatives in the Senate, in speeches marked by academic detachment, unenthusiastically supported the Republic of Ireland bill, the third, Professor J.W. Bigger, who had served during the war in the RAMC, alone in the house, opposed it. He wanted his country to be a free self-governing dominion rather than a republic. It was no use, he said, sneering at that loyalty to the Crown which was so strong in the six counties. 'I have ceased to regard the term "British" as a term of contempt. I remember when Britain stood alone, when free France was only a name, when Russia had not made up her mind on which side to fight and when America stood aloof.' This was a highly unusual note to sound in the Oireachtas.[65] In the following year (1949), when advising the General Synod to adapt the state prayers to a republican form of

---

63 *Irish Times*, 17, 19, 21 Jan. 1948; 9, 23 May, 13 June 1951.
64 *Irish Times*, 3 Oct. 1948.
65 *Senate Debates*, xxxvi, 101-5.

government, the Primate, Dr Gregg, referred to the letters he had received from all over the republic calling earnestly for the retention in Éire of the prayers for the King and royal family, the writers apparently forgetting that the Republic was a fact. 'Many dwellers in the Republic', he said, 'regret the loss of the familiar words, but what other way out is there?'

As late as 1951 a perceptive journalist referred to the 'exunionist vote', comprising 'Protestants, Commonwealth supporters, West Britons, Castle Catholics and immigrants'. He might have added, if not included in any of the above categories, Irishmen who, having had a career abroad, had returned to enjoy retirement in Ireland. But the general election of 1951 was certainly the last occasion on which it was possible to speak of an exunionist vote, ex-unionists being by then, according to another experienced journalist, 'a politically negligible minority'.[66] For a decade or so after the establishment of the Free State, some who had been proud to be in the United Kingdom saw the signs of an emergent statehood, a legislature, an army, legations in foreign capitals, as absurdities, not to be taken seriously. Others, who might be regarded as ex-unionists, realistically accepted the new regime but were intensely concerned that the Commonwealth connection should be preserved. By mid-century Commonwealth membership was no longer an issue, relations with the United Kingdom were reasonably amicable and the inhabitants of the Republic took for granted that they were citizens of an independent country, a full member of the community of nations – the boundaries of their nation's march being fixed by its membership of international organizations, more especially the European community. Paradoxically this growing national awareness has been accompanied by a weakening of those traits, beliefs, manners and modes of behaviour thought to be inherent in the Irish character. Industrialization, urbanization, improved communications, technology, tourism and television, have made Irish life less distinctive, less racy of the soil. Against the present go-ahead Irish background it is hard to realize that only sixty years ago important segments of the voting public were 'men driving their little donkey

66 B. Inglis in *The Bell*, xvii, no. 4, p. 19; *The Times*, 29 May 1951.

carts to market ... and turf cutters on the lonely brown bogs'.[67] Naturally many of the presuppositions which underpinned society in the twenty-six counties have been challenged, and in an age concerned with relations between high and popular culture, international influences in the literary and artistic spheres and global communications, the conflict between the Gaelic revival and anglicization, which aroused such brisk and angry controversy in the first half of the century, is clearly of diminished significance. The country, it is assumed, is to have both an open economy and an open intellectual and cultural life. If a pre-Treaty unionist was able to survey the scene he might deplore the attainment of complete political independence and a strong tendency in the Republic to under-emphasize its important economic, social and cultural links with Great Britain. But he might also reflect that most pre-Treaty nationalists, and indeed many nationalists of the succeeding generation, would not be happy with some significant *fin de siècle* developments.

To label oneself an ex-unionist in the second half of the twentieth century might suggest either extreme insensitivity to political change or a form of jacobitism, an archaic allegiance infused with fantasy. Nevertheless there are scattered through the Republic those who, though they conform quietly to the constitutional position, may be seen as modernized Southern unionists. From family tradition, upbringing, religion, education, from having spent a considerable amount of time in England or from choice, they resemble closely in their opinions, attitudes, pastimes and prejudices, their counterparts across the water. Regarding Ireland with affection, participating in many activities (though generally avoiding politics), they cherish their ties with Great Britain, which, they are convinced, enable them to regard and think about things in a wider context than that provided by the republic. Fortunately too in spite of their outlook and presuppositions they are not unhappily at odds with their environment. Almost all Irishmen are in a sense Anglo-Irishmen. That is to say they have an English or British component of varying proportions in their cultural make-up. They speak and read English and have innumerable

---

67 *The Times*, 23 Jan. 1933.

contacts with Great Britain. Thousands of Irish-born persons are living and working there. A large proportion of the Republic's trade is with the United Kingdom. Irish newspapers are full of British news and their columnists repeatedly comment on British institutions, developments and mores. Much of the comment is critical and not infrequently its tone suggests that the commentator is burdened by a resentful sense of inferiority – if only because the Republic is smaller. But criticism, even if harsh, indicates interest, and interest may ultimately generate a degree of liking. A common language, a common literature, and multifarious and multitudinous contacts ensure that Great Britain will continue to influence ideas, currents of thought, institutional developments and manners and modes in Southern Ireland. So life will remain tolerable for a neo-ex-unionist.

Memories: An Afterword

Because I was born in September 1913, working on post-1914 Irish history has revived vivid and, it is to be hoped, fairly accurate memories of well over seventy years ago. It should at once be admitted that the memories of a small boy, living in a comfortable middle-class home in south Belfast, cannot be of much historical significance. Nevertheless they may be of some slight value as reflecting experience rather than the knowledge derived from printed and manuscript sources.

The Great War (which I scarcely comprehended) was brought home to me by a series of striking incidents – meeting at tea a cousin in khaki (subsequently killed in France); handing out magazines to soldiers in hospital blue; asking why street lamps in the Lisburn Road were blacked out and being told, 'because of Zeppelins'; carrying away from the Bank Buildings or Anderson Macaulay's (both with immeasurable stretches of gleaming counters and deferential shopwalkers in cutaways) a cardboard toy, composed of three figures, the Kaiser, Hindenburg and Ludendoff, which joggled if hit by a pea from a pea-shooter; and crying bitterly when my grandmother gave her sugar ration to my baby brother (I believed in fair shares for all).

Shortly before the war ended I was involved in a major world catastrophe, the 1918 flu epidemic. I clearly remember one autumn morning lying back in a large chair in the morning room, feeling very ill (a new, unpleasant sensation), with my parents and the doctor looking down at me with deep concern. I next remember waking up in bed, wondering why my pyjamas had been slashed. I had been unconscious for days with double pneumonia, and on one occasion the doctor had been compelled to break the news to my parents that I would not survive the night. It has been said that in the absence of modern drugs good nursing was of vital importance in the 1918 epidemic, and, possibly because all the household with one exception were struck down, the doctor was fortunately able to secure for us two nurses – one fat, the other slim; the latter, an army nurse, who in the emergency had returned to work from convalescence, was most impressive in her uniform cape. It was the fat nurse who one morning helped me to the window and, pointing to a Union Jack flying from a house across the street, said, 'we have won the war'. This illness, followed by a series of minor but potentially dangerous ailments, had important long-term results. With precarious health, for about six years I did not go to school, having a governess, who by a wise choice of books awakened an intense interest in history. If in my early studies kings and queens loomed large, their succession provided a very useful chronological framework. When I finally did go to school, I was frequently absent through illness, serious or exaggerated, and did not take part in games. This meant a rather isolated, though not a lonely existence. Life at home was full and interesting and I had a fair number of friends of my own age. But I spent an unusual amount of time by myself, a pattern of life likely to promote individuality or, putting it in a less self-congratulatory form, to nourish idiosyncrasies – some of them probably rather tiresome.

Shortly after the Armistice I was playing on the dining-room hearthrug by candlelight (the gas was cut off), listening to my father and uncle who were crouching over a poor fire, and heard clearly the words 'Red Revolution'. What that might mean I vaguely grasped when soon afterwards, out shopping with my mother, I saw with dismay that the trams, part of the natural order of things, were not running (early in 1919 there were serious industrial disturbances in several United Kingdom cities, including Belfast). However, normality was soon restored with the return of gas and the trams. Sometime later there were signs of civil strife. At night I heard fusillades of rifle and possibly machine-gun fire, and on at least one occasion saw the sky lit up by a burning building (possibly a public house, a favourite target for aggression since destruction could be accompanied by consumption). Also, one bright evening I stood at a window, looking out at an eerily deserted and silent street – curfew was in force. Suddenly I heard footsteps and saw a patrol of B Specials, decent middle-aged men with police caps and armlets, carrying them-selves with solemn determination. I felt reassured.

Only once do I remember being near to violence. In Castle Place I saw a crowd gazing silently at stains on the pavement and was hustled away by my mother (I believe two policemen were shot at that point). Armoured cars and Crosley cars were features of the time, firing my imagination, and I was very pleased when a friend of the family, I think an auxiliary but he may have been army, arranged for four armoured cars (of the cage type), con-structed on the scale of a toy soldier, to be made for me. When I visited the army workshop it was gratifying to be saluted by uni-formed mechanics. At this time I had other casual contacts with the Crown forces. I remember well sitting by myself on the edge of a chair in the quite elegant Carlton tea place, eating small cakes, feeling I was really in the world, while my mother was dancing (presumably fox-trotting) with a partner in khaki. I have very pleasant memories (for long fortified by snapshots) of walks round Bundoran with holidaying army officers. I also paid a visit with my nurse to the Bundoran RIC barracks. All was going happily when there was a sudden alarm and we were bundled out ignominiously by the back door. The DI had unexpectedly arrived. In Londonderry my nurse took me to the RIC barracks near the Guildhall where I was allowed to play with a carbine and handcuffs.

It was a disturbed time in Derry but my memories are purely domestic – streets that always went uphill and crossing the Foyle by the most attractive of the three ferries. The only sign of trouble I saw was a sandbagged fort in the Diamond guarded by a sentry with a fixed bayonet. Donegal, where my grandmother had a house in Fahan, was more exciting. One afternoon my mother, my nurse and I went to a circus in Buncrana – still associated in my mind with a large tent, hard seats high up, noise and the smell of grass. When it was over we went to the station to catch the train back to Fahan. The train was there and we took our seats but it did not move. A military detachment was settled in one or two compartments and the railway men would not transport them. The scene is still vivid – the driver, fireman and guard standing on the platform, the soldiers sitting tight and laughing (it made little difference to them where they spent the time), and many passengers expressing vehement indignation. My mother was worried that my grandmother would be disturbed by our prolonged absence so in the end she decided we would have to walk. Very soon I realized that the walk (five miles) was endless; my nurse, a sturdy country girl, took me on her shoulders and the journey then was very enjoyable. After getting home I went down to the bottom of the garden to wait to see if the train would come. In time it steamed past but I never heard how the dispute was resolved. Probably on the same visit, when taking a walk with my father we met a large military patrol, putteed and bandoleered, resting on a bank at the side of the road. While the sergeant in charge and my father discussed local topography I was delighted to chat with the soldiers. That evening about dinner-time, the news arrived that people in the village who had heard we had been talking to the soldiers were coming to burn down the house. I was conscious of great perturbation. The maids were crying in the kitchen; my father, not easily dismayed, was probably preparing to see what could be done by tact; my grandmother, a Liverpool English-woman, a staunch Episcopalian who after fifty years still talked of 'the Irish' in a faintly pejorative tone, was, I am sure, bracing her-self to confront the King's enemies. My attitude, which must have accentuated the nervous tension, was that I must see the fire. When, after a long tearful resistance, I was at last forced to go to bed, I made a great effort to keep awake, but was overcome by sleep. The next morning I discovered nothing had happened. About a year later (in my grandmother's absence) the house was occupied in succession by refugees from Derry, by the IRA, by the Free State army and finally by looters. My grandmother – who must have regarded a newspaper reference to 'another loyalist lady's house plundered' as an accolade – then sold the house and moved to Belfast to be near her daughter, a step which, I am fairly sure, she had long wished to take.

A year or so after visiting Donegal, I was upset rather than mere-ly excited by political developments. Spending a summer holiday (1921 or 1922) in Portrush I detected that my mother was distressed and in the end found out the cause was 'the Boycott' (of Belfast goods in the south and west). I doubt if I exactly comprehended what this was but grasped that we might soon have no money. This made me so unhappy that my mother took me to the Bazaar and bought me a toy motor car to my delight. But the boycott may have permanently scarred me. By indicating that mysterious and malignant powers (I would now call them political and economic forces) could interfere with my well-being, it increased a sense of insecurity which to a limited extent was to influence my later life.

My mother's worries were certainly increased by the risk my father ran in keeping in touch with his customers in the west of Ireland. On one occasion three men stopped the car in which he was travelling, put him up against a wall and said they would shoot him. He asked for a few minutes in which he could state his opinion of the republican leadership. The men were so shocked by the uncharitable feelings he displayed on the brink of death that they started to argue him into a better frame of mind. During the discussion a bicyclist arrived with an order from the local IRA commandant that my father was to be released. One customer, a merchant in the west of Ireland, a Catholic and a strong constitutionalist, was determined to continue to obtain his tea from Musgrave's, my father's firm. Though he and my father agreed on not yielding to coercion they decided to 'camouflage' (a term the war had brought into vogue) their operations. The markings on the tea chests indicating a Belfast origin were to be covered by innocuous labels. These tactics created a moral dilemma for the merchant's foreman. A young man of character, he was a leading member of the IRA, which was wholeheartedly behind the boycott. In the event he decided that his duty to his master, whose service he had entered before joining the IRA, took precedence. When, as he explained long afterwards, he visited the railway station luggage office, he found the labels were so badly affixed that the Belfast markings were visible. Consequently, he spent a long, exasperating night replacing them properly. Some years later he set up in business on his own, ordering his tea from Musgrave's.

My father also had a brief *rencontre* with the Crown forces. One night when he was staying in the Gresham in Dublin, the hotel was raided by the military, there being imperative shouts of: 'every one down to the hall'. He continued lying comfortably in bed and soon the door was thrust open by a young army officer who asked him why the blazes he was not downstairs. My father suggested that he look at the bank-book on the dressing-table, adding, if the bank manager trusts me, surely you should. The officer opened the book, stared at the entries, remarked 'Good heavens Sir I should like an introduction to your banker', saluted and left (the overdraft was fairly heavy).

These rather flat anecdotes illustrate a noticeable tendency to emphasize in conversation the humorous side of 'the troubles' (a useful euphemism). There was an understandable desire to obliterate, or at least push into the background, the fear and the bitterness; and the strange inter-mixture of belligerency and normality that characterized the years 1919 to 1923 nourished the incongruous and the comic. Irishmen had, especially amongst themselves, a reputation for being entertaining raconteurs, which many of them strove to maintain with unflagging, competitive vigour.

Of course public affairs impinged only slightly and spasmodically on a small boy intent on household life, his family, children's parties and outings, Sunday School (intelligent and liberal), the cinema (*The Four Horsemen of the Apocalypse*, *Orphans of the Storm* – I was very worried that Danton would not arrive in time to save one of the lovely sisters from the guillotine), the gramophone (*Yes! We Have no Bananas!* and *Felix Kept on Walking*) and my growing armies of tin soldiers, their manoeuvres influenced by *Fights for the Flag* and Henty. But I was in touch with events in the wider world, reading avidly from about 1920 the *Belfast Newsletter*. It printed in deep black on the top left-hand corner of the front page a summary of the day's news, frequently then a diet of outrages and murders which encouraged me to read further in spite of gentle attempts at censorship. The *Newsletter* also printed regularly an extract from the day's *Morning Post* leader, so I steadily imbibed high toryism, expressed in sinewy prose. After some pleading I managed to secure as a present *Tales of the RIC*, having already read some of the chapters in *Blackwoods*. Based on the struggle between the Crown forces and the IRA 1919-21, it depicts the former as the courageous and skilful upholders of authority battling against cowardly, dishonourable and ruthless adversaries.

I had a fragmentary awareness of what was happening in the wider world and in a very rudimentary way I developed an outlook on affairs. It may seem ridiculous to refer to the political views of a boy of nine or ten but there has to be an embryonic stage in intellectual life and early impressions may subconsciously influence later conceptions. Living happily in a well-run home I early had a bias in favour of order, peace and stability and a dislike of insurgency, and in spite of the widely held belief that the young tend to be rebels I later met, as a schoolboy and an undergraduate, many contemporaries who were temperamentally conservative. My early instinctive loyalties manifested themselves on two public occasions – the visit of the King and Queen to Belfast in 1921 and the state entry of the Governor in 1923. Standing on a chair in Shaftesbury Square I saw the royal procession, the King in admiral's uniform and the Queen in white, sitting in an open carriage. The King's penetrating blue eyes seemed to look straight at me, establishing on the spot a strong, personal link between us. The entry of the governor, seen from a high window in Ann Street, was less dramatic. Clutching an elaborate programme of the ceremonial, I was much impressed by the escort of mounted police (rarely seen in Belfast).

If I may for a moment advance into my teens. With a fair number of books in the house, with access to two largish libraries, able to frequent Mullan's bookshop and a second-hand bookshop with a considerable stock, highly variegated in subject and quality and stimulated by intellectual competitiveness (in my case unexorcized by games), strong in my social circle in school, I read with greedy self-indulgence, often superficially widely and indiscriminately – Scott, Dumas, Wells, Thackeray, *The World Crisis*, Carlyle, the Russian novelists and Bernard Shaw with, for up-to-date literary news, the *Sunday Times* and the *Observer*. It was against this background that I was introduced to Irish nationalist literature. A visitor from the South, shocked by my ignorance, lent me Pearse's works and a lively-minded schoolmaster directed me to Davis, Mitchel and Lalor (adding as a corrective John Eglinton's *Anglo-Irish Essays*). I am afraid the nationalist writers failed to attract me. They seemed over-intense and, frankly, second-rate. I remained satisfied with the political and cultural context in which I had grown up, the United Kingdom. I may have been wrong-headed, but I am not seeking to justify myself, only to explain.

The Trinity I entered in 1932 (eleven years after the Treaty and shortly after de Valera came into power) was, I now realize, a remarkably self-contained institution. Though it was in the very centre of Dublin, it was 'juxta' rather than part and parcel of the city. Its tall, severe west front, with usually only a small wicket gate open, was uninviting and the college grounds did not provide a shortcut to anywhere, so the Dublin traffic, vehicular and pedestrian, swirled past Trinity's walls and railings, unregarding and unregarded. In the 1930s the universities, particularly the older universities, were somewhat aloof institutions.[1] The dons, fairly well placed financially, prided themselves on their independence, and the undergraduates were self-assured – Trinity men were occasionally to be heard proclaiming loudly, 'there is a way we have in the varsity that nobody can deny'. And the gap between Trinity and the Free State world was considerably wider than the customary divide between town and gown. The College still clung, so far as circumstances permitted, to its pre-Treaty loyalties, symbolized by the flying of the Union Jack on suitable occasions and a universal wearing of poppies on Armistice Day, the chapel being packed for the two minutes' silence followed by a lusty rendering of 'God Save the King' – the feelings expressed being deep and genuine, even allowing for a dash of youthful affectation.

It was soon brought home to me that the Trinity outlook was viewed with abhorrence by a section of the Dublin populace. Having heard that an anti-imperialist meeting was going to be held on the evening of 10 November 1932 in College Green, I went out to have a look at it. The Green was crowded, there were speeches and cheering, then suddenly there was an outburst of nasty booing. The target was myself. I was wearing a poppy, either through absent-mindedness or because I has never been in contact with bitter political feeling. I might have been badly battered but was saved by the intervention of half a dozen burly Dublin women, wearing their husbands' war medals, who were present to express vehement disapproval of the proceedings.

---

1 Within Trinity the phrase 'Oxford, Cambridge and Trinity, Dublin' was fairly frequently used. I doubt if it was current to the same extent in the other two institutions.

Under their protection I retreated back into College. Later that evening, hearing a loud menacing roar, I ran from my rooms to the Front Gate where two elderly porters were striving desperately to shut the wicket against an angry crowd. They were slowly yielding to *force majeure* when an undergraduate standing beside them, with a mighty swing brought a hockey stick down on the wrists of the assailants. They gave way and the bolt slammed home. Part of the meeting then swept out of College Green into Nassau Street. On the safe side of the College railings, in darkness, I kept pace with the crowd, fascinated and frightened by the savagery of their shouting.

Shortly afterwards in more sedate circumstances I was reminded of the gulf between 'loyalists' or ex-unionists and the majority. Having discovered that a 1916 exhibition had been opened in the National Museum I decided to visit it. Entering the museum I asked a sturdy, beetle-browed attendant the way to the 1916 room. He drew me aside and said that he was very glad that a young gentleman like me wanted to visit it. 'The people here,' he explained, 'don't like it – and do you know what they have done? – they have put a Minister Fusilier in charge of it and the other day when a young man wanted to see the relics of the martyred Pearse, he told him he would like to put his bloody head through the bloody glass case.' At that point I noticed that a small, sandy-haired porter with a row of medal ribbons on his tunic and a fat charwoman were staring at us with contemptuous hostility. 'He is the Minister Fusilier,' my acquaintance remarked, 'and she is another of them.' Involuntarily sailing under false colours, I left the building as soon as I decently could. Some weeks later I met at a cousin's a woman member of the Museum's staff, a staunch ex-unionist, who assured me how strongly members of the staff from the old regime resented the obtrusion of the 1916 memorabilia amongst their splendid collections.

Within Trinity the courses and teaching closely resembled those in a British university – I nearly wrote, 'in other British universities'. However, there was a school of Celtic studies and courses in Irish and the comparatively few undergraduates who studied Irish were prone to assert vigorously the immense value, especially to Irishmen, of their own subject. Their assertions left me cold or, on controversial occasions, heated. I felt no impulse to learn Irish. My ancestral connections with the language, if they existed, were very distant; I was not a good linguist and my slight acquaintance with Gaelic literature, gained from translation, did not stimulate me to attempt to master the language. There was, in the honor course in History and Political Science, a modest Irish component, covering Irish history from 400 to 1837. I concentrated on the post-1485 period but other sections of the course – British history, economic history, political science – interested me more. A conventional 1930s undergraduate, I enthusiastically and crudely applied the economic interpretation of history to a wide variety of developments, though I did not become a Marxist. By the time I read *Das Kapital* I had already by a conflation of Burke, J.S. Mill and Adam Smith become a liberal-conservative and a free-trader, Hobbes, whom I read with delight, providing an infusion of hard realism. All this may sound pretentious, but I readily admit that I only imperfectly understood much of what I rapidly ploughed through, missing subtleties of phrasing and dialectical complexities.

Beside the perennial questions on which undergraduates sharpened their wits, two topics loomed large in our discussions and debates: pacifism and socialism. Pacificism intensified as the threat of a war or wars that would leave civilization in ruins increased. Undergraduate socialism was continuously invigorated by the publications of the Left Book Club and weekly by the *New Statesman and Nation*, which, having a front half combining fervent political conviction with witty irreverence and a back half devoted to civilized living and thinking, greatly appealed to the consciously sophisticated undergraduate. Another facet of Trinity's intellectual life at this time should be mentioned. Owing to the size of the Divinity School and the calibre of some of its members, intelligent undergraduates were bound to be aware, if only in a superficial way, of theological issues – the influence of the Oxford Movement, Modernism and the teaching of Barth and Kierkegaard (talked about if not read). Incidentally, though some Catholic writers were certainly mentioned (Newman, Chesterton, Christopher Dawson and Bernanos come to mind), I do not recollect any Irish Catholic theologian being referred to except George Tyrrell, who after a Church of Ireland youth spent the rest of his life in England.

What all this leads up to is that the patterns of thought in Trinity during the thirties were far from being in accord with the predominant tendencies in Free State opinion. Even the Trinity nationalists were usually pacifists, socialists, internationalists, which meant that though their opinions might be quite coherent, their *Weltanschauung* differed markedly from that of the leaders, ecclesiastical and lay, of public opinion in Southern Ireland. I should add that this contrast in principles and prejudices between College and the surrounding world was stimulating for the Trinity undergraduate. It reminded us of the varieties of religious and political experience and encouraged us to examine our opinions, a salutary exercise, even if the result was a confident reaffirmation of inherent convictions.

At this point I should stress that Trinity was not a Laputa. Trinity undergraduates went to the theatre and cinema, were at home in Dublin restaurants and met the non-Trinity world in sport and games and to some extent in social life. I myself fortunately enjoyed the hospitality of two well-known Dublin hostesses – Lady Hanson (dinners, garden parties) and Miss Sarah Purser ('at home' with cucumber sandwiches). Both entertained a fairly wide spectrum of Dublin society, but I rather think that most of the guests, though happily at home in the Irish Free State and inclined to regard unreconstructed ex-unionists as anachronistic bores, had the style and some of the prejudices of the *ancien régime*. I met two indubitable nationalists at Lady Hanson's: James MacNeill, the former Governor General, and Hugh Law, a sometime nationalist MP. MacNeill had been for twenty-five years in the Indian Civil Service and Law was Rugby and Oxford. It was probably at one of these houses that I met the ubiquitous Professor George O'Brien of UCD, who kindly asked me to tea. My fellow guests, all UCD undergraduates, struck me as very polite and well-dressed. But, to the dismay of our host, we clashed violently over a political issue – the Spanish Civil War. They were all strongly pro-Franco and anti-Red. I, following the British government line, a non-interventionist, was driven by the spirit of contradiction into defending the Madrid government. About this time I belonged to the Contemporary Club, a discussion club founded at the close of the nineteenth century, which met in a large room in Lincoln Place. The discussion could drift over a wide field, the members, fortified by tea and barnbrack, contributing conversationally – though at least one member tended to indulge in flamboyant and repetitive rhetoric. Two outstanding members were Dr Rowlette, an exceptionally well-informed and worldly-wise medical professor, who once gave me a piece of invaluable advice – to curb my propensity to interrupt ruthlessly in conversation, and Harry Nicholls, a sometime mathematical scholar of Trinity, who was one of the city engineers. Nicholls, who would have taken part in the 1916 insurrection if he had not been arrested in advance, was often, at a Sinn Féin meeting, the embarrassed cynosure of all eyes when an orator, dwelling on how the movement embraced men of all creeds and classes, would declaim, 'And we have on the platform a Protestant from Trinity College!' A genial anecdotist, Nicholls resembled one or two other early supporters of Sinn Féin whom I met, in being mildly disillusioned by Irish developments though by no means disavowing his youthful idealism.

Trinity undergraduates were brought pleasantly in contact with the world beyond College by meeting, in College societies, distinguished visitors ('distinguished' at least for the occasion) from all over the British Isles. The Irish visitors ranged from the multilingual and excessively aristocratic Marquis MacSwiney of Mashanaglass to Peadar O'Donnell, the novelist and socialist agitator. On a November evening in 1936 I motored out to Clontarf with the auditor of the College Historical Society to try to persuade O'Donnell to speak at the opening meeting of the Society the following evening. O'Donnell accepted the invitation at once and swept us into a party he was giving. I would have thoroughly enjoyed it but for a nagging problem. Convention dictated that a speaker at the opening meeting should wear evening dress. Members of the Society took convention very seriously and the auditor had instructed me to remind O'Donnell of the custom. It was a delicate assignment but the conversational tide ran in my favour. O'Donnell began to weigh the merits of the different missiles that had been flung at him – for first place he hesitated between rivet bolts (Belfast) and potatoes bristling with razor blades (Glasgow). When he paused I casually remarked, 'Tomorrow night you will be in no danger, everybody will be in evening dress.' 'I won't,' he said and in fact he turned up looking very smart in a well-pressed blue suit.

President de Valera's first official engagement in Trinity, to address the College Gaelic Society in the Public Theatre, was a tense occasion. The hall was packed and as the tall dark figure, who represented for many of those present traditions they had been brought up to abominate, moved towards the platform, the atmosphere was electric. But de Valera was accompanied by the Provost, Edward Gwynn, and any incipient disorder was quelled by Gwynn's commanding presence and cold, apparently all-seeing gaze. A year or two later I met one of de Valera's leading opponents in a relaxed, charitable mood. He warned me not to criticize de Valera harshly – 'after all, the man's mad'. When about this time another of de Valera's opponents, Ernest Blythe, took the chair at a College Historical Society debate, one of the speakers was Noel Hartnett, a red-haired, fiery Kerryman, a strong supporter of Fianna Fáil, though on social policy to the left of the party. He delivered an impassioned attack on the Cumann na nGaedheal record, ending each clause of his indictment with the phrase, 'Another damned good bargain'. It was magnificent and I was much impressed. I was also impressed by Blythe's quite effective response to the philippic. In a highly competent summing-up, he simply ignored Hartnett and his contribution to the debate.

Hartnett's speech vividly illuminated antagonisms in Free State politics which we knew existed but rarely if ever experienced first-hand. Few Trinity undergraduates belonged to a Free State political party or were even emotionally involved in Free Sate political life. Nevertheless, we were in a detached way interested and often amused observers of politics. Though in retrospect the Irish Free State was after 1923 a placid, small country where nothing very momentous occurred and the pace of change was slow (witness the immense amount of almost unadulterated Georgian building which was still to be found in Dublin), there was plenty of surface excitement stirred up by, for instance, the Economic War, Anglo-Irish relations, the Blueshirts, de Valera's constitutional campaigns and successive general elections. Moreover, many people were, in the 1930s, loath to admit that drama had departed from Irish politics, that the romantic quality associated with the Land War,

Parnell, insurrection and civil war, was dead and gone. Political oratory was still somewhat high-flown, and while the constitutional parties debated vigorously, the extreme republican movement, challenging the legitimacy of established authority lurked in the shadows. One Easter Monday, perhaps in 1934, it was rumoured that the IRA was going to assert itself, and a number of groups of would-be spectators hung about O'Connell Street, waiting for the Post Office to be seized. Two or three years later I came in contact with non-juring Sinn Féin when I was trying to secure a ticket for a meeting at the Mansion House, to be addressed by speakers of widely differing views. I went to a house near College and climbed innumerable flights of stairs until I arrived at a landing in which there were three doors, inscribed respectively, *An Phoblacht* (the Republican magazine), Cumann na mBan (the women's movement) and The Government of Ireland. I knocked on the third door and was received by two pleasant middle-aged ladies who readily gave me a ticket. At the time I was amused by this *reductio ad absurdum* of Sinn Féin theory, earlier used against Crown authority in 1919-21. Now I am more conscious of the dangers inherent in political fantasizing.

At this stage I feel I should write continuously in the first person singular though I think a fair number of my contempoaries shared my views. Irish nationalism of the 1930s failed to attract me. It seemed strident, triumphalist, narrow, intolerant, self-righteous and far too quick to condemn English behaviour and English attitudes both in the past and in the present. Whatever youthful radicalism I possessed expressed itself in assailing Free State orthodoxy and the new establishment. Moreover, on my regular visits to England I did not feel an alien. My Irish relations who lived in London were happily at home there. I delighted in metropolitan life to the limited extent I could participate in it (an early memory is ham and veal pie in the chocolate and gold dining-room of the Holborn restaurant) and, though a shy boy sometimes suffering from an inferiority complex (a then fashionable problem), I never attempted to bolster my self-esteem by emphasizing my Irishness. My outlook can be summed up in a remark I made years later when chatting about foreign travel with a Trinity colleague who had a very nationalist background. We agreed that it was most enjoyable but that nevertheless it was pleasant at last to relax again in familiar surroundings. As I put it, 'I always feel a sense of relief when I see the Cliffs of Dover.' He was startled, not feeling at home until he saw Dun Laoghaire.

During the 1930s I grew to greatly appreciate many features of Dublin life – the reassuring Trinity routine with congenial company and conversation on tap; the libraries, each with its special flavour; the restaurants, the Bailey, a chop-house, the cheapest of the better restaurants, the Dolphin, wonderful value; walking in the hills; hospitable houses. But I remained politically unassimilated – partly because for years I spent much of my time as an undergraduate and research worker studying history, in an era when academic historians strongly emphasized the value of objectivity – and objectivity could promote detachment, tinged with superiority. What was far more important, my craving to feel I belonged to a greater entity, that I shared 'a partnership in all science, a partnership in all art, a partnership in every virtue and in all perfection', was fully met by my being a British subject.

A pessimist might expect that the persistence of this dichotomy, not to say conflict, between my political and cultural outlook and prevalent opinion in Southern Ireland would create disturbing and disabling tensions. But in fact I was scarcely conscious of any strain arising from this source. After all Trinity, where I spent much of my time, was very 'English' by local standards, and of the people I met outside college, many were highly anglicized. Others, who would regard themselves as indubitably Irish in outlook, were good-natured, broad-minded and argumentative, and we could talk about a wide range of topics, including of course politics, with gusto, without those deep-seated divergences which I have dwelt on coming to the surface. Or if they did emerge, they would be either ignored or welcomed as adding spice to the discussion. Semi-assimilation may seem an incongruous, even absurd condition, but it has existed and continues to exist in many countries, is probably inevitable and, if it has obvious disadvantages, it may sharpen the social perceptions and widen the sympathies of the unassimilated and be of benefit to a community that regards variety and a degree of dissidence as desirable.

Bibliography

MANUSCRIPT SOURCES

LONDON
British Library
  Bernard papers
  Long papers
Public Record Office
  Claims for compensation registers (CO905)
  Courts of inquiry in lieu of inquest (WO35)
  Criminal injuries – Irish Grants Committee (known until March 1926
    as Irish Distress Committee), 1922-30 (CO762)
  Midleton papers
  The Times archives
  Healy letters

DUBLIN
National Archives
  Cabinet minutes
  Department of Finance files
  Department of Justice files
  Department of the Taoiseach files
National Library
  Clonbrock papers
  Ireland Today London 1913 – annotated copy
Trinity College Library
  Bernard diaries
  Courtown papers
  Curtis papers
  Dowden papers
  Starkie diaries
Representative Church Body Library
  Papers and minutes of the Dublin Conservative Working Men's Club
  H.J. Lawlor correspondence

BELFAST
Public Record Office, Northern Ireland
  Carson papers
  Southern Irish Loyalist Relief Association minutes 1922-63 (in Unionist
    Alliance papers)
  Irish Unionist Alliance papers
Cambridge University Library
  Templewood papers
Oxford University Library
  Fisher papers
Wiltshire County Record Office
  Long papers

PARLIAMENTARY REPORTS

Hansard's Parliamentary Debates, 3 series (1830-91)
Hansard's Parliamentary Debates, 4 series (1892-1909)
The Parliamentary Debates (Official Report), 5 series, Commons,
  1909-; Lords, 1909-
Dáil Éireann: Minutes of the Proceedings of the First Parliament of the
  Republic of Ireland 1919-21 Official Record. Dublin 1994
Dáil Éireann ... Official Report 16 August 1921 to 26 August 1921 and
  28 February 1922 to 6 June 1922. Dublin 1922
Dáil Éireann: Suianna Priobhaideacha an dara Dáil (Private Sessions)
  1921-22 Dublin 1922
Dáil Éireann ... Díosbóireachtai Pairliminte – Parliamentary Debates ...
  1922-
Seanad Éireann: Díosbóireachtai Pairliminte – Parliamentary Debates,
  1922-

PARLIAMENTARY PAPERS

Return for 1870 of Landed Proprietors in each County, Classed According
  to Residence and Extent and Value of Property ... H.C. 1872, xlvii
Return for each County, City and Borough in Ireland ... of the Persons
  Holding the Commission of the Peace ... Cd20, H.C. 1886 (session), liii
Intercourse between Bolshevism and Sinn Féin Cmd 1326, H.C. 1921, xxix
Compensation Committee: Warrant of Appointment, Cmd 1654, H.C.
  1922
Relief of Irish Refugees: Correspondence between H.M. Government
  and the Provisional Government of Ireland relating to the Liability
  for the Relief of Irish Refugees, Cmd 1684, H.C. 1922, xvii

Compensation for Malicious Injuries: Letter to the Provisional Government of Southern Ireland, Cmd 1736, H.C. 1922, xvii

Royal Irish Constabulary: Disbandment Terms, Cmd 1618A, H.C. 1922, xvii

Royal Irish Constabulary: Revised Terms of Disbandment, Cmd 1673, H.C. 1922, xvii

Royal Irish Constabulary: Return Showing Rates of Pay and Compensation Allowances Payable on Disbandment Cmd 1719. H.C. 1922, xvii

Irish Grants Committee, Second Interim Report Cmd 2032, H.C. 1924, xi

Compensation for Injury: Memorandum Relating to Compensation for Injury to Persons and Property, Cmd 1844, H.C. 1923, xvii

Summary of an Agreement between H.M. Government and the Government of the Irish Free State Relating to Compensation for Damage to Property in Ireland, Cmd 2445, H.C. 1924-5, xxiii

Compensation: Report of the Commission Presided over by Lord Dunedin, Cmd 2748, H.C. 1926, ix

NEWSPAPERS AND MAGAZINES

Bell, The
Blackwoods
Catholic Bulletin
Cork Constitution
Daily Express
Derry Sentinel
Dublin Evening Mail
Edinburgh Review
Evening Mail
Irish Review
Irish Statesman
Irish Times
Morning Post
National Review
Nineteenth Century and After
Spectator
Studies
TCD
The Times

OTHER PRINTED SOURCES

[Ashtown, Lord], *The Unknown Power behind the Irish Nationalist Party*. London, 1907.

Bagwell, R., *Ireland under the Tudors*. 3 vols. London, 1885-90.

Ball, F.E., *The Judges in Ireland 1221-1921*. London, 1927.

Barry, T.B., *Guerilla Days in Ireland*. Dublin, 1949.

Battersby, T.S.F., *'A Modern Eye-Opener': Sixty Points against Home Rule*. Dublin, 1912.

Bence-Jones, M., *A Guide to Irish Country Houses*. 2nd ed. London, 1988.

Bence-Jones, M., *The Twilight of the Ascendancy*. London, 1987.

Biggs-Davison, J. & G. Chowdharag-Best, *The Cross of St Patrick: The Catholic Unionist Tradition in Ireland*. Bourne End Kensal, 1984.

Bolton, A.D., *The Criminal Injuries (Ireland) Acts*, 5th ed. Dublin, 1922.

Bowen, E.D.C., *The Last September*. London, 1929.

Bowen, K., *Protestants in a Catholic State: Ireland's Privileged Minority*. Montreal, 1983.

Breen, D., *My Fight for Irish Freedom*. Dublin, 1924.

Buckland, P., *The Anglo-Irish and the New Ireland 1886-1922*. Dublin, 1972.

Buckland, P., *Irish Unionism 1885-1923: A Documentary History*. Belfast, 1973.

Burke, R., *A Genealogical and Heraldic History of the Landed Gentry of Ireland*. London, 1912.

Carty, E., *The Irish Volunteer*. London, 1932.

The Case of the Irish Landlords. By One of Them. London, 1903.

Collins, M., *The Path to Freedom*. Dublin, 1922.

Comisiún na Gaeltachta: report. Dublin, 1925.

*Commission on the Restoration of the Irish Language ... Summary in English of Final Report ... *. Dublin, 1963.

Commission on Emigration, 1948-54.

Comerford, R.V., M. Cullen & J.R. Hill, *Religion, Conflict and Co-existence in Ireland*. Dublin, 1990.

Cooper, B., *Collar of Gold*. London, 1920.

Cooper, B., *The Tenth (Irish) Division in Gallipoli*. 1917.

Curtis, E. & R.B. McDowell, *Irish Historical Documents, 1172-1922*. London, 1943.

Daly, M.E., *Dublin, the Deposed Capital*. Cork, 1984.

D'Alton, L.L., *Death is so Fair*. London, 1936.

D'Arcy, F., *Horses, Lords and Racing: The Turf Club 1790-1990*. The Curragh, 1991.

De Blacam, A.S., *Towards the Republic: A Study of Ireland's Social and Political Aims*, 2 ed. Dublin, 1919.

The Disruption Bill ... Report of a Meeting Held on 14 April 1886. Dublin, 1886.

Dowden, E., *Fragments of Old Letters*, ed. E.D. Dowden. London, 1914.

Dowden E., *New Studies in Literature*. London, 1895.

Eglinton, J. (W.K. Magee), *Anglo-Irish Essays*. Dublin, 1917.

Eglinton, J., *Confidential, or Take It or Leave It*. London, 1951.

Eglinton, J., *Irish Literary Portraits*. London, 1935.

Eglinton, J., *Memoir of A.E.: George Francis Russell*. London, 1937.

English, R. & G. Walker, eds, *Unionism in Modern Ireland*. London, 1996.

Falkiner, C.L., *Studies in Irish History and Biography*. London.

Falkiner, C.L., *Essays Relating to Ireland, Biographical, Historical and Topographical*. London, 1909.

Farrell, M.J., *Mad Puppetstown*. London, 1931.

Figgis, D., *The Gaelic State in the Past, the Present and the Future*. Dublin, 1917.

Fitzgerald, B., *We are Besieged*. London, 1946.

Fitzpatrick, D., ed., *Ireland and the First World War*. Dublin, 1988.

Fitzpatrick, D., ed., *Revolution: Ireland 1917-1923*. Dublin, 1994.

Gaughan, J.A., *Austin Stack: Portrait of a Separatist*. Naas, 1977.

Gillespie, R., *Cavan in the Era of the Great War 1914-18*. Dublin, 1995.

Godley, A.D., *Reliquiae*, ed. C.R.L. Fletcher, 2 vols. Oxford, 1926.

Gregory, Isabella, *Lady Gregory's Journals*, i, 1916-24, ed. D.J. Murphy. Gerrards Cross, 1978.

Hickey, T.F.W., *Easter Week*. London, 1933.

Hickson, P., *The Ladies Road*. London, 1932.

Hone, J., *The Life of George Moore ...* . London, 1936.

Hone, J., *Ireland since 1922*. London, 1932.

Implementing an Irish Policy. 1972.

Ingram, T.D., *A Critical Examination of Irish History*. London, 1900.

Irish Unionist Alliance: Publications. Dublin [1893-1913].

Jennings, I. & C.M. Young, *Constitutional Laws of the Commonwealth*. Oxford, 1952.

Jackson, A., *Colonel Saunderson: Land and Loyalty*. Oxford, 1995.

Jones, T., *Whitehall Diary*, ed. K. Middlemas, iii: Ireland 1918-25. London, 1974.

Knight of Glin, D. G. Griffin and N.K. Robinson, *Vanishing Country Houses of Ireland*. Dublin, 1988.

Kotsonouris, M., *Retreat from Revolution: The Dáil Courts 1920-24*. Dublin, 1994.

Lawless, E., *Hurrish*. Edinburgh, 1886.

Lecky, E., *A Memoir of the Rt. Hon. W.E.H. Lecky*. London, 1909.

Lee, J., *Ireland 1912-1985: Politics and Society*. Cambridge, 1989.

Leech, H.B., *The Continuity of the Irish Revolutionary Movement*. London, 1887.

Leslie, S., *Doomsland*. London, 1923.

Livingston, P., *The Monaghan Story*. Enniskillen, 1980.

Lyons, F.S.L., *Culture and Anarchy in Ireland 1890-1939*. Oxford, 1979.

MacCarthy, M.J.F., *Priests and People in Ireland*. Dublin, 1902. 4th edition 1914.

McDowell, R.B., *The Irish Convention 1917-18*. London, 1970.

McNeill, R., *Ulster's Stand for Union*. London, 1922.

MacNamara, B., *The Clanking of Chains*. Dublin, 1920.

Macready, C.F.N., *Annals of an Active Life*. London, 1924.

Maguire, T., *England's Duty to Ireland*. Dublin, 1886.

Maume, P., *'Life that is exile': Daniel Corkery and the Search for Ireland*. Belfast, 1993.

Meath, Lord, *Memories of the Twentieth Century*. London, 1924.

Meenan, J. *The Irish Economy since 1922*. Liverpool, 1970.

Miller, D.W., *Church, State and Nation in Ireland, 1898-1921*. Dublin, 1972.

Moore, G., *Letters* ... ed. by J. Eglinton. London, 1942.

Moran, D.P., *The Philosophy of Irish Ireland*. Dublin, 1905.

Murray, R.H., *Archbishop Bernard, Professor, Prelate and Provost*. London, 1931.

Newspaper Press Directory ... [issued annually] London.

Nolan, W., L. Ronayne & M. Dunlevy, *Donegal, History and Society*. Dublin, 1995.

Nolan, W. & T.G. McGrath, eds, *Tipperary: History and Society*. Dublin.

Nolan, W. & T.P. Power, *Waterford: History and Society*.

O'Brien, K., *Prayer for a Wanderer*. London, 1938.

O'Connor, J., *History of Ireland 1798-1924*. 2 vols. London, 1925.

O'Donovan, G., *Father Ralph*. London, 1913.

Phillips, W.A., *The Revolution in Ireland 1906-1923*. London, 1925 2nd ed. 1926.

Rolleston, C.H., *Portrait of an Irishman*. London, 1930.

Rolleston, T.W.H., *Ireland, the Empire and the War*. Dublin, 1900.

Ross-Lewin, The brothers, *In Britain's Need*. Dublin, 1917.

Samuels, A.W., *Home Rule, Fenian Home Rule; Home Rule all Round; Devolution. What Do They Mean*. Dublin, 1911.

Sexton, B., *Ireland and the Crown 1922-36*. Dublin, 1989.

Solomons, M., *Pro Life?: The Irish Question*. Dublin, 1992.

Somerville, E.O., *The Enthusiast*. London, 1921.

Somerville, E.O., and Ross, M., *Irish Memoirs*. London, 1917.

Stanford, W.B., *A Recognized Church: The Church of Ireland in Éire*. Dublin, 1944.

Stanford, W.B., *Faith and Faction in Ireland*. Dublin, 1946.

Starkie, E. *A Lady's Child*. London, 1941.

Tales of the R.I.C. Edinburgh, 1922.

Tovey, H., Hannon, D. & Abrahamson, H., *Irish Identity and the Irish Language*. Dublin, 1989.

Townshend, C., *The British Military Campaign in Ireland 1919-1921: The Development of Political and Military Policies*. Oxford, 1975.

Unionist Convention ... Report of the Proceedings. Dublin, 1892.

Vaughan, W., *Landlords and Tenants in mid-Victorian Ireland*. Oxford, 1994.

Walker, B.M. ed., *Parliamentary Election Results in Ireland 1801-1922*. Dublin, 1978.

Walker, B.M., ed., *Parliamentary Election Results in Ireland 1918-1992*.

Walsh, B.M., *Religion and Demographic Behaviour in Ireland* (Institute of Economic and Social Research, paper 55). Dublin, 1970.

Waugh, E., *Work Suspended*. London, 1942.

Webb, B., *Diaries 1924-32*, ed. M. Cole. London, 1956.

Webb, T.E., *The Irish Question*. Dublin, 1886.

West, T., *Horace Plunkett, Co-operation and Politics: An Irish Biography*. Gerrards Cross, 1986.

Whyte, G.K., *A History of St Columba's College*. Dublin, 1980.

Whyte, J.H., *Church and State in Modern Ireland*. Dublin, 1971.

Wilmot, J.E., *Historical Review of the Commission of Inquiry into the Losses, Services and Claims of the American Loyalists ...* . London, 1815.

Yeats, W.B., *Essays*. London, 1961.

Yeats, W.B. *Letters ...*, ed. R.J. Fenner, G.M. Harper, & W.M. Murphy, 2 vols. London, 1977.

Index